Broken Child

Mended Man

Adam Starks, Ph.D.

WYZ PUBLISHING HOUSE

PHILIPPI, WEST VIRGINIA

Wyz Publishing House, September 2016

Book design by Streetlight Graphics, LLC.

Edited by Sara D. Thomas

The origami-style owl logo and Wyz Publishing House are trademarks of Wyz Enterprise, Ltd. www.wyzenterprise.com

Published in the United States of America by Wyz Publishing House, a division of Wyz Enterprise, Philippi, WV.

For more information, please visit www.adamstarks.com

Cataloging-in-Publication data is on file with the Library of Congress

Library of Congress Control Number: 2016912234

Paperback ISBN: 978-16345-2290-8

10 9 8

Contents

Dedication

To my beloved wife, Emily, my brilliant children Jayden, Isaiah, Susannah and every person who has positively touched my life. You have all inspired me to go the distance.

Author's Preface

I prefer to be true to myself, even at the hazard of incurring
the ridicule of others, rather than to be false,
and to incur my own abhorrence.

Frederick Douglass

As long as we define ourselves in terms of our pains and problems,
we will never be free from them.

Eckhart Tolle

I can be changed by what happened to me, but I
refuse to be reduced by it.

Maya Angelou

Men judge more from appearances than reality.
All men have eyes, but few have the gift of penetration.
Everyone sees your exterior, but few can
discern what you have in your heart.

Niccolo Machiavelli

Thank you for purchasing my memoir. This book isn't another story about a black boy who managed to survive the streets. Those accounts of overcoming urban plights are admirable, but this is a nonfictional story about the struggle I endured before and during my years in foster care. Conversely, my survival tactics originated in rural Rappahannock County, Virginia as a poor country boy who was destined to do more than be defined by my circumstances.

The preamble of my decision to write this book has to be accredited to the positive people who have come into my life within the past couple of years. It was their initial push to bring my story to light that motivated this process. At first, I reluctantly nodded in agreement knowing that I was afraid to confront a past never dealt with accordingly. I had to "get over it" as so many unknowing people illogically stated and make a viable life for myself.

I grew up determined to end the cycle, but not before nearly becoming a victim of my self-destructive behavior during the process. Throughout my writing progression, I discovered the depth of my resilience and laid much of my burdened past to rest. I fought back tears for a lost, broken child throughout the first few chapters, as I relived the life of that lanky, nappy-headed, ashy kid who took on more than his fair share of sorrows. Nevertheless, I was able to overcome those obstacles and break the generational cycle of grimness afflicting the Starks family. That's not to infer that I'm better than any other Starks in Rappahannock County. The evidence put forth in this book will convey my poor judgement calls and character flaws as a fatherless child coming of age in the foster care system.

Fast forward to today and I'd undoubtedly tell you that I'm a tremendously privileged man. In my past, there were plenty of chances for my life to divert into drug addiction, alcoholism, or even imprisonment. Instead, I find myself expressing the most vulnerable details of my childhood, which in turn made me the resilient man I've become. Today, I'm a proud husband, father, community volunteer and find myself full of aspiration to do more.

In short, I refused to be a victim of my circumstances. With the support of my Rappahannock County and Eastern Mennonite University communities, I turned out to be a contributing member of our society. For their peace of mind, I've protected the identities of everyone involved in my life by using alias names throughout the book.

Back to the original point, the kind of upward mobility I experienced is becoming rarer in our country, so it's important for me to convey that the secret to my success lies within an insatiable desire for knowledge and embracement of community. Education proved to be my saving grace, and my communities provided the necessary foundation.

I deliver this story to the best of my recollection, not to garner sympathy, but to give others inspiration to overcome and cope with hardships. I interject humor and other lightheartedness when I can. Though truth be told, some of the reading is emotionally heavy and requires time to digest. In addition, the explicit language throughout the book is not intended to purposely offend anyone. This language was just an everyday part of my life. If you can understand that, then I encourage you to continue. If you're hypersensitive to such language, then you're going to miss the overall point of the book. Notwithstanding, I've since learned that there's a time and place for swearing. Seeing the world for what it is; cursing is the only thing I can manage to do some days.

With that in mind, navigating through the peaks and valleys of life, I have determined that lessons from my triumphs and struggles may provide value to others trying to process the hardships and risks that inevitably come with life. By way of reviving tucked away memories and extracting them into a worthwhile read, I hope you will discover both solace and resilience. I encourage you to let your hardships manifest into valuable lessons for your future. I don't have all of life's answers and probably never will, but coping with life's ups and downs will strengthen you in the present moment, thus sustaining your will to succeed in this uncertain world. It's also important to remember that the definition of success is different for everyone. It arrives at different points in our lives based on myriad reasons.

With the completion of my memoirs, I close the book on a troubled past to embrace the present and accept the future. Ultimately, that is how we survive and learn to cope with the tribulations that may negatively affect us. In short, embrace the hardships in life by learning from those instances. That was my path to contentment and self-realization. One of my foster mothers once said, "Regardless of your circumstances, no one owes you a damn thing." The message wasn't elegant by any means, but it stuck with me over the years. Instead of being a victim of my past, I had to realize my potential and accomplish something meaningful during my lifetime.

If you're struggling with life in general, then this book is for you. I encourage you to face your hardships head on, accept the outcome, and know that life will indeed get better from the lessons you gather along the way. As you continue on your journey, I don't recommend walking it alone. Seek those who will remain a positive force in your life and lean on them in times of need. Pay it forward as much as possible by reciprocating that same compassion within your community. Helping others will alleviate your pain, but more importantly, you'll discover a sense of empowerment by realizing how important you are by making your piece of the world a better place. I couldn't have accomplished anything without the three foster families who stepped in when they did, or the mentor who guided me through the college and financial aid process, or the high school track coach who encouraged me to think about college in the first place or the teacher who handed me a novel that would ignite a love for books that I never knew existed. You get the idea. Stand on the shoulders of the influential people in your life and take your rightful place in this world. Only then will you be able to walk tall and withstand the hardships while blazing your trail. The beauty and the curse of life is that it isn't scripted, but it's ultimately you who will determine its narration.

Hard-Knock Origins

*Hardships often prepare ordinary people
for an extraordinary destiny.*

C.S. Lewis

*Out of suffering have emerged the strongest souls;
the most massive characters are seared with scars.*

Khalil Gibran

*Be patient and tough;
someday this pain will be useful to you.*

Ovid

*When I hear somebody sigh, "Life is hard,"
I am always tempted to ask, "Compared to what?"*

Sydney J. Harris

*Although the world is full of suffering, it is also
full of overcoming it.*

Helen Keller

*The two most important days in your life are
the day you are born and the day you find out why.*

Mark Twain

Chapter One

California Born

The simplicity and strength that comes with the name Adam didn't resonate during my formative years. The name itself, meaning *first man or man made from the ground,* adequately describes my journey thus far. From a more positive viewpoint, the strength and resilience signified in my name may have forced me to dig deeper to hone in and rely upon my keen survival instincts. If I managed to survive my childhood, the simplicity of it meant I would not have to fight the undetectable stigma and unnecessary battles so many black individuals have to endure throughout their adult years. However you decipher what's in a name, I can say with certainty that the name itself was part of the reason I internalized its strength throughout the latter part of my formative years. Regardless of my mother's shortcomings, I eventually came around to thanking her for this name. Even though my mother chased an impractical dream of becoming a songwriter, heavily drank alcohol during my womb occupancy, and managed to lose us to the foster care system, she managed to bless me with a name that would not hinder my future attempt at achieving the American dream. In essence, I would become grateful to fight one less societal battle.

I was born August 26th, 1980 in Burbank, California at St. Joseph's Hospital, and spent the first years of my life living in an apartment complex. I can only imagine that it was the standard-issue cookie cutter of every other apartment high rise in West Hollywood; tan-colored exterior, five or six stories high, and topped with red-orange clay roof panels. I remember the interior consisted of vibrant red and white. Red had to have been my mother's favorite color. The only picture of my mother from that period had her donning a solid red wardrobe from head to toe. As for the apartment; red carpet, red furniture, red and white striped walls; throw up a couple of green elements in the space and our place could've been a year-round Southern California Christmas lounge.

It was the perfect scene for a little boy who liked vibrant colors, but the best memories with my mother had to be dancing around the room to a variety of music from the Temptations to Dolly Parton. She introduced me to the diverse genres she grew up with, so I had early access to good music. My favorite song was Marvin Gaye's *I Heard it Through the Grapevine.* Mom had that classic on heavy rotation in her record player. The California Raisins were my first Saturday morning heroes. Anytime that commercial came on the TV set, I had to do my rendition of the grapevine song then ask Mom to buy me some raisins. She did one better and managed to get me a set of stuffed California Raisins for Christmas one year.

Looking back, my patchwork of memories during the first five years in California revealed a much simpler life compared to the challenges I would face moving cross-country to Virginia. My earliest recollection is falling out of my stroller onto a Hollywood Boulevard Star Walk of Fame when I was around two years old. Whether that meant I was destined for stardom or my mother needed to make sure I was buckled in more tightly next time remains to be seen. My mother already had another child, my sister Eve, five years earlier with the only man she would ever marry. Her alcoholism coupled with her blind, unproductive ambition led to their divorce well before I was born.

While we were in Hollywood, she managed to have relations with two more men who produced my other brothers, Noah and Christopher. Surprisingly, I don't remember much about either one of my brothers or their fathers during our time out west. According to Mom, Noah was born at Hollywood Presbyterian, and Chris was born at UCLA. Mom said she decided to give us biblical names since she was told by a doctor in the early 70s that she would never have children. Supposedly, she continued to pray throughout the years, and was blessed with my sister Eve, then me six years later and Noah in 1984. While Christopher is not a biblical name per se, *it began with Christ* was Mom's logic. The rest of us, including Moses and Matthew, who would arrive much later, were given solid biblical names. Some refer to it as luck; however, the biblical names may have been our saving grace since all of us managed to make it out relatively unscathed by the possible fetal alcohol symptoms infants can face when expectant mothers drink heavily during pregnancy. I've tried to find some logical explanation, but luck doesn't even begin to describe how all of us managed to make something of ourselves later on in life.

My father was absent from the get go. I don't have his side of the story since I never met the man, so I can't offer a guess as to why he chose to abandon me. The blank line where my father's name should be on my birth certificate represents the same void I still feel today. I cannot help but think that life would have been so much easier if I had the ability to ask him for advice. Of course, that assumes he would have been stable enough to provide sound guidance. Although I don't know his side of the story, I always considered him a coward for escaping his responsibility. Ultimately, I could only hold him accountable by being a dedicated father to my children. His absence had the opposite effect on my psyche. Instead of a continuation, I chose to break the cycle and start anew. I made that vow early on as I was watching an episode of *The Cosby Show* one night. I wanted to be just like Dr. Huxtable and have a huge family that looked up to me. Gratefully, my sister's father went above and beyond to provide that foundational example. Although I struggled with false memories during my adolescent years, my father never existed during my stay in California. I have no recollection of Peter Miles McKissack, but according to my mother, he came around a few times after I was born before venturing off to Vegas to pursue music stardom.

The redeeming memories from my early childhood involved my sister and her father, Caesar. Although we didn't live together, my sister always seemed to be by my side. She even nicknamed me Chachie after the *Happy Days* character. To this day I have no idea why, but the name stuck during my stint in California. As for Caesar, I couldn't have wished for a better father figure in my life. Our travels together granted me the fatherly insight my little inquisitive mind needed at the time. Whether it was my wonderment as to why the moon was following our car or pondering why those basketball-looking globes were stuck on the electrical lines, Caesar always had a straightforward response. Typically, I followed up with an "Oh!" and kept humming to the tune on the radio or whatever Mom had stuck in my head.

Caesar always treated me to McDonalds, and I may have owned every Happy Meal toy from 1983-84. At mealtime, I'd pretend to be the Hamburgalar with chicken nuggets in one hand and fries in the other while doing my little version of a happy dance. Afterward, I recall Caesar dropping me off with Mom and just entertaining myself with a skit featuring the

Hamburgalar on a skateboard and Grimace chasing him along the carpet while they argued back and forth. They never thought I was listening, but most of it had to do with Caesar lecturing my mother about her drinking problem. Caesar would eventually leave, and I would continue to entertain myself amidst empty Busch beer cans until Johnny Carson came on. Yes, his show was on way past a normal child's bedtime. However, one of my favorite sayings as a toddler was, "Heeeeere's Johnny!"

Although the moments were cherishable, I faced a lot of adversity outside of the comfort of Eve and Caesar's affection. There was never a doubt in my mind that I would always be safe in their presence. Unfortunately, Mom didn't always leave me in their care, so I could only hope to hold my own when she sent me to spend the day with Gladys. Anytime I hear the music of an ice cream truck, I still think of her three girls who took joy in locking me inside a closet while they bought ice cream to eat in front of me. I remember sitting in the dark with a glimmer of light coming from underneath the door helplessly plotting my revenge, yet never carrying through with it since I was always outnumbered. However, there were times when karma would take place. One time I got the idea to pee off of the balcony and show off my rainbow-shaped stream to the three sisters. One of them was impressed and got the bright idea to try it herself. She pulled her pants down, aimed, but the stream proceeded down her legs. I had a good laugh with the other two girls, but that was the extent of my ability to divide and conquer. We teased her until I left that day. The girls lived in the same apartment complex, but I never knew how their mother, Gladys, came to know my mother. All I remember was being dropped off and the torture that ensued. Besides having all of the Twizzlers and Kool-Aid I could consume, Gladys was usually oblivious to the torment and dared any of us to disturb her while watching soap operas. Her girth and big hair curlers were intimidating, so I didn't dare test her command. As soon as my mom left, I couldn't wait for her return. I always wanted to open one of the windows to see if I could just fly away. The destination did not matter; anywhere but with those three demon spawn would suffice.

My mother never held a job, so I never knew where she went during the times. Upon returning to our apartment, I anxiously awaited Caesar and Eve to take me away, even though I knew it would not be forever like I always wanted. Some days they would arrive as I had wished and sometimes they didn't. Occasionally, Caesar would just drop Eve off for a few hours. Like every toddler, my mind conjured up the idea that I was at the center of everyone's universe and completely oblivious to the fact that they had lives outside of my self-absorbed bubble. Although we played gleefully, I mostly remember Eve commanding Mom to stop drinking so much alcohol to no avail. In an effort to look out for her brothers' well-being, Eve was constantly critical, but she hardly penetrated my mother's steadfast denial. I never fully understood the problem until I came to resent my mother for her alcoholism a few short years later.

All of that denial led to inevitable consequences. Due to Mom's addiction and never holding down a job among other reasons, we ended up being evicted from our apartment during the spring of 1985. I recall looking at our belongings Mom had piled up in the center of the family room for storage. She bent down to my eye level and assured me that everything would eventually be delivered to Virginia. I was only allowed to take a book bag full of clothes and some of my most prized Happy Meal toys. Whatever I had in that bag was all that ever made it to the eastern countryside.

The night we had to leave California, Eve was sobbing and hugging me tightly in her arms as our mother led my uncooperative body to the back of the plane. Pulling away from her was the earliest emotionally painful moment in recollection, and I cried myself to sleep during the one-way trip to Virginia. I remember the sick feeling in my stomach and shaking from the fear of leaving everything I'd known behind on the west coast. Whether I wanted it to or not, life would have to go on without my beloved sister. Mom's dreams of becoming a successful songwriter in Hollywood quickly faded away. Our memories of California would eventually fade as well with every picture and belonging, which were confiscated by storage due to failure to pay for the unit. In essence, the first four years of my life were hopelessly discarded.

Although I received a handful of letters from my sister throughout the years, I wouldn't reconnect with Eve again until she moved across the country to attend her graduate program at Duke University fifteen years later. I was at a track meet as a collegiate athlete representing Eastern Mennonite University in 2000. Beforehand, we went on to lead two completely different lives. Fortunately, Caesar won custody of Eve after divorcing Mom years earlier. Her father's involvement proved to be her saving grace, and my father's absence would only lead to an unsettling childhood.

Chapter Two

Virginia Raised

I eventually forgot about my abandoned stuff in a California storage space as the struggles and phobias from country living started to consume my thoughts. As a frightened five-year-old child, I don't remember arriving at the airport or who picked us up, but I can recall the culture shock pulsating through my mind as I stepped out onto my Uncle Doy's farm. The Rappahannock countryside was filled with so many unknowns. The unfamiliar sounds of chickens and cows left me with an overwhelming longing for cars humming down the road in West Hollywood. I clutched my mother's leg as a plump white-feathered chicken came toward us. Uncle Doy assured me that there was nothing to worry about and invited us inside my Aunt Lilo's house. I looked around the unfinished home and realized that there was no television, which meant no Johnny [Carson]. The unwelcoming stare from Lilo was a precursor to my first three years in Virginia.

Everything from taking a splashing bubble bath in an acrylic tub to using a toilet with in-house plumbing was taken for granted in California. Bathing in a large galvanized wash tub to using an outhouse were completely foreign to me. Both proved to be the bane of my existence; especially during the winter months. Even the food they ate was different. Fish cakes out of a can and corn on the cob were entirely new to my palate. Sometimes Uncle Doy would have a sit-down with us and remove his tightly curled straw cowboy hat. It was one of the few times I ever saw him take it off to dig into his plate. He didn't waste any time when it came to scarfing down his meal. While eating corn, he gnawed through each row with buzz saw-like precision. I recall trying to mimic his eating habits only to manage a chomping motion and getting most of the ear stuck between my teeth. I spent the better part of that evening picking it out.

From getting caught in thorn bushes to barbed wire fencing to cutting myself on rusty metal in random junk piles around the yard, everything seemed to draw blood. Nature was also foreign to me, so anything I came in contact with was intensely dreaded. Uncle Doy did not help my anxiety as he retold the old wives tale about snapping turtles not letting go until the next thunderstorm if I happened to be bitten by one. As far as I was concerned, we had left planet Earth; I had officially stepped into the Twilight Zone – another favorite show of mine. In what would later be known as my haunted castle, the inside of the thermal insulation-exposed home was eerie, but I feared outside even more so. The slightly leaning two-story home with weathered wood siding appeared to be more suitable for the Addams family.

Uncle Doy had a way of teasing that made me want to hide under our bed and stay forever, but he also let Noah and me ride on his lap while steering his tractor to tour his tens of acres of farmland. There wasn't much to it with the exception of sloped hills, scattered hay bales, and cows freely roaming about. Those rides helped quell some of the angst, but then he'd put me on top of one of his hay bales, and I'd throw a fit if I saw a cow coming toward us. *What if the cow couldn't tell the taste difference between little kids and hay and ate me*, I thought to myself. I'd plead for him to take me down, and he'd wait until I either started crying or the Black Angus cattle were close enough, and he would make me pet it. It may as well have been a dinosaur since I couldn't imagine a worse fear at the time. The first time he tried to make me pet one, I squirmed from his grip and darted across the farm. I crawled underneath the barbed wire fence, burst through the door and hid under the sheets for hours. The next time, Uncle Doy kept a firm grip on my ribs until I extended my hand to pet the cow. Unless I stepped in a patty out in the field, I was cool with the cows after that point.

Whether it were the rooster attacks on the way to the outhouse or the swans reacting to the threat they felt as I threw rocks in the pond, my lanky, fragile frame was fair game for the nasty critters. My fear of animals was legit, and after scanning the bites and scratches to validate my fear, I gathered the courage to carry one of Uncle Doy's sickles anytime I had to go somewhere. I was rarely, if ever, at ease during my first three years in Virginia. Everything I was familiar with seemed to disappear with one fateful plane ride. I quickly decided that the country life wasn't for me. California occupied my dreams and thoughts often. My mother continually promised that we would make it back home; but our dream would never come to fruition. She still believes it to this day, but I lost that hope by the time I turned six years old.

Being escorted around the countryside to visit family or go grocery shopping allowed time to collect my feelings and temporarily escape reality. Although I was only five years old, I was very aware of my surroundings. The sunshine was different here than in Burbank. Burbank's piercing sun rays made me want ice cream or to play in the pool all of the time. My underwear was always the wardrobe of choice. However, the sunshine in Woodville, Virginia seemed to gently kiss everything it touched. The one thing that always fascinated me riding through Woodville and all throughout Rappahannock County were the number of trees alongside the mountaintops. Open meadows and modest homes scattered along Route 211 complemented the untamed mountain ranges and rolling valleys that would finally give way to the historic Skyline Drive – a natural escape where the wilderness spoke softly with a wind-aided cadence of birds, insects and rustling tree leaves. While I missed the brokered pattern of trees and city living in southern California, the untouched, pristine Rappahannock countryside awoke my childlike curiosity. The mountain ranges and valleys were covered in foliage that appeared to touch the clouds crossing the unspoiled blue sky. The horizon gifted me with an abnormal sense of peace and allowed me to momentarily forget the strife of hunger and my mother's worsening alcoholism. Plus, I always looked forward to the local gas station since it always had so much neat stuff.

Anytime we'd go to one of the gas stations, I'd usually pick up some candy cigarettes and caps for my toy pistol. I'd go home, rip open the package, load my chamber, put my six-shooter cap gun in my pocket and practice drawing it out against the chickens with a candy cig in my mouth just like the old westerns Mom used to watch in California…sort of. Coupled with that imagery, one could easily assume I had somewhat redneck aspirations. After getting a roll-back STP toy car for a Christmas present one year – the only Christmas gift that year – I had a dream of taking Richard Petty's place when he got too old to race. I would play with that car for hours and even added a Dukes of Hazard element by building improvised ramps to jump all over the floor. The cars didn't last very long after that, so Mom or my cousin Jaevon would buy a replacement for me. I talked about it so much my Mom even managed to get a couple of race car outfits for me. While living under that roof on the farm that was the closest I got to seeing my first-ever dreams come true. More often than not, most of my dreams were food related.

Perpetual hunger was the biggest challenge I faced during my first years in Virginia. There were too many days when my stomach pains refused to subside; like a cut being continually reopened. Mom seemed to have a special stomach that could feel full after a 6-pack of Milwaukee's Best beer, but that was not an option for me or my brothers. Food constantly occupied my mind, and I went to any length to get it. During the summer months we had periods of relief when my Uncle Doy brought a bushel of crabs, fresh grapes or apples to the farmhouse. Although he did so on random occasions, it was always a nice surprise.

In between random deliveries, I had to be somewhat devious. I took the time to get to know a grandma-like lady who lived on the lot adjacent to Shade Road. Aunt Annie had a big ol' cherry tree and strawberry patches as far as my little brown eyes could see. I picked the sweet fingernail-sized berries for hours and made sure we didn't waste a single one. The cherry tree was easily one of the tallest trees I can remember. Standing in the middle of the strawberry patch, I wondered if the leaves were tickling the clouds. Despite its towering height, I climbed it with surprising ease, determined to pick every reachable cherry. Of course, I made sure Aunt Annie received her share of the bushel. It was the least I could do since she was always so gracious to us.

The blackberry bushes behind Uncle Doy's house were fair game. I didn't have to get pricked too many times before becoming a little pro at weaving my skinny arm through the thorny, crisscrossed stems. After rinsing, I rolled the berries in sugar to experience a moment in heaven. Of course, I shared with my brothers; it was only right since I had a big helping while picking. Eventually, I convinced Noah to be my picking partner; however, he seemed to take on a lot more scratches and tangle ups than I ever experienced. There was nothing to do for it but let the hurt wear off and record another scar on his skin. Blackberries always bring back good memories for no other reason than I ate them without a care in the world. Even fighting the junebugs off the fruit was fun, as I would tie fishing line around them to have a flying pet. The berries were always a dependable food source when in season and they were plentiful.

Then there was a last-resort crab-apple tree. I knew the punishment that would result in eating them from prior experience, but it was always a dependable backup plan if the junebugs and birds picked the best of the berry harvest. Noah loved them, but I never really cared for the sour, bitter taste that proceeded with a race to the outhouse. A late summer afternoon in 1987 would be the last time I would climb this tree. I sprang up there just like every other time during previous seasons, but this time the top of my head connected with a hornet's nest about halfway up the tree. I remember swinging and being afraid to jump from so high. Noah ran into the house to tell Mom, but the last thing I remember was swinging by the back of my legs on a branch and waking up in a hospital room. From that experience, I'm still terrified of hornets as a grown man.

It was during the dreaded fall and winter months that our vulnerability was truly exposed as our fruit-filled oasis turned into a cold, food desert. Periodically, especially around Christmas time, we would receive food catalogs, and I would hide them under the mattress so I could touch the food on each page as if it were real. No matter how many times I told Mom how badly I wanted a ham with pineapple or a cheese platter, none of the items ever showed up on our porch step. Nevertheless, I'd continue flipping through glossy pages wishing for the nicely dressed ham and cheeses to appear in our mailbox, but those pipe dreams were out of reach for a hungry little boy. I didn't know what cheese tasted like at the time, but it sure looked good on those pages. On other occasions, I would make bread sandwiches. Three slices of bread and a vivid imagination of a McDonald's cheeseburger in the middle of that dry heap got me through some tough stretches. There were always random packs of ramen noodles sitting around that I'd pour the flavored salt on and eat dry since I couldn't use the stove. At some point, Mom was granted WIC and food stamps, but food rarely ever made it onto our plates.

I had no idea what Mom did with the food stamps. At one point she told me Aunt Lilo took them as rent payment, which was believable since she knowingly hid food in compartments throughout the house. Occasionally she would cook us fried chicken, mashed potatoes and green beans but only when she was in an extremely good mood. It did not happen often enough for me to remember more than a handful of times, and she certainly didn't overcome her resentment toward us.

One day Aunt Lilo underestimated how much attention I was paying to her moving grocery bags through the house, and I saw her go into a room. After unloading the haul into her bedroom, she locked the door and began shuffling the bags. At this point, we had torn the thermal siding throughout the house so bad, it was fairly easy for a pint size like me to get around through walls and exposed floor studs. I took this opportunity to spy and plan to get a share for me and my brothers, and started to explore in Aunt Lilo's part of the house. I had been living in the home at least six months by this point when I was traumatized by the sight of a sick, elderly woman lying on a stained mattress with a bunch of pads underneath of her. It turns out that this person was my grandmother! The smell was so rancid that I had to forcefully refrain from vomiting. Somehow, I managed to hold up, tucked my nose under my shirt and watched Aunt Lilo store some food in a box under some sheets. That was all I needed to see, and I quickly backed out as the pungent odor started to penetrate my thin shirt. I quickly ran back to tell Noah of my new secret plan to get us more food.

This newfound sustenance would provide a consistent source for a few months until I got greedy one day. My routine consisted of waiting until Aunt Lilo left for work then squirming through my path that led into her room. My grandmother never moved, and at one point I wondered if she was dead. I never stuck around long enough to check because the smell was bad enough to kill the cows outside. I took a daily ration for me and my brothers and endured the sneers from Aunt Lilo to avoid starving on any particular winter day.

That all came to an end when I heard Aunt Lilo screaming at Mom; "One of those little niggers of yours took all of my God damned cookies. I'm tired of this shit already and you all need to find a place and get the fuck out of here!"

Mom retorted, with her usual, "We're going back to California" bit, and that was the end of it. I got to steal one more day before I found a new box with a lock on it.

The only thing consistently left outside of Lilo's door was a box of off-brand cereal. I resorted to this but not by choice. The tasteless flakes came with an assortment of roaches and eggs that I had to sift through. That part I could always stomach out of desperation, but I could never overcome the times when I'd have to substitute water because the milk had spoiled in a refrigerator too old to keep perishables cold. Nevertheless, I would always sort through the roaches and fix a bowl for Noah. He never seemed to mind and always seemed grateful for whatever I could find for us.

The other two items that always seemed to be left out without much explanation were sardines and my youngest brother Chris' baby food. I was the only one who would eat the oil-soaked sardines. They were okay, but I did not care for them until my cousin Bryce showed me how to dip them in vinegar and put them between saltines for better taste. Bryce also introduced me to pork rinds, pig feet soaked in vinegar and frog legs. However, he didn't show up often enough to be a dependable food source.

As an adult thinking back, WIC checks or food stamps explain the baby food, but, to this day, I have no idea why there were sardines left out while mostly everything else remained locked up. Noah and I always looked forward to getting our hands on our baby brother Chris' banana and peach flavored food jars, but we would leave them alone if the supply was getting low. I didn't want Chris to feel the constant hunger pains we felt.

As mentioned before, my recollection of Chris is somewhat hazy. The one prominent memory that sticks out in my mind was when Mom was feeding him a bottle at Aunt Sun's (Bryce and Jaevon's mom) house. She had done this many times before, but Chris was spewing black substance and helplessly wailing. My mother was sitting on a stool desperately trying to hold him still while continuing to force the bottle to him. I noticed that she was holding him in an awkward position, but what caught my eye was the blue bottle of motor oil on the counter. I instantly ripped the bottle from Mom's hand, opened it up and sniffed motor oil. My drunken mother had mixed up the oil and the baby formula on the counter. I told my aunt and grabbed Chris to wipe his mouth out with paper towels as he continued to spew remnants of oil from his stomach. I gave Mom the sternest look I could, but she barely noticed and slumped over the table. I held Chris tight throughout the night. Thankfully, he rebounded the next morning, and I fed him regular food while savoring a couple of bites.

Luckily, school provided a solution to our malnourishment. In the fall of 1986 at the age of six, a year late, I started Kindergarten. I began mid-fall, so I was escorted to my classroom by the secretary. I can't recall anything other than feeling anxious as I coasted through the taupe-colored hallway. Mrs. Brightland was interrupted as I was nudged into the lively and colorful room. With a big 80's hairdo complemented by a big smile, she signaled for me to come to her in the front of the room. She introduced me to a bunch of kids who didn't look like me, but I couldn't quite put my finger on it. Mrs. Brightland was a sweet teacher, but she didn't tolerate my flippant mouth. I wasn't in class five minutes before I was in the dunce corner.

I was placed in the back of the room beside Rachel, took two sniffs of the air toward her, and yelled, "You stink!"

Mrs. Brightland snapped, "Adam, you come here right now. That was not nice. When we're not nice, you come here and sit in the corner." I got to know that corner very well throughout the year.

Mom's alcoholism was getting increasingly worse and feeding us was not even in her top-five list of priorities. The summers were okay because I could forage for berries, but it was still a struggle to get Mom to do her part. I didn't know how to write back to Eve, so I gave up on the thought of her rescuing us. I quickly realized that survival fell on my shoulders, and I was going to get our food by any means necessary. Lunch time was my favorite part of the school day. Eating chicken nuggets, macaroni, pizza, and even green beans put me in a euphoric state of fullness. However, that feeling was short lived once I became determined to make sure my brothers knew that same feeling.

After I became comfortable with the Kindergarten routine, I began studying the cafeteria process and found a lot of kids throwing away untouched food. Touched or not, I learned to ask if I could have whatever they had left over. I qualified for the free-lunch program, so I spent a lot of that thirty-minute window trying to acquire other kid's food to stuff into my pockets to transfer to my book bag. I had two race car outfits that I tried to wear as often as possible because each set had the most pockets of any clothing I owned. I worried about my brother's all day in school and could not wait to get off the bus to feed them. Mom had stopped breastfeeding Chris by this point, so it was up to me to feed him his jar of baby food or fix his bottle when I got home. He was always happy to see his big brother. He always pronounced my name "Annung," and I just proudly rolled with it. Noah never wasted any time getting into my book bag to see what I had managed to get my hands on that day. This became my after-school routine in our battered Woodville, Virginia home.

At night, the living situation was much more complicated. Regardless of our nocturnal needs, Mom was going to get a space on the queen-sized mattress shared with me, Noah, Chris and later, Moses. She would also get a sizable portion of the thin blanket issued to us. I could usually rip most of it off of her once she was asleep and cover up my brothers. However, Noah and Chris would sleep sidewinder on the opposite side, leaving little room for me to sleep. The most important thing was making sure my brothers were warm. Some nights, I'd find enough space to allow me to curl into a fetal position to lie at the foot of the bed, but it wasn't often. Even without covers, I preferred this to the alternative. Most nights, I laid any available clothes into a pile for a pillow and would make do with the cold, rigid plywood on the floor. It was hard for me to get to sleep, so I'd watch television until the national anthem played and the color swatches signaled the shows were ending for the night. That was my routine, and I accepted it as the man of my family.

Fortunately, we never had to share the bed with any of the strange men mom brought in on so many nights. They would occupy the room for a while but never spent the night. I was grateful for this break from her selfishness, but it didn't mean I could completely avoid them. When Aunt Lilo refused to watch me, Mom took the liberty of showing me where she picked up most of her men at the local dance hall called the Pine Knot. From what I can recall, the club scene was as basic as possible for the middle-aged crowd looking to have a good time. The wood paneling, white cinder block walls and off-white dropped ceiling tiles didn't create the most *happening* atmosphere. However, the 60s and 70s funk and disco music were on point for that crowd. Through the smoky haze from cigarettes, women were pulling men off the wall to dance the night away. I would just watch the ladies' hips gyrating and guys snap their fingers barely stopping just long enough to enjoy bar drinks. Meanwhile, I would be chewing, in tune, a tasteless piece of Bazooka Joe bubble gum that had long since lost its flavor.

My mom would escort and place me in one of the bench seats against the wall while she danced the night away. Some of the women would come over to check on me and tell me how cute and handsome I was, but I never said much. When Mom would come over for a break, I couldn't look at her

- 31 -

because the short skirts openly exposed her genitalia in an effort to attract more men. Her short skirts always made me feel uncomfortable, so I managed to keep my head down most of the night and get lost in my imagination. I'd witnessed her private area more times than I ever wanted to endure. Her method of attraction always enticed the wrong kind of men.

Mom finally met a man who didn't initially use and abuse her; however, it was not at Pine Knot. Uncle Doy had hired some seasonal help for his carpentry business, and she caught the attention of José, who was from Mexico. I didn't understand a word that came out of that man's mouth, but he seemed nice enough to Mom, so I didn't give him too much trouble. He came around frequently, and it was nice to have a consistent man around the house if they had to be there.

Like I stated before, we didn't communicate well, so he wasn't an influential figure in my life. I remember resenting him when he would eat food in front of us and fail to bring anything home. He didn't even bring stuff home for Mom, so we relied on our usual tactics to find sustenance to maintain throughout the day. He became more and more of a nuisance as the months went on. Eventually, Uncle Doy didn't have work for him, but he managed to stick around and began pestering us. More importantly, he began sleeping in our only bed and snored so loud that none of us managed to get any good sleep. He may have been good enough for Mom's needs, but he was essentially worthless to me in my everyday pursuit to eat, or so I thought.

One winter day after recovering from pneumonia, I told him I was hungry. José repeated it back in his broken English, and I nodded in reassurance, so he proceeded outside, grabbed a chicken by the neck, swung it around his head, and separated the head from the body. Snap! The chicken fell to the ground stumbling around without a head for at least ten seconds before falling over. I was awestruck by his strength after that moment. He taught me how to pluck the feathers and boil it in a pot with pepper and salt. That was probably the most meaningful thing he ever did for us. However, that didn't last long.

As José's weeks of unemployment turned into months, he began drinking Milwaukee's Best alongside Mom until they both passed out. *Great*, I thought to myself. *Now I have two fucking drunks to deal with.* The excessive drinking led to abuse, initially out of our sight until one blustery winter day. With just under two feet of snow on the ground, Mom and José managed to get into an argument over something, and out of nowhere, he clenched his fist and struck Mom across the face. As the blood dripped from her lip, I remembered the promise to protect her, but I also recalled José effortlessly snapping that chicken's neck. As I felt my scrawny neck, I noticed some soup cans were within reach. As José was lunging toward her, I quickly grabbed two cans and struck him in the back with one and the face with the other. He turned around with emblazoned eyes and staggered toward my direction. I quickly ran out of the front door to take advantage of the head start Mom gave me by holding him back. I immediately noticed the thickness of the snow slowing me down considerably. It was enough time for José to overpower Mom, tightly pack a snowball into ice form, and strike my right shoulder. I slumped over face down in the snow unable to get up. The next thing I recall was being wrapped up in Mom's arms under a blanket. José didn't come back around for several months after that incident.

September 8th, 1987, José and Mom brought Moses Veliz, into our world. I don't know why my mother kept my sister's father's last name or why she granted Moses with that same name, but the hospital and state of Virginia let her have it. Unfortunately, I don't remember a lot about Moses. He looked a lot like Noah with his light complexion and curly black hair. I was somewhat happy by this revelation because Chris and I were dark complexioned, and now Noah had someone that looked like him. Mom was breastfeeding him, so I didn't have to worry so much initially about how he would get fed. I did recall dipping into his Gerber food supply when no one was around.

After a year, the responsibility once again fell upon me to take care of another little runt. I wasn't sure where I'd heard the term, but the nickname fit. Just like Chris, less than two years earlier, I changed his diapers and fed him baby food when he would cry as Mom regressed back into her drunken state. The last memory I have of Moses being in my care was when Noah was very sick and vomited on the floor. When I went to get something to clean it up, I returned to see Moses slapping his hand in it and licking it. I'd hoped that throughout this process more would come to my recollection of Moses, but sadly this is it. I loved him, but he was just another addition to my routine.

I cannot recall my first, second, or third-grade teachers because I was always either severely ill or thinking about Noah, Chris, and later Moses. I was also growing, so hunger interfered with most of my thoughts during those three and half years. My only escape off the farm was going over to Scott's house in Castleton, Virginia. I don't remember how we became friends, but I looked forward to the Saturdays when I could visit him. I don't know if he knew how good he had it, but everything I had always dreamed of: a loving mother, an attentive father, an older brother, a completely finished house, cars to go wherever they needed, television, a full fridge, and toys from wall to wall were his to take for granted. First thing I always went for were the G.I. Joe soldiers and armory. We quickly assembled our arsenal and prepared our basement battle strategies and began throwing figurines everywhere.

After having our fun, his mom would tell us, usually multiple times, to take a break and get a bite to eat. We would pick up the room and retire to his huge sofa to watch Thunder

Cats and He-Man. I loved his mother. The thought of her bringing me food and juice that I didn't have to steal from the school cafeteria made me feel like a normal child. I always contemplated ways to stay, but knew I had a bigger responsibility to my brothers at home. I'd think to myself, *face it; there's no way to convince anyone to take me and my brothers.* Besides, I never talked about my life to them. I only took those moments to be selfish and just enjoyed being an ordinary, stable child. Ultimately, I'd return to the farm in time to search for dinner to feed the boys.

Memories of the farm were not necessarily all bleak. There were times when I got to be a rascal. When I was chronically ill from multiple bouts of pneumonia, I recall Mom holding my limp body closely and singing *Jesus Loves Me* repeatedly to console me. She also taught me the ABC song before Kindergarten and told me she loved me often. She just couldn't go through the normal motions any loving parent would. Looking back, I credit my need for action over words to her saying that she loved us but rarely displayed with motherly actions. The most meaningful way she expressed her love was buying us something at one of the little country stores – usually candy or a cheap toy.

Sometimes, Mom would meet a worthwhile man who would bring useful things into the house. In late 1986, one of Mom's various boyfriends bought a TV for us, which was complemented by my cousin Bryce's brand new Nintendo shortly thereafter. I was ecstatic because I had something to talk about with Scott and didn't have to wait to see the next level of Super Mario. I could also practice Duck Hunt and Hogan's Alley so I could be as good as Scott. I quickly became obsessed, which landed me in trouble with Mom. She wanted to watch her soap operas, and I told her that I was playing the fucking game. Without saying a word, mom broke a twig off of one of the bushes near the house, came back in, and wailed it across my legs yelling, "You ain't gonna speak to me that way! Now y'all get outside and do something!" After the initial shock wore off, I realized that it was the first time my mother had hit me. The welts over my legs and arms had been a constant reminder for a week before I was brave enough to go near the video games again. Of course, it helped that I used Bryce as my shield and stayed in his lap.

However, Bryce didn't help to suppress my fears for long when he brought his collection of horror flicks into the house. As a six-year-old, self-proclaimed man of the house, I wanted to be brave like Bryce, so I kept my eyes open for as much as I could. *Friday the 13th* and *Nightmare on Elm Street* movies were his favorites to watch with his girlfriend, LaShaunda. I often interfered with their couch time, but they didn't seem to mind. In most of those instances, I was left gripping the covers and occasionally staying hidden underneath them until the gore subsided. LaShaunda would grip Bryce as he confidently held her until the movie was over. I was terrified for weeks at a time after watching those movies, but never turned down Bryce's offer to watch. Afterward, Bryce and LaShaunda would often disappear, and I'd search for Mom to console me. If she was drunk, I'd check on my brothers to assure myself they hadn't been hacked to pieces. My vivid imagination always ran wild after watching those movies. Thankfully, Jaevon would take the initiative to convince to venture outside when he visited.

My cousin, Jaevon, would visit every so often donning camouflage and black boots to take us on new adventures around the farm. He was proud of his service in the Army, and he wore that standard issue uniform with absolute pride. I don't ever recall seeing him in another outfit. He was the only reason I ever set foot in the wooded area of the property. Like I mentioned before, I was terrified of the farm in broad daylight, so I could only imagine the horrors that lurked in the woods. However, Jaevon's military skills came in handy when it was time to face the natural environment with its snapping turtles, snakes, or frogs around the pond. I was much less fearful when he was around.

The pond was yet another area that kept my anxiety keyed up. A simple body of water that would be serene to normal country children stoked my imagination in the most negative way. The pond was on the left side of the driveway coming in, so I made sure to steer my legs into the right-side grass to avoid the ducks, swans, and any other animal that would pay a visit to the waterhole. Almost every time I threw a rock into the pond to enjoy the ripple effect, bullfrogs and peepers would seemingly pop out from underneath the cattails. I was always terrified of frogs, which Noah always took pleasure in chasing me around the farm with one squirming between his little fingers. Like Uncle Doy, Mom pointed out snapping turtles tending to their own affairs and decided to share the old wives tale about how if they get a hold of you, they won't let go until the next thunderstorm. I steered clear of all turtles to avoid any risk whatsoever. That wasn't even the worst of it. The misinformation from my mother that scared me the most was her guidance about staying away from black snakes; they were bad luck if they crossed your path, and their poisonous bite would likely kill us. I wouldn't uncover the truth about snakes in general until my tenth-grade biology class eleven years later.

However, Jaevon's marksmanship with his rifle eliminated my anxiety altogether. When I watched him blow a black snake's head off as it slithered across the gravel driveway, I had to run toward it to watch it squirm uncontrollably during the last moments of its life. He also managed to pick up others with his bare hands and move them away from us. Over time, I felt that this was probably the best thing since I never had a good feeling watching animals die. Nevertheless, Jaevon would find other ways to impress me with his marksmanship. One time, he saw a snapping turtle floating across the middle of the pond, lifted his rifle up and severed its head with a single, effortless shot. The rest of the body spun around in a circle spewing enough blood eventually turning the pond a beet red color.

Our greatest expeditions with Jaevon led us to the river on the back end of the farm. With our makeshift fishing poles and worms, we set out to catch some rainbow trout and catfish. I didn't catch many fish; probably because we were some noisy little kids, but I'll never forget the majestic flow of the river. Playing alongside the bank was among some of the most joyful and free expressions I had as a child on the farm. Without a doubt, our explorations with Jaevon set the stage for my adventures with Noah as my sidekick.

Most of these excursions didn't have good outcomes. As children without too many boundaries, we set out to do whatever we wanted while rarely expressing any sort of caution. Correction; Noah was the risk taker, and I was somewhat more cautious. Noah had a thing for teasing the swans and geese. One random summer day, I eventually warmed up to skipping rocks in the pond when Noah got the bright idea to throw gravel toward the flock to stop them from honking at us. Little did we know that honking was a warning to steer clear of their eggs. Nevertheless, our throws were coming up short, and Noah wanted to get closer. Just about that time, they were midway across the pond in full attack mode before we could get moving. Naturally, I outran Noah with my longer, more developed legs, and he bore the brunt of the attack. There was nothing I could do for him, but run to the house to get Mom. Uncle Doy and Jaevon came out to assist, but Noah's bare back and legs had several abrasions. For most children, this learning moment would've developed a reasonable sense of fear, but we would always go back for more. I never got caught, and Noah had to learn to throw harder and run earlier. Yes, we were brats, but we didn't know any better at the time. Bored kids will do just about anything to make the time pass.

Uncle Doy eventually put us to work to make some of that time useful. Noah and I eventually learned to pick up eggs from the chicken coup. I hated that job. My over exaggerated panic level when I encountered a hen might as well have been a close up with an ostrich. Plus, there were only a few things that smelled worse than chicken manure on the bottom of my shoes. My shirt-covered nose defense against the stench rarely provided any relief from the reeking fumes. Nevertheless, I had a job to do, so it was get in and get out for me.

While I managed to fear the chickens like every other farm animal, Noah had an affinity for them, especially the little downy chicks. Anyone raised on a farm knows you don't mess with a hen's chicks. Time after time, Noah would come in the house crying with his bowl full of eggs, face, arms, and legs bloodied because he always had to pet those chicks. I have to admit that they were cute but only from a distance. Noah never made the connection, no matter how much I told him to leave the babies alone. I always knew to run whether he made it out unscathed or not. Noah's fearlessness always got the better of him in situations that required speed on foot, but he was the bravest kid I knew. However, I always resented him for chasing me with those critters. That led to a lot of payback once I caught my breath from running.

Like any other pair of brothers, we constantly fought over nothingness. Some of the time, I just wanted to be alone, and he kept pestering me. Most of the time what we fought about had to do with the snake, frog, worm, salamander, bug, or whatever other creature he could get his hands on to chase me with around the farm. My revenge always ended up with us in front of the television and catching him off guard to smother him with our bean bag. I took advantage of being stronger than him, so I would sit on it and give him just enough air to apologize before letting him up. We repeated this until one day I decided that I wasn't going to let him up. I had no concept of being smothered since I hadn't experienced it, so I continued to scare him until I heard him wince. I laughed while he started to cry as he was leaving the room. He came back with a pair of orange-handled scissors and threatened to throw them at me if I didn't leave. It was night time and being terrified of the dark, I held my ground and stood in the exact same spot. Without hesitation, he threw the pair of orange-handled scissors with a precision that lodged the blade into my right hand. I had my head turned, so when I looked down to see scissors sticking out of my hand; I released a scream that silenced everything going on in the house. Mom strolled in drunk and pushed Noah to the ground yelling and grabbed my hand while I was crying. She just yanked the scissors right out. I continued to bawl as she held me in her arms. Noah and I had an unspoken truce after that incident.

The dumbest thing my brother and I did was teasing a dog named Bear. Fittingly, he was the size of a full-grown St. Bernard but had a yellowish-orange fur coat with a grizzly-like face and was as mean as the devil himself. The day Uncle Doy brought him home, he warned us never ever to go near Bear. I don't know who or what the farm needed protecting from, but if this dog ever broke loose of his chain, he'd certainly get the job done. All of the fear I had designated for the other farm animals suddenly vanished and concentrated on this one freak of nature.

That healthy level of fear subsided when Noah and I got the idea to make the beast bark. We were overconfident the chains would hold him, but we stayed near the door with our handful of gravel. We traded turns chucking a few pieces of gravel his way and watched him extend his chain to the point of standing on his hind legs. We had done this multiple times before but never really hit the dog.

This time was different. Both of us managed to get multiple hits and piss him off something awful. The drool running from his mouth and white foam spewing from his flaps weren't enough of a warning sign for two dumb kids to stop. The chains came loose from around the crab-apple tree, and he charged directly towards us. Wide-eyed, I dragged Noah in and slammed the screen main door as he charged into it. Mom, drunk again, was listening to us scream incoherently, but she managed to hear, "Bear got loose!" I'll never understand why she decided to go outside, but she did and in seemingly no time, she was back in with a chunk of her upper arm missing. Uncle Doy managed to come to her rescue and tie Bear back to the tree. My memory fades, which probably stemmed from the shock of seeing so much blood flow from Mom's arm onto her clothes. When Mom returned with her arm bandaged up, I apologized and promised never to tease or go near that dog again. Seeing mom hurt always took an emotional toll on me.

Unfortunately, this wasn't the first time I saw my mother hurt. In addition to being an alcoholic, she was a victim of domestic violence from multiple men. I never understood what my mom saw in all of the men she brought home. I was only hurt by one, which I explained earlier in the chapter, but for the most part the men didn't interact with me or my brothers very much. Instead, they shared cans of beer together, disappeared for a while back to the bedroom and then left. Most of the beatings took place while I was at school. One of

Mom's eyes would be swollen shut, or her lip would be busted wide open. I added worrying about my mother to the routine.

Getting off the bus one first-grade day, Mom came rushing down the driveway. Some days she was at the bus stop to greet me and other days she wasn't. I didn't think much of it since I was on my own most of the time. However, this time was different. I stopped almost immediately, my eyes widened as she came closer with blood running off her chin. This time she had been beaten worse than any time I'd seen before. Her wig was half removed from her head, her nose was crooked, some of her teeth were missing and her lip was split, which created a waterfall effect of blood streaming from her mouth. She reeked of beer and was covered in blood, but I knew I had to hold her. I told her it would be okay and that I would stay home to take care of her until she got better.

My wonderment escaped my silent thoughts to ask, "Why do you let people do this to you, Momma?"

She replied, "Because I love them, Adam."

I didn't understand, so I retorted, "But they don't love you back." I missed the next few days of school making sure that bad man didn't come back to hurt her. I remember starving while tending to Mom's needs since my easy access to cafeteria food was gone.

During that time, Kat Hardy, a social worker came by to introduce herself. Luckily, my mom was sober and recovered from her beating with the exception of some scarring, so she must have appeared somewhat reasonable. It was a rather quick visit since my Mom didn't welcome her into our home. She appeared antsy afterward, but being a youngster; I couldn't make the connection as to what would make her feel that way. Looking back now, I missed nearly two months of Kindergarten, mainly due to chronic illness and disliking school, but somehow managed to be passed along. First grade was proving to be a similar trend, and I can only guess that the county decided that it was time to intervene. It was amazing we got to stay with Mom as long as we did, but I guess the case against her was irrefutable in the end. This tense relationship between Kat and my mother would continue for a couple more years before she would be embedded in my memory.

A new addition to our tumultuous routine included looking out for any strange cars coming down the driveway. Anytime we saw cars; we either had to hide in the house, duck down in the fields or stand by in one of the nearest sheds until Mom appeared to tell us it was safe. Mom informed us that these bad people wanted to take us away, but she was going to make sure that never happened by getting us back to California. Kat usually arrived in a blue or white car, exchanged assertive-toned words with Mom, and always left empty handed. A walk around the house would have exposed unlivable conditions for first-world children, but Kat always made a beeline back to her vehicle and sped off leaving a trail of dust as her heavy car barreled down on the dirt driveway.

The closest call came toward the end of my second-grade year. I knew I was different because I wore the same unwashed, undersized racecar jumpsuits all of the time, so I avoided school as much as possible. Kids who used to play with me were complaining of my smell, which was a foul mix of body odor from bathless weeks and clothes that sat on the line too long after the rain and mildewed. My brothers and I were satisfied living on fruit, but I would manage to attend school for no other reason than to sneak food from the cafeteria.

By this point, Kat had had enough of my mother's games and was likely aware of her alcohol abuse. She made a habit of coming by unannounced and snooping around the property. On one occasion, Noah and I discovered trash bags full of women's clothing in one of the abandoned sheds and began trying each article. As I stated before, bored kids will do anything to make the time pass by, so we put the clothes on and hopped all over the stacked, untorn trash bags. Kat stealthily arrived, and we knew the drill; hide until she left. The portions of torn, rusted tin from the roof exposed light, allowing us to peek at the familiar car roaring down our dirt road. There were no formal greetings this time. Kat stormed out of the car and demanded to see each of us. Mom had Moses, who was crying uncontrollably, and I had no idea where Chris was. Mom lashed out saying that she had no right since she wasn't related to us. At about this time, I looked back at Noah, who had uncovered a snake under a tire. Naturally, I froze but managed to overcome it when Noah smilingly reached for the snake. This was no ordinary black snake like those that crossed our paths nearly every day. The golden scales and head standing forced me to protect my brother. It was the first time I had managed to overcome my zoophobia, but I still had to balance between flight and staying put. As the snake closed in on us with his creepy tongue directed our way, I was never more relieved to hear Kat's car making an exit. I didn't wait for her to completely make it down the driveway before grabbing Noah's hand and darting out the back as fast as I could. Mom heard me screaming, "A gold snake tried to kill us! Help!" Mom directed us into the old house and calmed me down. Of course, Noah was all smiles and laughing. Then Mom asked us why we had on girl clothes. We glanced over our attire, took the clothes off without explanation and stayed indoors for the rest of the day.

At this time, I was an eight-year-old in third grade and Noah was in Kindergarten. Mom took Kat seriously after that heated exchange. I no longer called the shots about school. Mom took a forceful tone and even threatened to whip me with a switch from the blackberry bush if I tested her. By now, I was constantly worried about Chris since he would have to fend for himself until we returned from school. At least when

Noah was there, the two could occupy each other, so I wouldn't have to worry. Chris and Moses consumed most of my thoughts that year. I knew they were going hungry, and weren't being tended to since Mom's drunken stupor was becoming more and more her normal state of mind.

Although I hadn't managed to train Noah to gather food at school, I continued my cafeteria ritual. Negotiating and taking food kids wouldn't eat (except hush puppies; not a single one of us liked those damned things) was the norm, and I became known for it. My pockets and book bag were stuffed with the daily rations to split between my brothers or to spread out over the weekends. However, one day my daily drill was noticed by our principal, Mr. Chester. I was stuffing green beans in one of the pockets of my racecar outfit when he approached me with a friendly greeting. My eyes widened since I knew he must have seen me, but I didn't notice his presence. He smiled and looked down into my eyes, "Adam, can I buy you some ice cream and talk to you for a little while?" Excitedly, I accepted his offer and picked out a creamsicle. We sat down at one of the tables, and he encouraged me to talk even though the bell rang for the next class. In between savoring my orange delight, he asked me to tell him about my home life. My mother never mentioned anything about talking to strangers or school faculty, so I naively revealed some of my routine over the course of about a half hour. However, I excluded the part about stealing food from the school cafeteria. I can't recall everything I told him that day, but he smiled, patted me on the back and escorted me back to class. That was probably the beginning of the end of life as I knew it.

Section Two

It Takes a Village...and Then Some!

*One day, in retrospect, the years of struggle
will strike you as the most beautiful.*

Sigmund Freud

*Not everything that is faced can be changed,
but nothing can be changed until it is faced.*

James Baldwin

*When peoples care for you and cry for you,
they can straighten out your soul.*

Langston Hughes

*There is always one moment in childhood
when the door opens and lets the future in.*

Graham Greene

Chapter Three

White Foster

October 6, 1989: After months of threatening,
Rappahannock Social Services finally did it. Up to that point,
I'd missed 142 days of school including 57 days in
Kindergarten and 12 days before being taken away early that
third-grade year.

Social Services Report:

> *This child was brought into care on an Emergency
> Removal Order. The child's mother is allegedly
> alcohol addicted and she has refused to enter
> treatment for this problem.*
>
> *The child was physically neglected. The home
> environment was a detriment to the child's health and
> well-being.*
>
> *...At the time this agency assumed custody, the child
> was living in a two-bedroom house with his natural
> mother and three siblings. The home was extremely
> unsanitary and physically unsafe for a young child...*
>
> *The child did not attend school regularly and his
> school performance suffered.*

Most of us often take the people who have had the biggest impact in our lives for granted. For better or worse, I will never forget the day our local social services finally retrieved my brothers and me from an otherwise normal school day. It wasn't too long after that get-together with my principal that Noah and I were intercepted at school. Chris and Moses were taken directly from our shanty farmhouse.

Kat Hardy arrived at the elementary school to pull me out of my third-grade classroom one early Friday afternoon. I was called to the office and told to pack up my stuff to leave for the day. Kat greeted me at the office door and escorted Noah and me out to her car. We buckled our seatbelts as instructed and naturally inquired as to where we were going. This wasn't the first time I'd come in contact with Kat, but this was definitely the first time I'd been inside the car I spent so much time avoiding. She nonchalantly told us we were going to see a movie. When I asked if Chris and Moses would be coming too, she replied that they would be alright. I guess she told the fib to keep us calm during the ride to the opposite end of Woodville. I didn't immediately know where we were, but when we arrived at a huge white Victorian home on the side of a hill with a white woman and two of her children standing at the end of the sidewalk, I knew we weren't at a damned movie theater.

Kat prompted us to get out, so we nervously obeyed her order. Amber, my new foster sister, was the first to greet us with an enthusiastic, smiling "hi!" She was donning a long dress, straight blonde hair and piercing blue eyes. She looked different somehow, so I decided not to respond out of caution. Next, Madeline, our new foster mother, introduced herself and cordially ended with, 'It's so nice to finally meet you boys." Again, I didn't know how to respond. She reminded me of the little Southern ladies I'd seen in the cookbooks at the supermarket. Then I started wondering if she cooked like they did in the magazines. The awkward silence was broken when Darren, our new foster brother, invited us to play with him. We saw toys, so we quickly followed the little red-headed boy to his intricate construction site. He was in the process of bulldozing a road to get to his other pretend town. I was impressed with his layout and tried not to intrude with the dump truck I chose. Kat exchanged words with Madeline and gave us a brief good bye before heading out. Just like that, she left. We wouldn't see her again for a few weeks.

Later on that evening, Matthew, our new and oldest foster brother, introduced himself as he entered the house that evening. He managed a quick *hi* and went straight to his room. That *hi* was the extent of our conversations with him for the first week. He spent most weekends with his father, so I don't recall much about him. However, he always wore a coon skin cap, which I constantly sported when he wasn't around, and fringe leather jackets with matching moccasins. The dude was always in full mountain man mode. He also sported a curl in the front center of his forehead resembling the Superman from the old comic books.

James, our new foster dad, entered from work just in time for dinner. He sat down and looked at us, said hello and started shoveling food toward his mouth. His entrance will forever be seared into my memory. His stained button down shirt exposed his hairy belly and his burly physique clumsily bumped into chairs and other furniture around the house. That feature alone made him intimidating. He was by far the largest man I'd ever met by that point in my life, but his revolting odor was something I had the hardest time getting used to. He was a seafood manager for a supermarket chain, so his malodorous profession trailed home in the evening. That first night I nearly lost my appetite from the smell of raw seafood permeating through the dining room.

Eventually, we were led to our room, which had bunk beds. I beamed and stared in disbelief at my very own bed. For the first time in my life, I was finally sleeping without negotiating bed space between mother and other siblings. For the first time in months, I didn't have to worry about getting crowded out and sleeping on the floor. Madeline made us brush our teeth, which was something new and coaxed us into bed. To say it was a long day would be a gross understatement. It was downright traumatic once I realized that we weren't going back home. As the lights went out, worry deleted that brief period of elation as I stared into the dark. I always kept the lights or television on to keep watch over my brothers until the Star Spangled Banner played in the middle of the night, and color swatches took over the set.

I didn't sleep much that first night. I felt betrayed by Mom and Kat, and didn't trust my new family. I was afraid for Chris and Moses. I thought they were on their own, unprotected and unfed that night and nights leading up to our first visit with one another. I don't know why I possessed an innate nurturing capability, but my life seemingly came crashing down that night as I decided it ultimately wasn't enough to keep my family together. No one could convince me otherwise. I blamed myself for getting sick too often and failing to protect my mother. I eventually cried myself to sleep that night, but I would carry that burden around until my collegiate years.

The next morning was the official start of my new life. I was still hoping it was all a bad dream, and when I opened my eyes, I'd arise from the cold-wooden floor and find my family in bed. I peered out from underneath my blanket to find Noah still asleep while still in my very own bed. For the first time since I could remember, the smell of breakfast saturated the house. It didn't take much to impress me in the way of food, so eating a normal breakfast that I didn't have to scrounge around for was a welcomed change. Noah and I sat at the table with the Resnick family in a dining room equipped with tables and enough chairs for everyone. This was a first for me outside of the cafeteria table at school. I stared again in disbelief at the intact walls, doors, and bathrooms. It would take several months before I would be used to not peeing outside wherever I pleased or holding my excrement for days at a time because I didn't want to walk in the blustery cold to go to the outhouse.

Madeline spent a good part of that weekend trying to fix us up. She took the allowance that social services provided her and bought us new clothes and shoes. I wouldn't have to wear the same outfit for an entire week. My pants came down below my ankles. My shirts fit. My shoes fit. I wasn't familiar with name brands, so I was genuinely grateful for the new wardrobe.

Next on the agenda was addressing our hygiene issues. While Noah wouldn't have been too bad, I was as funky as could be. I hated the bucket of cold water we bathed in at Aunt Lilo's, so I had avoided a bath for months before we arrived at the Resnicks. In addition, Noah's biracial lineage blessed him with long, black curls that just draped from his head. My hair, on the other hand, hadn't met a comb, brush or pic since I arrived in Virginia. I can't recall my hair care in California, but I can recall with absolute certainty that nothing touched my head in Virginia up to that point. I was nappy, happy, and that's just how I rolled on the farm. As a result, the matted mess on my head was suitable for a bird's nest. This put Madeline in panic mode because she had never taken in black kids before. Luckily she lived next to an interracial couple with two girls of their own who were able to give her some pointers on black hair care. Unfortunately, the only thing that could relax the demonic patch that sat atop my head would've been a full-blown exorcism. After a whole bottle of detangling shampoo, a failed attempt with scissors, a broken clipper set and a face full of tears; I had my first haircut.

The haircut was the worst of it, but my skin was also extremely dry and ashy. I'm not referring to the ashiness that occurs when being out in the cold too long, or from dehydration. I'm referring to the alligator skin, looking like I'd been dipped in a flour bucket ashy! Lotion and other oil-based body rubs were non-existent to me. Mom used to apply Vaseline on me, but she had to catch me to do it. Madeline went into full Greased Lightning mode and rubbed me from head to toe with coconut oil that her neighbors recommended. I probably looked and smelled like a Bounty candy bar when she was done with me. While my skin probably sung her graces, I was distressed from the swift transformation. I probably lost a couple of pounds in sheer dirt that came off my body that weekend. Regardless, I was going to have to learn how to accept this new direction my life was headed.

That following Monday, Noah and I hopped on a new bus and continued with our school year at Rappahannock Elementary. Matthew, Amber, and Darren were homeschooled, so they didn't have to get on the bus. I don't remember much else other than uneventfully completing my third-grade year. Conversely, there wasn't a single day that went by without thinking about Chris and Moses. The overpowering sadness took its toll on me during the weeks following our transfer into a stranger's home.

Within a month after intercepting us, Kat coordinated a visit for Noah, Chris, Moses and me to meet one last time at a centrally-located McDonald's. I looked, smiled and looked again. It was the best feeling I had had in weeks. I got to hug Chris and heard him pronounce my name "Annung" one more time. Chris, Noah, and I would reconnect in a couple of years. However, that would be the last time I saw Moses. My chances to reconnect with him since have been unsuccessful. I can recall giving Moses a teddy bear hug and telling him that I missed him. I touched his tight, black curls, and he smiled in recognition of me. Then he was placed in his car seat and returned to his new family. That visit alleviated a lot of my stress to know my brothers weren't locked in cages. No one told me anything specific, so I could only imagine the worst. That was the unfortunate side of having such a vivid imagination.

That summer of 1990 gave us time to get associated with each other and establish some sort of pecking order. It wasn't recognized on paper, but I was going to be damned if Noah and I were at the bottom. Discipline was rarely dished out by Mom, so boundaries didn't exist from our standpoint. Madeline changed all of that, mainly with the help of Darren. I quickly learned through Noah that he was going to tattle tell everything we uttered and did in his presence. Noah had picked up a bad cussing habit from me, which was considered acceptable language in the Starks' household. The difference was I knew when to shut the spigot off, and he didn't. When Noah dropped a "fuck" or "shit" in his conversation, Darren jumped up to inform Madeline. Noah would get called into the kitchen to sit down while she wet a bar of soap and stuck it in his mouth for five minutes or so depending on the severity of the word. So, rule number one for me was absolutely no swearing at the Resnick's house, or at least not in front of their kids. Noah never quite picked up on that. I lost count of the number of times that boy was reprimanded with soap tastings. Poor Noah even got to the point where he stuck that nasty bar in his mouth by himself. It only happened to me once when I yelled a bunch of obscenities at Amber and finished with, "Now stick that in your pipe and eat it!" It made no sense whatsoever, but it was enough to taste test a bar of pink soap for ten minutes.

I really tried to help Noah, but I did more learning than assisting. He kind of kept to himself after a while because he was always in trouble for something. One area I could help him was at the dinner table. I was a recovering survivalist, so they could have laid table scraps in a dog bowl, and I would've made pretend exquisite cuisine with it. Noah, on the other hand, rejected any vegetable put in front of him, especially brussel sprouts, green beans, and lima beans. His punishment was to sit there until he cleared his plate. While we got up to play Nintendo or watch a movie, he would sit there in that hard-ass chair until it was bed time without even sniffing in the plate's direction. After a few nights of this nonsense, I would sneak back into the kitchen and clear his plate so he could get up and be a normal kid. I hated to think what would have happened had I been caught, but it was worth the risk for my brother. This devious little deed continued throughout our stint there.

I wasn't always sneaky enough though. Some old habits were hard to break, so when I got caught stealing food from the cabinets and tucking a stash underneath my bed, Madeline explained to me that there would always be enough for all of us to eat. She made me promise never to do that again and reassured me that I would never go hungry in her care. I accepted that lesson since there were always three meals a day, but I never quite got the hang of the rest of the rules. I received my share of spankings, but rules were for kids who gave a damn about being civilized. For better or worse, I'd set my sights on being a hellion from the get go.

Spankings were just an addition to the routine. I wanted to see how far my boundaries extended, which were not very far for Madeline. She did not play that. Her small frame had no qualms about bending my lanky frame across her knee. Hangers, wooden spoons, a shoe, bare hands or whatever she could get her hands on whilst bent over her knee. No one was spared if we stepped out of line, but I never kept tabs on who was being spanked. Once, I heard the first whap connecting with skin, I got the hell out of dodge. The worse spanking I ever received was during a wet, bare ass-to-ping pong-paddle episode. The paddle ridges gripped my ass like a needled mitt and the hole in the center suction cupped what little meat I had to call a behind back in those days. After that incident, I never wanted that torture device reserved for my hind parts ever again. It was the last straw for Madeline who told me night in and night out about staying in the shower too long. It was nothing for me to stay in for twenty to thirty minutes at a time and run the hot water out before anyone else had a chance to get in. After I recovered from the initial shock of being clean, I enjoyed the concept of the shower. It reminded me of playing in the rain and splashing in puddles without being stuck with the mildew smell afterward. That reminiscent memory was over the night Madeline met me outside the door with that paddle. I've never been able to play a game of ping pong since without thinking of that moment. I had about as much luck avoiding discipline for my unashamed mischief as I did with animals around the house.

Darren introduced me to Snuggles, the pudgy and grumpy family pug, by shaking his foot in the dog's face and letting him snap and tug relentlessly at his shoes while being dragged around the floor. I wasn't amused as much as I was cautious.

To be truthful, I was terrified of Snuggles. I thought he was an alien cat with a gremlin-like face. He constantly sneered, and I steered clear of him at first. Eventually, I warmed up to shaking my foot and letting him tug at it.

The worst conflict with the alien dog occurred when Amber got mad at me over taking something of value from her and she yelled, "Sic 'em, Snuggles!" while I was sitting on the living room couch. That pint-sized demon spawn charged full steam ahead, but I was comfortable enough by that point to not to take his stubby little legs seriously. However, I wrongly doubted his ability to jump as he used my legs as a springboard to jump up and snag my upper lip. I pushed the little shit away from my face and shrieked in pain as my cupped hands began to fill with blood. Madeline ran in to grab me and demanded to know what happened. Fighting through crying, hyperventilating and a swollen lip, I yelled, "Snuggles bit me because of Amber!" Madeline escorted me to the bathroom sink trailing blood throughout the house. When she was done washing and bandaging, the bathroom looked like a murder scene. The last thing I remember was holding an ice pack to my lip for the rest of the night. To this day, I'm reminded of that scar every time I shave.

Madeline and James bought other dogs, and they were more bashful and less scary than Snuggles. Matthew was an avid hunter, so he liked beagles. Darren looked up to him, so he naturally wanted what Matthew had access to. Darren's birthday fell on Christmas Day, and I'm almost certain that's when he received his first dog. Darren chose the name Jubidoo for his beagle. That poor dog was run over by a passing car right in front of the house and had to be put down. Darren was so torn apart by it that his parents replaced Jubidoo with another beagle.

Darren and I played with that dog all of the time and one day got the idea to let him practice swimming in a rain barrel. We were tossing him from close range before I got the bright idea to back up and see how far I could toss him. Well, I backed up too far, and Jubidoo's back hit the rim of the barrel breaking his spine instantly. He couldn't even make it across as Darren pulled him out before he sank. Darren carried him inside, and once again his beloved dog had to be put to sleep. Darren decided that the name Jubidoo was bad luck and never bestowed another pet with that name. It was the first time I expressed a sense of genuine guilt for my poor behavior. For some reason, Madeline decided it would be a good idea to get me a bird to teach me about responsibility.

My gentler side emerged with the arrival of a yellow and green parakeet I named Spanky. I took pride in watering it, daily feedings and changing its cage on a weekly basis. I was getting the hang of the routine and started gaining some confidence in myself until he decided to escape while I was cleaning the cage. I can only assume I'd left the gate open. Nevertheless, I finished putting his cage back together and kept the gate open in hopes that he would fly right back in. After a few minutes, I grew impatient from sitting in a corner and waiting. I tried to coax the parakeet into the cage by chasing him around the room to no avail. Amber came into the room to investigate the commotion and joined my fray trying to help me catch him. While she was chasing it around, I got a broom to hopefully trap it and grab it. I didn't envision what that plan looked like beforehand, but I saw the perfect opportunity when Spanky flew through the center of the room and swung for the fences. The broom connected with the fragile bird plunging him into the wall. That was the end of Spanky. I tried to explain to Madeline that he flew into the broom, but I'm pretty sure she didn't buy it. We buried Spanky in a shoe box, and that was the end of my bird caring days. I was simply going to have to find other ways to occupy my time without animals at my mercy.

In the midst of those tough lessons, I was still dealing with anger and uncertainty that I couldn't quite manage to convey to anyone. I didn't even fully understand it, so there was little if any hope of articulating it to Madeline. I accepted the fact that I was now a ward of the state and the Resnicks were my family. They wanted me to act and dress differently. There were so many rules and commands that I couldn't seem to function. Aggravated by my plight in life, I acted out constantly. However, Madeline refused to give up on me and included us in everything her family had the opportunity to do.

There were a few activities other than eating that would allow me to reach a more mellow state of mind.

Any trip in the big Buick always felt like an adventure for me. The red interior reminded me of our apartment back in California. Pretending to drive from the backseat was one of my favorite things to do. Her kids always fought over the window seat, but I liked the middle so I could see where I was pretending to drive. Long trips and family vacations were always a blast with the Resnicks; especially the one to South Carolina visiting Madeline's sister. She had a great big pool, and the warm breeze was enough to calm my tensions. We enjoyed fresh seafood that tasted better than the stuff James brought home from his job and splashed around in their in-ground swimming pool.

Of course, before we arrived, I got on one of my stubborn streaks at a rest stop. It was one of our first stops, so Madeline encouraged everyone to get out to use the restroom. I claimed that I didn't have to go. She tried to convince me, but I was adamant about not going. Well, no less than 10 minutes on the interstate, I really had to go badly. The next rest stop had to have been at least another two hours and away, so I crossed my legs, held my breath or daydreamed anything I could think of to take my mind off the swelling urge. We finally arrived at another rest stop, and I took off cross-legged toward the restroom signs. I made it to the self-imposed finish line, fumbled my fingers trying to untie my drawstring and wet my pants right in front of the urinal. Sullenly, I returned to the car with a big wet spot seeping down the front of my pants. Madeline made sure to give me the I- told-you-so lecture while unpacking my pants to change. So there I was with the reeking stench of piss the rest of the trip down. Thankfully, the fun went on as planned afterward. Regardless of how difficult I was at times, Madeline never gave up on making us feel included.

Madeline also made sure Noah and I felt special on our birthdays and Christmas. Birthdays with cake and candles didn't happen every year with Mom, so I tried to be extra good on those days to show my appreciation. Come to think of it, I was probably very good leading up to those days as well just to ensure my presents didn't get sent back. Once Madeline introduced me to coconut cake, there was no substitute. Maybe it had to do with constantly smelling like a Bounty bar, but eating it was a much better experience than putting it all over to avoid looking like a flour child.

To this date, Thanksgiving is my favorite holiday. One of my warmest memories comes from my first Thanksgiving with the Resnick family. As a nine-year-old child who was grateful for a piece of bologna between two slices of bread that I had to pick the mold off of, seeing that big turkey at the center of the table surrounded by green beans, corn, gravy, mashed potatoes, stuffing, biscuits, cranberry sauce, and ham with pineapple on top, which made me feel like a little prince at the head of the table. I didn't blink the entire night because I didn't want my catalog dreams to vanish. It didn't seem real until I sunk my teeth into that bite of turkey complemented with cranberry sauce. I ate three full plates that night and burped to make room for her homemade apple pie. Once the turkey bones were exposed, Darren and Amber fought over who got the wishbone and all of us rowdy kids tried to get a hand in to break it in our favor. That first Thanksgiving was my most euphoric holiday memory, and there hasn't been a Thanksgiving since that has passed without remembering that celebration.

Christmas at the Resnicks was even better. It wasn't just a cheap toy from the gas station I'd manage to tear up within a matter of days or a granted wish of not freezing to death. Instead, we were warm and had several presents under the tree including one big gift for each child. Madeline knew how to put on a show at Christmas time. I recall being mesmerized by the lights and angel atop the Christmas tree. Before foster care, I only saw Christmas trees in the Sears Christmas-edition catalogs, but the Resnicks' tree was even better than those; theirs was real to the touch! On Christmas Day, Darren would wake us up around 4AM, and we'd dance around the Christmas tree hoping to make enough noise to wake Madeline and James out of bed. Before we did anything though, Madeline would have one of us read the story of the birth of Jesus Christ followed by the recital of a thankful prayer. She reminded us about the true reason for the season and the importance of being grateful for what we had. I may have appreciated the spiel as I grew older, but that wrapping paper was distracting almost to the point of hypnosis. After Madeline rested her case for Jesus, we probably looked like a barrel of monkeys tearing into those boxes.

In between holidays and birthdays, video games proved to be my great escape. I could get lost for hours playing Nintendo or Sega Genesis and felt like the rest of the world didn't exist. I obsessed about beating every game and managed to do so within a week or two. Unlike Bryce, who took his Nintendo when he went to spend the night at his girlfriend's house, the Resnick's game systems were permanent fixtures. Of course, we didn't have the luxury of saving our spot in the game back then, so when it was time to go outside or go to bed, that was it. I would get terribly angry and go stomping out of the room mumbling vulgarities under my breath. However, at bedtime I came up with an idea to cover the Nintendo's red light power indicator with a hand towel right before bed. When Darren caught me, I was afraid he was going to tell, but he stayed up and played with me until the wee hours of the morning. We were definitely bonding by that point, but that was probably not one of my more positive influential moments.

It wasn't until I started off the year failing courses in the fourth grade that my obsession with video games caused problems. When I revealed my first report card Madeline asked, "How can you figure out how to beat these games in a matter of weeks, but you can't figure out your reading, writing, and arithmetic?" She would remind me that I was failing every subject and how important it was to get good grades in school. I brought her a second report card that was almost an exact replica of the first. That's when she had had enough and decided to take what I considered drastic action. I could have handled a spanking for every bad grade, but when she decided to take the video games away completely, I once again thought my life was over. I bawled and ballyhooed, rolling all over the floor trying to get her to reconsider, but when I looked to see if she was buying it, she hadn't budged from her original cross-armed position; so naturally I tried again. I got to wear myself out trying to cry throughout my pathetic attempt at a negotiation. However, Madeline wasn't playing around. The next report card showed improvement, but it wasn't good enough to earn my games back. I cried again, but I had to accept the fact that I was going to have to apply myself in a world I had absolutely no interest in occupying. I hated the rules.

The other issues I had with the home were Madeline's persistent demands to use manners and doing chores. I wouldn't come to appreciate either until much later in life, but I'm grateful for her effort. Today, cleanliness provides me with a sense of consistency in a seemingly chaotic environment. My mannerisms have helped me land opportunities that otherwise wouldn't have been available, but that's for another book.

As her child, I had to do the dishes a few times a week and initially tried to cheat by washing and rinsing with a half-assed approach. Matthew would always provide a pre-inspection for Madeline reminding me to do them right, but I rarely listened to his recommendation. Madeline would enter the kitchen and do a spot check and made me do them again or until I did it right. I eventually learned that it was just quicker to do them right the first time. Unfortunately, my stubborn streak blinded me from realizing this early on. I could've saved so much time, but I usually had to learn the hard way.

Manners were also a hard concept for me to grasp. Yes ma'am. Yes sir. Please and thank you. *"This stuff wasn't for kids like me,"* I thought to myself. Outside of Madeline's purview, I disliked and distrusted authority. As far as I was concerned, authority, specifically grown-ups, had betrayed me throughout my young life, so the last thing any of them deserved was my respect.

One of the biggest betrayals came at the hands of a pencil-necked counselor. I continued to struggle with anger, so the forces that be thought it would be good for me to visit a therapist on a regular basis. At first, I didn't speak to the man because I had nothing to say to him. He broke my silence by stating that I could trust him and whatever I said would be kept a secret. Being a naïve child, I reluctantly trusted him and told him how much I hated living with the Resnicks in hopes that he would be able to get us back with Mom. If we were all back together, then everything could return to normal. Of course, most of this had to do with my own selfish comforting, but I would unleash a spiteful rant during each session to convince the therapist that Noah and I needed to be removed from the home and returned to Mom. Of course, I had no idea my brother Moses was in the process of being adopted, and Mom had been committed to Western State Hospital for treatment of her paranoid schizophrenia diagnosis. Outside of my world, everything was standing still, and I just had to find a way to make it back to what I considered a state of normalcy. After about three months of this charade, I walked right into the trap I had set. The counselor told either the social worker, Madeline or both everything I revealed and my stories pretty much fell apart. *That sorry fucker*, I thought to myself. He lied to me. While I gave myself a pass for blatantly lying, he didn't keep his promise to keep it between us, and that was somehow different. Consequently, my twisted logic landed me on Madeline's watch list for some time afterward. I wasn't easily forgiven because I had betrayed her.

The other behavioral antidote Madeline tried to use to quell my anger was attending church every Sunday and reading the good Holy Bible. Even with my vivid imagination, it was hard for me to grasp the concept of sitting in a pew, for what seemed like an eternity, listening to a man tell me what to do and what not to do in order to please God and Jesus and sometimes they were one in the same. I went along with it if for no other reason than I didn't have a choice in the matter. My fuck-the-world attitude needed Jesus' healing touch, so I was going to church every Sunday for the foreseeable future. James was the only one who didn't have to go, but he even managed to get off the couch some Sundays long enough to hear the devil be damned. The trick to getting him off the couch was football season had to be in recess.

Eventually, I started to question my anger as I learned more about the value system associated with our Sunday school lessons, but it led to more questions than answers. For example, the moral of the Noah's ark story was that when God is mad, he can drown everyone. Well, I wanted that kind of power. I had a shit list of people who needed to be drowned immediately, and I silently prayed to God to help make that a reality. I didn't find out until later that God usually doesn't grant prayer requests for killing people. However, He never granted my request for my family to get back together either. That was the underlying reason I had trouble being a true believer.

I also took everything our pastor bellowed or read out loud literally. How else was a child supposed to absorb the all-important guidance from the pulpit? The most memorable sermon was when he tried to convince us that demons were coming out of our television. I thought to myself, *Now that's some shit. I've been watching TV all my damn life and ain't no demons ever come out of it.* I wondered if he was referring to the color swatches that appeared on the screen after the Star Spangled Banner at one o'clock in the morning. Nonetheless, he encouraged the congregation to forfeit their televisions for a more sin-free lifestyle and less temptation. None of that ever made sense to me, but no one ever questioned anything that supposedly came from the holy book. However, Madeline interpreted it differently and cut our television privileges way back. I was not too happy with the preacher's message that day.

There were parts of attending church that I enjoyed. I remember singing along to the song "Amazing Grace," but was bored with a lot of the other hymns, mainly because I had no idea what they were referring to. The blood-of-the-lamb hymns were creepy to me as I envisioned the pastor knifing a lamb while its blood spewed everywhere. Also, every time he would ask us to join in communion, it just wasn't very appetizing way to present food in my young opinion. He would recite 1 Corinthians 11:23-26, "...This is my body, which is broken...this cup is the new covenant in my blood...this do in remembrance of me. *"Ain't he dead?"* I thought to myself. But I really liked grape juice and cracker, so I went along with it. However, I preferred a big cup instead of the teaser shot glass and at least one whole cracker if we were going to commit to this ritual, but it wasn't my place to bring it up.

The other ritual I took issue with was the offering plate. Madeline would give each of us a quarter to put in the plate as it passed alongside. I contemplated keeping it since I was poor but didn't want to risk rotting in Hell, so I reluctantly placed it in the pan hoping my riches would come another day as promised. Noah and I would get a kick out of being directed to return to our pews. Pew was the word we used anytime we smelled something malodorous or stepped into a wet cow patty on the farm, so I couldn't help snickering during those jovial moments as a nine-year-old.

The more I listened to the stories about Moses and Jesus and other biblical heroes, the more I started to believe and question the direction my life was headed. I was growing fearful of Hell and didn't want to end up there for being a bad kid. I wanted to at least try to straighten up in case this stuff was actually true, so I approached Madeline one night and told her that I wanted to accept our Lord and Savior Jesus Christ into my heart. She was so proud as we recited verses in Romans 10:9 and the Salvation Prayer right in the middle her living room. Madeline hugged me afterward, and just like that I was a saved child. Jesus had forgiven me for my sins. Although I continued to be a hellion, I felt an abnormal sense of relief to be forgiven for all of the wrongdoings in my life. Later on, I was baptized in a river near an overpass and gained a closer relationship with our pastor as we continued to pray together for my family. Praying seemed to help dial back the intensity level of my resentment. However, we may have been too close together during our prayer time. Our pastor eventually told Madeline that the scent from the coconut oil reminded him of an Almond Joy bar.

Although we attended church every Sunday, I never got into the habit of sitting still. I was always antsy and downright bored since I had the attention span of a junebug. However, all of that changed after church when we'd sit for hours on end watching football. The Resnicks were split as Redskins and Cowboys fans, but Noah and I didn't care for either team. Noah eventually picked the Chicago Bears, and I picked whichever team was winning. One time I switched teams in the middle of the game and Madeline had finally had enough. "Just pick a team and stick with it!" Taken aback, I looked at the screen as they were showing highlights of Dan Marino tossing a touchdown pass to Mark Clayton, so the Miami Dolphins became my team.

Once I finally decided on a team, Madeline bought us football cards, so we could learn more about the terminology of the game and the players associated with each team. I managed to collect several Dolphin players' cards including Marino, Duper, and Clayton. I began absorbing the stats and memorizing the back of the cards. I flipped through my set so many times that many of the cards became worn. When we began going to a hobby shop, I learned about the importance of keeping cards in mint condition. I eventually became bored with them since I couldn't touch them like I wanted to, but that didn't stop me from enjoying the games. For being as far away as we were from Miami, our local channel picked up nearly every Dolphins game throughout the year. Like everything else, I took it to the extreme and hinged my moods on their wins and losses. Even with great players, they were only an average team, so my mood was about half and half during football season.

Madeline also got us interested in baseball cards, and I enjoyed getting those packs for the stick of gum inside. I couldn't watch the sport on TV for more than a couple of innings, but I became fascinated with the stats. The local team was the Orioles, so logically I picked the Houston Astros as my team because I liked their star logo. I knew everything there was to know about Craig Biggio and Jeff Bagwell, but never got a chance to watch them play on TV. Collecting and trading the cards helped Darren and I connect on a more brotherly level. I had to use other means to connect with Amber.

Amber and I watched a lot of movies together mainly because I was always waiting to insert a different movie in between her Dirty Dancing marathons. She adored that movie and watched it with a great big grin on her face each and every one of the thousand times. It piqued my nerves after a while. I just got tired of it after I could recite every line from memory, and the songs would never leave my head. It was fun dancing to it in the middle of the family room, but we didn't try to mimic the on-screen moves though. She was my sister after all, and I just wasn't really into girls at the time. Besides, she sat down beside me for countless hours watching The Shakiest Gun in The West or Milo and Otis. To this day, I don't know what fascinated me about the Don Knotts movie, but it was on heavy VCR rotation when it was finally my turn to pick. It filled the void left from having the video games taken away for so long. Plus, it was probably the only thing that convinced me to finally ride a horse.

Amber loved to ride horses and had a friend named Sarah, who rode my bus and owned several on her farm. I would venture out with her from time to time but just to their house. Neither Amber nor Sarah could convince me to jump on any of her horses. They seemed taller than cows, and I had no intention of going near one. One evening we went over after I had been watching the Don Knotts flick, and I finally decided to hop on the saddle. I patted the white and brown speckled thoroughbred before gently tugging on the strap, and in Don Knotts-like fashion I fell off immediately almost getting trampled in the process. My left shoulder and ribs hurt from the fall, so that was the first and last time I ever rode horseback.

From then on, I remember visiting Sarah's house and dancing to Vanilla Ice and MC Hammer. My living room lounge moves were on point; at least in my mind. Being with

Sarah's family broke up the monotony of the everyday with the Resnicks, so I appreciated the time we spent over there. On the other hand, I was going to be begging for the monotony soon enough because my semi-balanced world was about to become unstable once again.

When Madeline broke the news that we were moving to neighboring Culpeper County, tremors reverberated throughout my body. Outright resentment sent my senses into overdrive, and I just snapped. My world went black; devoid of hope for a light that would end the persistent uncertainty that consumed my thoughts. Almost immediately, I decided that I couldn't stay with the Resnicks. I couldn't move away from the only familiar setting I had left, so I conjured up a plan to escape their home and stay in Rappahannock.

I turned to one of my best friends in fourth grade, Cameron. When I told him about my plight, he decided that he didn't want me to move either. It was early spring when Madeline broke the news, so I knew I didn't have long to plan. My friend, Wally overheard us and also joined in on the planning by providing a map of Rappahannock County. There was no distance too far, so we figured out the road system that would lead me back to my house on Shade Road. I decided that I couldn't directly return home without my brothers, so I asked Cameron if I could stay at his house while I made a plan to get Noah, Chris, and Moses back. Cameron excitedly agreed that I could live with him in nearby Flint Hill for a while but shared his concerns about the distance being too far to walk. Without hesitation, I took him up on his commitment and devised a blueprint to sneak to his house. Over the coming weeks, we had details down to food supply along the way and a shortcut through the mountains. I considered how frightened I was of dark forests but had to push all of that fear aside for the sake of getting my family back together. Plus, I'd figured out that Jason and Freddy weren't real, but thanks to Mom's superstitions, I made sure it wasn't Friday the 13th just in case. I prearranged my only stop at my friend Tyler's parent's gas station before heading into the mountains. I had some candy and random snacks from Madeline's cabinets, but Tyler offered to load my bag with food from his parent's store. Plus they had those cherry suckers that I liked. That's what I was looking forward to the most. The plan was in place, and I was confident as an unhinged child would be under those circumstances.

The Friday arrived. It was an otherwise normal school day with all of the kids excited about the weekend. I was just hoping to survive through the expedition. When the bells rang to indicate the end of the school day, it signaled the queue to initiate my plan of action. The starting point was behind the bushes at the left front end of the school building. When the buses were coming to pick us up, I would just wait to go out of the building last, slip in behind the bush and wait for the buses to leave before moving forward. As the bell rang, I walked slowly toward the doors and about five of my friends stood by to see if I was going to actually go through with it. I initially chickened out and decided to walk past the bush at the last possible second, but Cameron pushed me in. Already dirty and bleeding on my forearm, I was fully committed now and thought to myself, *I'm gonna kick Cameron's ass later.* From his standpoint, Cameron told his mom that I was spending the night, so I guess he didn't want to be a liar. Or maybe he really wanted me to spend the night; who knows? I peered through the bush to see the buses, hoping no one could see me. After the line of busses left, I sat behind the trimmed evergreen for about five minutes trying to regain my composure. About the time I decided to leave, Sarah's mom, the bus driver, came back around asking teachers if they had seen me. She was good friends with Madeline, a point I didn't even consider, so I had less time than I thought to get moving. Now I was terrified because I was less certain that I could pull it off. Nonetheless, Sarah's mom pulled off with her load of kids wanting to go home, and I waited for her to be far enough in the distance before taking off.

Now, I was absolutely committed. With my hands trembling and heart pounding, there was no option to turn back. I calmed myself with the imagery of Cameron embracing me as I arrived at his front door and convinced my numb legs to push forward. I started up the hill, through the baseball field and finally onto the main Route 211 stretch of road. I was only a half mile in before deciding that the effort was more tiring than I'd expected. I started noticing little details I hadn't noticed before on the bus. There was a lot of trash alongside the road. There were also a lot more cars than I expected. Oh, and there was a dead bird. Something about seeing its exposed ribs or the smell of rotting carcass incited another level of fear in me that helped propel my legs to move faster down the road. Madeline had always said when I was scared to think of Jesus. So for the first time my vocal chords belted out *Amazing Grace* and *This Little Light of Mine* without a hymn book. As the image of the bird seared into my memory, my thoughts fast forwarded to my possible demise somewhere in the mountains. Meanwhile I kept repeatedly singing the only two church hymns I'd rarely ever paid attention to with more conviction.

Finally, I made it to the gas station unscathed, at least physically. I opened with a friendly hello to Tyler's parent's hoping he had already stolen the goods he promised me, but he was nowhere to be found. I looked through every corner of the store, but he never showed. I couldn't wait any longer. I was no stranger to hunger, so I decided to take the risk as I looked into the wooded area and up into the mountains across the street. I just hoped Cameron's mom could cook. As I walked toward the door, I was greeted by a burly police officer.

"Hi, are you Adam Starks?"

"Uh, yes sir," I replied. I momentarily thought about lying but didn't want to risk going to jail. "I got some people looking for you, so why don't you go ahead and come with me."

Fuck, I thought to myself. It was over that quick.

I spent the night in a different foster home before being returned the next morning. Madeline and I had a long discussion before she decided that I would be grounded for a month. That meant extra chores around the house, no TV and no video games. The following Monday in school, everyone knew what'd happened, and they surrounded me for every last detail at the lunch table. From that point, I uneventfully passed fourth grade and finally earned my video games back on a regular basis. None of it mattered much as I faced the inevitable move to Culpeper. If I would've been able to look into a crystal ball to see the future that lay ahead for me, I would've given serious consideration to Hell before Culpeper, Virginia.

The home we moved into was much smaller than the fourteen-room Victorian the Resnicks were partially renting in Rappahannock. The overwhelming number of differences didn't bode well for my swelling angst. One of the first instances at the new house occurred when I threw a ball and it broke James' side view mirror on the truck. I went in the house and started to throw a fit. Madeline tried to calm me down, but I guess I was too far gone by that point. I started banging my head against the door frame in an attempt to punish myself while Madeline continued to talk to me.

I stopped long enough to blurt out, "Are you gonna stop me from doing this to myself?"

She replied, "If you're stupid enough to keep banging your head against the doorframe, then I'm stupid enough to stand here and watch you!"

She had a good point. It was hurting really bad, so I eventually stopped for my own sake. There were likely more moments like that throughout the summer. I would eventually get back to being a normal kid again, even if it were for just a short while.

Darren, Noah and I had plenty of new land to dig up with our construction toys, so we began bulldozing and hauling dirt for our new settlement. We even had a forested area to play in, and Matthew helped us build forts. Amber played along as well. Two kids next door, Lyle and Martin got acquainted with us and joined in all of our self-amusement. After they grew more comfortable with our family, they began spending the night after a while. Apparently their father was an abusive alcoholic, so Madeline would let them escape his wrath until he sobered up. I recall a few scuffles with both of them but for the most part, I enjoyed having them over. However, most of our time that summer was spent in Madeline's natural product shop that she decided to open up right in the heart of town. We tested toothpaste, mouthwash, pills, cookies, and even candy, but those days were much longer than the Sundays at church. We helped where we could, but most of the time we were an annoyance pestering Madeline for something to do. Also, James' job was closer to the new house, so he was home more often. He'd still lie around like a lump on the couch, but he was a presence more often. James enjoyed basketball, and if I'd sit still long enough, he'd teach me about the ways of the game. I liked the Seattle Supersonics for no logical reason whatsoever other than I liked the combination of their green and yellow colors. If it wasn't football season, we were watching pro basketball to fill the void. James never really moved from his spot unless it was time for bed, work or hunting season.

During deer season, we would help process the venison in the form of loin, steak, burger, and jerky. Although the smell was horrid, the most quality time I had with James was around that meat processor. Once I acclimated to the area, it didn't seem to be such a bad place. Maybe it wasn't just shy of Hell after all. After shopping for another school year, I was cautiously optimistic about the possibility of making new friends at a new school.

Fifth grade was a pivotal moment in my life for many reasons. I can pinpoint that year as the timeframe that clearly defined my views on race from an outcast's perspective. I'll never forget my first day of fifth grade no matter how hard I try. Floyd T. Binns Elementary, a predominantly black school, would prove to be a toxic, uninhabitable environment for an awkward black boy. Similar to Rappahannock, I entered through the front doors to see the dull, lifeless beige color on the walls. However, this school was jam packed with students trying to make their way; each with their own set of struggles. I note this since there was an immediately noticeable dark aura within Floyd. Most of the students sneered and had their own slang unlike the country jargon I was used to. Once again, I was out of my element. All of the black boys seemed to have the same threads on. Baggy jeans, high top kicks, a ball jersey, or a shirt two sizes too big for them – I didn't see anyone dressed like me in a striped polo and tight jeans or any prospective friends.

The second floor in the school only represented another level of intimidation for me. I was anxious, but if I was going to survive their mob mentality, it was time to take the dreaded risk of introducing myself. At recess, I tried to interact with potential new friends only to be met with immediate rejection. That day, I got a rude awakening to the unwritten code of blackness. With a jacked up haircut, off-brand tennis shoes, and Wrangler jeans, I was a target from day one.

Roderick and Antwon circled around me and exchanged put downs while the crowd of in-network black kids laughed at my expense. "Dis nigga talk like a white boy! Can you balee dat? Why you talk like that? And look at dem Safeway sliders. And dat fucked up head cut. What da fuck happened to yo' head, nigga. Shit look like someone chopped it up with a lawn mower." I stood still and probably looked clearly shaken until Antwon decided to slap me upside the head. I pushed him back and paid dearly for that mistake. Roderick and Antwon doubled up and pushed me to the black top scraping both of my elbows. Roderick stepped over me to reassure his status and mine, "Welcome to Floyd, bitch nigga!" They swapped high fives over top of me and walked away. The other students just stood there laughing. I was numbed by being out of my element with their style of roughness. Instead of being that boy who had survived up to that point with pure grit, I convinced myself that no amount of it was going to get me through this year. I thought they were going to kill me.

Having white parents proved devastating to my budding reputation once the word got out. Thanks to Taren, the whole school would eventually know my circumstances. Taren couldn't have been more out of place as a white trash product, but she was tough as nails, wore motorcycle shirts, jeans, and cowgirl boots with nasty metal tips. She also rode my bus and made my thirty-minute ride hell on wheels. Every day, she made it a point to tell me that she was going to make me her nigger followed by I had a white honky for a momma. I'd retort with a "Fuck you, dirty little bitch," only to receive an evil laugh and a reiteration of making me her nigger. I was definitely intimidated by her, and often conspired to get my revenge. However, I never carried it out since it involved killing her. Lucky for her, blood made me squeamish.

One day, I finally had enough of Taren. For no reason, she kicked me in the shins and crotch with her metal-tipped boots as I walked down the hallway. I'd vowed never to hit a girl after seeing my mother get beaten to a pulp, but this was different. Plus, I convinced myself that God would forgive this one instance. Once I recovered, I plotted to find her and catch her off guard. At recess, I marched onto that blacktop, approached her from behind and yelled, "TAREN!" She turned around wide eyed not expecting to hear her name. Before she could react, my sidewinder fist was heading toward her face. I'd never hit anyone before so the hand-eye coordination appeared to be somewhat off as my right hand connected with the top of her ear and side of her head. Feeling the sting from my sharp, bony knuckles, she went down grabbing her ear and crying. As I ran, she yelled, "I'm gonna make you my nigger, you little mother fucker!"

Unfortunately, that punch only made her more resolute. She spent that afternoon projecting spitballs at me while the class laughed. Even Mrs. Lawson joined in on the laughter and told me that I was hopeless. By this point my desk, clothes, and surrounding area were covered with spitballs. The one that set me off was made mostly of her rabid drool dripping from my cheekbone. I stood up yelling any obscenity I could think of and flung my desk two rows up, just narrowly missing

Taren's head and crashing into the wall. Mrs. Lawson, shocked by my actions or the sudden super kid strength, demanded that I go to the principal's office. I faced the class and retorted, "Fuck all y'all" before heading toward the office.

The principal wouldn't accept my side of the story for my actions and decided to call Madeline to inform her that I would be sent to in-school suspension for the next three days. When Madeline heard my side of the story, she asked the principal what would happen to that girl. The principal replied with no intent of punishing Taren and reminded her that I was the one who threw the desk. Madeline retorted with a threat to take them to court over the matter. After that conversation, I was back in class the next school day. Madeline made sure that they couldn't mess with me without dealing with her. Unfortunately, that led to having no recourse for the reoccurrences of tag team bullying.

Roderick and Antwon cornered me the day after that incident to inquire how I managed to get out of trouble. I told them my foster mom called the school. Roderick, asked, "Yo' mamma white right?" I didn't fully understand what that had to do with anything, but this information was gold for Roderick and Antwon. It gave them all the justification they needed to round up others to take out their insecurities on me.

Whether it was being pushed down a flight of stairs after an assembly meeting by a random kid in a Lakers jacket or catching a beat down by a gang of five while using the urinal, my routine consisted of defensive stances. The only education I received that year was learning how to grow eyes in the back of my head and make friends with the few white students in my class.

Marshall and Harvey were my saving grace at that school. They were the only two kids who would sit with me at the lunch table and play with me at recess. Harvey was a scrawny, laid back character with cartoon-like dirty blond spiked hair ascending from the back of his head. Marshall was more of a cool cat with a porcupine-like spiked, white blond hair and a short stature. His zeal for life was contagious, and he took the liberty of coaching me to be more in line with black culture. His affinity for black culture intrigued me, so I gratefully went along with it. Funny as it seems, he introduced me to some harder rap like N.W.A., KRS-1, and LL Cool J, playing basketball, and even went as far as getting his mom to shape up my head when I spent time over at his house. It still didn't help since I was the only black boy hanging around white dudes. Roderick and Antwon still managed to embarrass me at any given moment, and Marshall and Harvey couldn't protect me from the random beatings I received in the bathrooms and during gym class. All of that changed when Jeffrey came to town.

Jeffrey was introduced to the class about midway through the year. He was by far the stockiest kid I'd even seen; akin to a bull with shaggy hair. Seeing an advantage in my favor, I immediately introduced myself and invited him to sit with Marshall, Harvey, and me in the cafeteria. We instantly hit it off and even found a similar interest in baseball and football cards. I even managed to trade off some of my favorites with him to show my commitment to our newfound friendship. I figured it was a small price to pay to have my own personal bull for protection. These mother fuckers were going to be sorry if he ever got a hold of one of their frail body frames. That strategy eventually paid off immensely when he saved me from what would've been my first swirly with a stool floating in the toilet.

I was minding my own business using the urinal when a couple of boys jumped me from behind and started pounding my head into the urinal and wall. Once I fell to the ground, I was kicked several times before being lifted. Usually, they just let me lay there as they abandoned me while laughing their way out of the restroom. This was different, but it wasn't a good kind of different. Another kid came out of the stall without flushing and directed the two to flush my head in his stall. With renewed strength, I squirmed out of their hands forcing them to drop me. Then I kicked in every direction until another set of hands got ahold of my feet. As they reopened the stall door, Jeffrey yelled, "Hey, what the fuck are you guys doing to Adam? Put him down now!" As he charged toward them, they dropped my limp body to defend themselves. He ended up knocking one to the ground and pinning two to the wall in one fluid motion. The two against the wall managed to wriggle away from his grip and escape, but I was satisfied with the outcome. He helped me up and put his head under my shoulder to escort me away from the stalls. I took one more look at the stool that could have been mushed into my hair and thanked him repeatedly. The smell alone could've killed a horse. He was my personal bodyguard after that incident. Low and behold, once the word got out, the attacks suddenly stopped; at least on school grounds.

The bus was a different story. I was always being pushed around and tormented by the other kids. I generated the courage to tell the bus driver that they kept hitting me. I needed to work up the courage because he was always telling us to "shut the hell up, or he was going to throw us off on the side of the road." After knowing what it felt like to be alone on the side of the road, I couldn't take that risk. In response to hitting me, the bus driver grumbled, "Well hit her back, you pussy." I didn't know what a pussy was in reference to a boy, but I added him to my hit list because it didn't sound good. I explained that I couldn't because it was five against one. Sarcastically, he replied, "Well, I can't help ya!" I ended the conversation with, "Well fuck you too, ya dumbass redneck." We exchanged squinted eyes, but he didn't do a damn thing. That gained me enough respect to keep those demon spawns off of me for the last ten minutes of the ride home.

Luckily, Noah came away largely unscathed while I bore the brunt of attacks. He was young enough that no one cared about his appearance. His light bronze complexion and loose black curls gave him a pass that eluded me. Plus, some of the black girls on the bus designated him as an honorary Puerto Rican and nicknamed him Pretty Ricky. I have no idea where the name came from, but I was grateful that I didn't have to protect him. I just had to worry about being branded as too dark and ugly. The nappy tar baby nigger jokes from Taren and black kids alike eventually shattered my soul to the point where I'd lost the will to even get on the bus. My only determination to do so was thanks to my first crush, Maxine.

One of the most illogical moments I can recall from that year was going after a girl with my tattered reputation. Maxine had everything going right for her until I approached her. Her auburn hair, pretty smile, and caramel complexion made her attractive and noticeable, but I seemed to be the only one interested in chasing girls at that ripe age of ten. Conversely, Roderick and Antwon found out that I had a thing for her and had other plans instead. They decided to embarrass me in front of her by launching a spitball assault on me throughout the entire class. As I sat there imagining beating both of them into a bloody mess, the entire class including Ms. Lawson began laughing at me once again. Not to be deterred, I went into the bathroom after class to clean myself off and muster up the courage to ask Maxine to be my girlfriend. I can't recall the exact words I used, but I'll never forget her saying, "You're just too black. I mean come on; you're the same color as the black top." I looked at the black top on the playground and just stood there in disbelief as she walked away. How could something so ugly come from such a beautiful girl? She was always so nice to me, and I couldn't believe she was just like everyone else in school. It hurt, but I had to keep going. I had no choice but to put my guard up to survive the rest of my school year. After that episode, I didn't express strong interest in girls again until several years later.

Thankfully, I managed to have some positive experiences, too. I landed a spot in a school play and won the in-class spelling bee to represent my class for the whole school. I thought if I could win, maybe the kids in school would respect me for being good at something. After winning the chance to represent my classroom, I stood on stage in front of the entire student body and nervously spelled F-O-R-G-E-T-A-B-L-E. The moderator said, "That is incorrect Mr. Starks. You may be seated." I was stunned. How could I have been so stupid to misspell the word *forgettable*? Numbness began to set in. I couldn't believe my chance to secure respect at Floyd T. Binns was gone the very instant I stood up. Roderick approached me afterward and teased, "See; you still ain't shit, nigga. I knew you would fuck that shit up for us." I closed my eyes in a hopeless attempt to make my stint at Floyd forgettable. Right then, someone pushed me down the flight of stairs. I was clearly hurt, but instead of someone stopping to help me up, some of them kicked my dangling legs to the side and continued along their way. I limped to the principal's office to tell her what happened and described the person who did it, but she told me that I was making it up. I just couldn't catch a break in Culpeper's inept school system.

On a more positive note, aside from Jeffrey, Harvey, and Marshall, discovering my ability to draw was the best self-education that occurred that year. My newfound talent got me noticed and finally accepted by my peers, even if it was only for brief moments at a time. I could draw every professional football, baseball, and basketball logo from memory and charged twenty-five cents per page to earn money. Even Roderick and Antwon were envious of my work, so they began taking it easy on me during those final months at Floyd. They were Redskins and Lakers fans, so I made sure to do my best work to impress them. Both of them even placed my work in the clear parts of their trapper keepers to expose my artistry, which brought in more business. My art didn't stop every instance of the random torment, but recess and using the restroom became easier tasks thanks to my newfound talent.

More importantly, transferring my focus to art allowed me to drift into a depth of peace no therapist could ever afford me. It allowed me to see the world through a different set of eyes that went beyond the confines of color boundaries. Society was teaching me that I was nothing; just something to be tormented until it withered away. While I rejected the notion that I was nothing but a nappy-headed nigger, I accepted my role as an outcast from the black race as I knew it. This cast away status allowed me to flourish later on in life. Art allowed me to defy the odds and expose my bloom amidst a sea of concrete emotions. That sense of command positively overwhelmed me. The transfer of my joy and angst to paper made me feel invincible at times. Conversely, my late discovery of this talent wasn't enough to overcome the months of bullying from the Floyd students. The psychological damage inflicted over the nine months at Floyd had permeated my soul. I was beyond healing; beyond hope.

After discussing my situation, Social Services and Madeline mutually agreed that attending Culpeper schools was not in my best interest. I had slipped into a deeply depressed state of mind and had given up by that point. Even though the sense of aloneness overpowered my psyche most days, I yearned for the solitude and tranquility in Rappahannock. At least people, mainly friends, understood and accepted me. My black difference was only pointed out by blacks who rejected my skin tone and dialect due to my outsider status. Alternatively, my friends in Rappahannock embraced me without the intrigue of my dark skin. I didn't have to contest to be respected. I was openly accepted. I wouldn't have survived another year in Culpeper. When Madeline told us were going back to Rappahannock, Noah and I couldn't contain our excitement. We happily left with our bags fully packed, while Madeline remained tearful of our parting from her life. We didn't reconnect until twenty plus years later.

As for the Resnicks, they did the best they could with the limited resources they had. The notion of strangers taking kids into their homes signifies a rare abundance of love. They loved us the best way they knew how, and looking back; it was good enough for me. Reminiscing with Madeline over the course of writing this chapter, it was revealed that she shielded me from racism within James' side of the family. During one instance, we couldn't go to a Christmas party with his family. When inquiring as to why, she was told that it was because of the little nigger boys. The Resnicks were not allowed to come unless they "left the little niggers at home." Madeline chose us over them, and I had no idea how dedicated she was to our well-being.

For a foster child, there's no such thing as an ideal home; only ideal love. White or otherwise, they were family in my book. It was the best possible thing that could have happened to us given our neglectful situation beforehand. They couldn't have foreseen the challenges that came with raising black children. The unwritten materialistic black code those kids expected was unattainable for me, given the Resnicks inexperience with the burgeoning hip hop culture. Nonetheless, I was able to forgive them and even understand the benefits of the way she raised us much later in life.

Chapter Four

Black Foster

At the ages of nine and five, Noah and I were being moved to our second foster home. Life was supposedly going to be much better here. Aligning Noah and I with a black family that had our brother Chris appeared to be an ideal situation for us. With a little help convincing Miriam, our new foster mother, to take the plunge, Rappahannock County Social Services managed to get us back to my safe haven community. Miriam's sister, who everyone referred to as Nana, had taken Chris into her home during the onset of our foster care years. Like the Resnicks, these families were avid churchgoers, and that's where Noah and I reconnected with Chris. I can only describe the experience as someone moving just one of the weighted worlds off of my shoulders when I saw that he was doing okay. It was Nana, along with their sister nicknamed Granny, who convinced Miriam to take us into her home. On the surface, they appeared to be a tight knit, functional family unit, which alleviated some of my stress during the initial transition that summer. It was a nice change to be welcomed throughout the neighborhood. I didn't take in as much scenery here as I had in the past when I'd arrived at a new place. Instead, I took direct notice of the families.

With the exception of church and family gatherings around holidays and birthdays, we didn't visit with Nana and Chris as much as I had hoped. Like every household, they had their own schedule to maintain and set of challenges, including distance that didn't warrant accommodating my every whim. Conversely, Granny, Miriam's older sister, and Granddaddy lived next door, so we visited their brood every day. They reminded me of the Huxtable family. From what I observed, they were perfect in every way. Over the years, they had the ideal home filled with what seemed like an entourage of kids running around spanning from infancy to eighteen. They had taken in scores of unwanted children and cared for them like they were their own. Their biological sons and daughters were grown and had their own families, but managed to visit often.

Granny always made sure we felt welcomed at her house right along with all of the other shades of kids who came through during my time on the hillside. Granddaddy had a wise, cool cat kind of vibe about him. He rarely raised his voice, and he was a wealth of knowledge willing to share it with anyone who would bother to listen. He was the ideal father figure for the step, foster, and adopted children throughout the hillside. All in all, it was an idyllic change to be around black folks who didn't treat me like unwanted garbage.

I genuinely liked Miriam at first. It's hard to tell what exactly convinced a single, working woman to take on two boys, especially one my age, and welcome them into her home. She worked hard for everything she had, and took a great deal of pride in that. Miriam was always well-kept from sun up to sun down. She had high standards, and untidiness wasn't something she was willing to tolerate. Although she reiterated during our stay there that we would drive her to drankin', I can't recall a time when she ever took a sip of anything in front of us. She kept an immaculately clean home and managed to work full-time as a deli manager at a major supermarket chain before switching careers to become a shoe store manager.

One of the first memories from entering that home in Amissville, Virginia was her model dining room and living room. As soon as you enter the foyer area, the two pristine rooms surrounded my entrance view. To the left, there was a dark walnut-stained dining room table set with pillowed chairs covered with plastic, a walnut-stained wall table and matching china closet with flowered decorative plates and crystal-handled cutlery. To the right was a cream-colored living room with a walnut-colored accented sofa and chair set also covered in plastic with a fancy coffee table placed at the center. One of the first rules made very clear to us was that we were not allowed to play in either room. They were for guests only, even though she may have only had guests over a handful of times during our tenancy.

Still, she seemed to be satisfied with her decision to become a foster parent and initially took absolute pride in our well-being. She may have gone overboard by having us discard our off-brand clothes, but I didn't mind tossing my Safeway sliders. Within a week, we had a brand new wardrobe, brand name shoes, and a precision fade haircut with a defining part on the side. I was officially black in style. Miriam spouted a seemingly unending stream of money to more closely align us with society's expectations of black culture.

After those tasks had been accomplished, it was time to meet her adopted son, Damon. By every standard, Damon was a very successful man. Miriam was very proud of him and often spoke of his accomplishments. He had a big townhouse in northern Virginia and drove a new SUV. He was climbing the corporate ladder within a major global firm and had a wife and two kids. After that initial visit, his wife, Lisa was nice enough, but I was unsure how I felt about Damon. However, my new cousins, Marcel and Donte, seemed likable.

My uncertainty settled as the drama-free summer of 1992 made foster care life seem like a breeze. There were no chores, all the video game time I could muster and playing on the hillside with a group of boys who didn't have a care in the world. Upon reflection, the term drama-free may be inaccurate, but given what I had been through up to that point, the notable moments from that summer serve more as comedic relief than any source of real stress.

Everyone in the neighborhood went by some other moniker than their original name. To better fit in, Miriam wanted us to choose our own nickname to be referred to throughout the hillside. Noah came up with John out of the blue. I couldn't immediately come up with anything that I liked. Chachie was an option, but that name was reserved for Eve, so I rendered it off limits. I began to pace the floor as Miriam waited impatiently for my response. I panicked and chose the name Spikey. I knew immediately that is not what I wanted, but I didn't want to disappoint Miriam by changing my mind so quickly. That's what I called my friend Marshall because of his gel-induced blonde spikes all over the top of his head. It was fitting for him but terrible for a black kid without the appropriate chain and collar gear to give it some sort of relevance. Plus, the way Miriam said it sounded forced like she was calling a bulldog over for his dinner. I hated it. After a few weeks of forced effort, I finally told her that I didn't want a nickname after all. I think she was as relieved as I was. However, Noah's moniker still sticks with him to this day.

I wish that would've been the strangest occurrence during my first summer with Miriam, but the oddities were far from over. As noted before, the three sisters dutifully went to church every Sunday. Coming home one day after a grueling three-hour church session, Miriam asked Noah and me if we had been saved and baptized. I uncaringly replied yes but explained that Noah hadn't been because he was too young. However, Miriam wasn't satisfied with my response. Seemingly without justification, she wanted me to be re-saved at church, and the only reason she gave was that the white church didn't do it right. She may have been partially right from a cultural perspective since I didn't feel so out of place in the black church. I didn't have anyone petting my head or telling me how good I smelled. So I reluctantly agreed that the church was different since it was an all-black congregation, but the two fire-breathing Southern Baptists preached the same material from the same book. The following week, I went through the motions again, feeling no different than the first time around. Ultimately, that involvement made me take the process less seriously and eventually come to resent organized religion.

The most redeeming aspect of the church that summer was a trip to King's Dominion amusement park. The sounds of kids screaming, long distance sightings of roller coasters going in loops, and the smells of the sweet temptations that awaited me inside ignited my sensory overload before I even set foot in the park. I can recall my first experience with exhilaration, going from coaster to coaster without any sense of fright. The Shockwave happened to be my favorite ride at the time. Luckily, it was a slow day, so Noah and I would hop right back on to experience the front, middle, and back of the ride. That day more than made up for the boredom of sitting in pews for so many hours.

The most somber moment occurred when Miriam decided to take us to visit her imprisoned son, Demarius. I can't recall what he was in for, but it didn't matter. I saw firsthand how much stress that situation put on her. It must have been a low-level offense since we were able to visit him at a designated table for about an hour. Miriam introduced us, but Noah and I didn't have much to say. Again, I wasn't sure what to make of him in his dark blue jumpsuit. The one-hour allotment quickly passed, and we were on our way back home. Miriam was silent the two-hour ride there and the two-hour ride back. I was curious what was going through her mind, but I knew it wasn't my place to ask. She eventually opened up and talked about his wrongdoings once we got home, but I didn't relate it to her trying to teach me my first lesson until much later down the road. That warning message would come during my life crossroads facing the same fate years later.

I was grateful to be back in Rappahannock County and looked forward to reconnecting with my friends. However, I couldn't help but see the world through a racial lens. I can only assume that the stress of returning to school that year triggered the resentment and anger that had largely receded during that blissful summer. After enduring the bottom-feeding black culture within Floyd T. Binns Elementary School, I developed a cautious mentality, but not in the way they had hoped. While

I was grateful to have a haircut and clothes that would deem me acceptable by the larger black community I, in no way, felt beholden to my race. As far as I was concerned, the black community at Floyd T. Binns sought to destroy me for being different and somehow more underprivileged than they were. Instead of embracing me, they were taught to reject boys who didn't fit the model narrative based on the illogical notion of trendy materialism and appearance. God may have forgiven them, but I was going to be damned before I did. I had served my punishment for a lack of blackness that had nothing to do with my obvious black skin.

When I returned to school, my self-exile led me to several stopovers around the school cafeteria. When I entered the room and scanned the long brown folding tables, I usually sat with the nerdy white kids who were my friends before I moved to Culpeper. However, it wasn't unusual for me to venture over to the popular kids, redneck boys, girls only, or the black table. There was no rhyme or reason for which table I would gravitate to, but I felt comfortable being home again. It wasn't due to any sort of resentment for other black boys who had nothing to do with my prior experience, but a way of diversifying my friends to ensure I would never experience rejection on that level again. By that time, I had developed a me-against-the-world attitude, so a sense of belonging wasn't as important to me as having different types of people to rely on should I need them.

The first couple of months of school were a struggle to regain my sense of worth and normalcy. I didn't particularly miss the Resnicks, but there were subtle reminders throughout the day that made me consider the lessons I'd learned from Madeline. I rode the bus with the Bostick kids who attended church with the Resnicks, but Miriam didn't want us hanging out together. It mostly had to do with Miriam being skeptical and not wanting to risk any type of updates to the Resnick family. Adjusting to Miriam's style of parenting proved to be a challenge after the newness of our relationship wore off. There seemed to be more chores including cleaning dishes, vacuuming, dusting, sweeping, and even cleaning her car. Instead of five kids helping with this laundry list of chores, now it was just down to me and Noah. After a while, it seemed like all we were getting done was homework and cleaning. The rules, along with the routine, were pretty much the same. Everything had changed, yet managed to remain the same. Our first break arrived during our first Halloween celebration with Miriam.

The Resnicks didn't celebrate Halloween because it was believed to be the Devil's day. Halloween wasn't celebrated with Mom either because we were either too broke, she was too drunk or both. This year was the first that I had paid attention to the holiday in terms of having kid-like fun. Miriam took us to Damon's townhouse in a Manassas suburb. Rows and rows of cookie-cutter townhomes were decorated for the event, and we lined up with our new cousins, Marcel and Dante, ready to visit as many as possible. The rows seemed endless as we trekked through the neighborhood for hours of door-to-door solicitation. By the time we made it back home, each one of us had a thirty-gallon trash bag half full of candy. Overwhelmed by the joyful sight of the haul, I dived into the bag and tried to swim around in it like Mr. Scrooge paddling through his money on the Duck Tales episodes. There was more candy than any one kid could eat, but I was more than willing to try. After Miriam and Lisa had inspected our inventory, we were given the green light to dig in. I spent the rest of the night jazzed up on Pixie Stix and Smarties

Almost every time we visited Manassas, Miriam would take us to the mall on Sudley Road. Going through Manassas was big city livin' for me. The retail row along Sudley Road seemed to stretch endlessly for miles with every type of store and restaurant imaginable. I always saw clothes and things I wanted, but Miriam would always say that she didn't have enough money for all of my wants. I didn't make too much of a fuss over it since I was grateful for what she had done for us in such a short amount of time. However, that didn't mean I could refrain from coveting the brand name gear any less. I obsessed over my wants to the point of listing them on paper, memorizing the prices and in order of hopeful purchase. In essence, I was creating a new Christmas list every couple of weeks. My next obsession became money. That Halloween night I decided to start a candy shop selling sweets right out of my book bag.

I returned to school with my candy-filled sack and pockets jam-packed with change. I made my sales pitch during homeroom, in between class, lunchtime and the bus lines at the end of the day. My first week of sales were slower than I had hoped, but once the niche caught on, my classmates were lining up with pennies, nickels, dimes and quarters to get their stash of sweets. My slogan was, *"Why wait to go to the store when you got me right here?"* It was hard to argue with that logic. Without any prior sales knowledge, I strategized to increase the inventory once my candy supply was getting too low for comfort. I dug into my pillowcase full of coins and dollars to make new purchases. I also made a new price list and added candies kids asked for but didn't have on hand at the time. Bazooka Joe gum and Dum Dum pops were popular, but I couldn't keep Frooties in stock because I sold them so cheap. I had to raise the price on those along with Jolly Ranchers. My friends were going crazy over Blow Pops, so I made sure to carry extra. Miriam was supportive and was glad I was finally coming out of my shell as she would say. She even took me to different stores to buy more bags of candy. When I explained how I split the bag up and made a profit, she found it hard to resist my newfound interest.

Business was going so well that I decided to add a partner. Wally was one of my most loyal friends at the time. He had expressed interest in the beginning, but I wasn't exactly sure what I was doing. Once I had it figured out, he was the first person who came to mind. We partnered with a handshake, and I agreed to split the profits on sales. Wally turned out to be the perfect partner because he had access to the old Boston and Sperryville corner stores I used to visit when I lived with Mom. When he bought those cherry red suckers with the dimpled center and Topps bubble gum in the one-ounce juice cartons, our inventory was complete. Instead of change, we were counting dollar bills, and I was well on my way to buying some of the things I wanted when Miriam took us to the mall.

The operation had continued for about three months before our principal Mr. Sanford brought it to an abrupt end. He simply told me that I wasn't allowed to sell candy on school property, so that was the end of Adam and Wally's Candy Shack. I ended up giving my excess inventory to friends, but I ultimately blamed the sixth-grade teachers for getting shut down. That was the extent of my sixth-grade adventures. I didn't really care to learn anything and couldn't wait for the school year to end. The last days of being content as a child were thanks to the boys on the hillside.

My favorite memories from that time were our play in the forest directly behind our backyards. I never felt more alive than venturing into the woods or playing in our wide open field with the boys on the hillside. It was me, Noah, Roderick, Randall, Glenn, and later on Dax, and Dee who eventually formed the Hillside Gang. We were more or less a little sandlot group who did everything from playing baseball on our makeshift diamond to listening to our stereo while hanging out in our fort. For the most part, we played well together; about as well as one could expect a bunch of boys left to their own devices.

Our histories were similar in many ways. Roderick and Randall's father abandoned them early on, and their mother lost them due to drug addiction. Granny and Granddaddy adopted them just before we came to live with Miriam. I always envied them because they had presents piled halfway up to the tree at Christmas time, their birthday bashes were bigger, and they went on awesome vacations. Living in a single foster mother household, those things just weren't in the cards for us. When they left, I always thought of taking my future family to those beach destinations.

Glenn lived in a trailer at the tail end of the hillside with his mother and drunken, verbally abusive father. When Glenn spent the better part of the day playing video games or asked to come inside the house for a while, it was a good bet that his father was down the hill drunk and cussing his mother. I sympathized with Glenn since he didn't have a way out of his situation. He looked up to me when his older brother wasn't in town and even chose the Miami Dolphins as his football team. We always discussed our dreams and how we would one day make something of ourselves. His older brother would come down the road from Manassas to provide some temporary relief from his personal hell. I was always happy for him when he could get away, but I would also imagine what it would be like if I had an older brother.

Dax and Dee came along later. I may have been in eighth grade when their father married Granny's daughter who eventually lived next door to us. Truth be told, I didn't like them at first for no other reason than that they were from Culpeper. Although they had nothing to do with my past, I tagged them as Culpeper trash since I assumed they were all the same. It took a while before I trusted them, but their dad cut my hair for free. Everyone on the hillside kept a nice fade thanks to him, so it was easy to be around them. Plus, they were always good for a laugh. I don't know how they dealt with being separated from their mother, but neither one seemed to let it faze them.

More than anything else, we loved to get a baseball game going. Our diamond was outlined by dirt spots and uneven distances between the bases. We'd break out the gloves, bats, and balls, and I'd take the all-time pitcher position. Unless there was a cookout, we never had enough players, so we would have ghost men take a runner's place to have enough continuous hitters. I have to admit that it was difficult keeping up with ghost men, score and innings played. It was easier when Marcel and Donte would come down to visit or the girls in the neighborhood would play.

Football, on the other hand, was easier with an all-time quarterback going from one end of the field to the other. We played rough as boys usually do, but looking back I probably hit them harder than they deserved when they intercepted me. We always came in dirty and headed toward the closest fridge in the neighborhood. We were definitely country through and through.

Most of the time was spent in forts between abandoned trailers and later on in the woods. Our first fort was made out of reclaimed wood from all over the neighborhood. We had a wooden floor, albeit unleveled, table, chairs, a functional door, and even drawings tacked on each wall. No secret codes were necessary, so we'd park our bikes out front, drink juices boxes, and tune into the Washington, D.C. rap stations.

I also spent a lot of time alone in hiding. Solitude was important for me, but it was hard to come by. Influenced by letters from Mom, I spent a lot of time writing movie scripts or just processing an argument with Miriam. Mostly, I just dreamed about being famous one day. The latter thoughts led to my idea to coerce the boys into acting out my Black Ninjas script. If I was going to be famous, they had to come along with me.

As the de facto leader of the group, it didn't take much to convince the boys to take the roles I had assigned. Everything was going so well until a third of the way through the script. I was directing Roderick on how I needed him to jump from the roof with his makeshift bo-staff across his chest while kicking through the air. Just as I lunged forward, the entire shack came crashing to the ground. All of us just stood there looking at the ruins in disbelief. Almost immediately, we went inside Miriam's home and started planning for the next one. I put the script aside for the time being. I eventually ended up sending it to Hollywood with a sequel, and we never finished acting out the rest of it since the studio took about four months to return the original script.

For the next hideout blueprint, we decided to go without wood floors since we needed the extra wood to replace the broken boards we couldn't salvage. We managed to find some old rugs in the abandoned trailers to cover our floor. When it was completed, we reassured each other that this was an ideal location. There was seemingly nothing that could convince us to doubt our accomplishment. It was more durable since it was supported by two trees. We didn't have wasps or yellow jackets to deal with, and the new location was much better shaded. Aside from the ants that were only attracted to our food we constantly left in there, we had it made. Even the ants were collected into glass jars, and we would watch wars ensue between black and red.

One uneventful summer day, a black snake came crawling from underneath the rug and sent all of us screaming and scrambling for the exit. We dashed out of the woods, but once I realized Noah wasn't with us, I had to go back against my will. He was sitting down calmly talking to the snake. "Noah, get your crazy ass out outta here! Come on, man. That thing could kill you!" Once I got him out of there, we didn't return for a couple of weeks. Thankfully, there were other places to take our adventures.

Past Glenn's house was uncharted territory for us. The private property signs didn't deter us; although, it probably should have since we didn't know the people who owned the land. Beyond the brick home and the dead end road was an untouched mountainous forest range that stretched beyond our eyesight as we climbed the highest rocks and tallest trees. I, along with the rest of the Hillside Gang, ventured into the unknown excited to see what we would discover.

After what seemed like an all-day hike, we arrived at a massive river. I took a moment to be in awe of the similarities to the river I used to fish in with Jaevon. It was the first vivid memory I had of home since moving in with Miriam, but it was interrupted by the presence of eyeballs piercing the back of my head. I felt like the boys were looking to me for what to do next, but I couldn't swim. The river was too muddy and wide to cross safely, and the currents were too strong to risk taking a dip. I wasn't interested in dying or playing rescue, so I picked up a rock and threw it sidewinder across the river. Impressed with my number of skips atop the water, the boys followed my lead selecting their own smooth rocks, and we were in a full-fledged rock skipping contest.

It wasn't long before we were worn out and ready to head home. We were also hungry and thirsty, which was going to make the trip back that much longer. We did everything in our power to keep our minds off of the long distance and the fact that we had run out of water. We daydreamed out loud about building a tree house overlooking the river, but the thought of carrying boards and tools for hours back and forth nixed that idea real quick!

When we finally returned home, we were dirty, tired, and near starvation according to boys who were used to snacking on something nearly every hour. We would only attempt that trip one more time with more food and water before deciding that it was just too far back to see the river. However, that didn't stop my passion for exploring beyond the hillside.

The forest behind our neighborhood was ideal for trailblazing. There were very few hills that posed a challenge, and the trees were great for climbing. One day, I convinced the boys to go to the edge of the forest to see what was on the other side. Trekking for hours on end, it's a wonder we didn't get lost or eaten by a pack of animals. I even convinced myself that we had gone in a big circle the entire time since every radius looked exactly the same. We climbed trees, played freeze tag, flung rocks, and played sword fighting ninjas with sticks, but we began to lose interest after a couple of hours with no end in sight. After boredom set in, we got the bright idea to race each other home. Most of the boys ended up crawling to the fort a few hundred feet from the house. Randall had to ride piggyback on me since he was the youngest and his legs just eventually gave out. We took a nap inside the fort before returning home to the comfort of video games and juice barrels. Moments like this made it easy to forget my plight and just enjoy being a child while it lasted.

The weekends and summers were filled with music, cookouts, video games, trips to amusement parks, and Granny and Granddaddy's pool. We also had the three-hour church marathon every Sunday and a week-long church camp. I'd usually blank out that week. Eight hours of that was enough to drive any already anxious child to the brink. I was always grateful when the camp counselors let us outside to play basketball or kickball. However, it wasn't as easy for me to assume the de facto leader position, and I had trouble handling other kids calling the shots. One year, Roderick and I even got into a knock-down fistfight over whether I tagged him out or not. We were a wild bunch to control, and I can only guess that was why the instructors tried so hard to instill the fear of God in us. That day came for many when one of the older deacons arrived in a red devil costume with horns, a tail, and a pitchfork.

To this day, I'm not sure why someone thought it was a good idea to have a full-grown man dress up as the devil and come through the back of the church to approach vulnerable children. As the youngsters looked back to see the horned, red-tailed demon roaring at them and waving a pitchfork, absolute chaos ensued as they scrambled to get away. I stood up and watched in complete disbelief as one of the little girls defecated all over herself and tracked it across the aisle. The camp leaders instructed the man in the devil costume to get out in an effort to calm the kids down, but it was too little, too late. All of the small ones were hysterical by that point, and many refused to come out from under the pews. There were a lot of little ones who went home with wet shorts that day. For me, if I can pinpoint the day that I lost my faith in organized religion that moment would have to be it.

The only person who kept me from fully rebelling against going to church was our new youth choir director, Monica. I don't recall how she became involved with our church since she lived all the way in Manassas, but she arrived with a burst of happy energy that was instantly contagious. When she came up with the idea for a children's choir that would sing every second Sunday, I don't think the deacons and our pastor Fred had the heart to do anything but approve her request.

Her unorthodox style was probably why I liked her so much. Listening to our uplifting gospel choir was undoubtedly my favorite part of church, but Monica's idea to put a beat to the music added a new element that definitely brought the music to life for me. During our practices and designated Sunday performance, she wore a constant smile across her whole face, and I'm almost certain that she never stopped clapping. She had us up there with tambourines, maracas, and even had a set of bongos for me! All I did was show her my hand drumming skills on the offering table one practice, which she encouraged in order to add some extra beat to our music. Beating my fists to the music came naturally, so we went along with it for every song. That was my thing every Sunday, which made me happy because I was the only one who didn't have to sing as often. However, she had at least three of the children sing solos every month. I dreaded my turn at the microphone since I knowingly couldn't carry a tune in a bucket. In what I can only describe as an attempt to boost our self-esteem, each one of use had to do a solo at some point with the youth choir backing us up with clapping, swaying and chorus. I dismissed the whole ordeal as being kind of wacked out because the crowd forcefully clapped to our tone deaf verses. Dax was the only one who could sing in my opinion. He was obviously blessed with angelic vocal chords that must've been inherited from their father who would also perform solos for the church upon request. Marcel was a close second with my brothers following in third. The rest of us needed to stick to the instruments! Nevertheless, I was no exception. I knew from my attempts to rap in front of a mirror that singing or rapping wasn't my forte, but there I was singing Amazing Grace or Lean on Me. The random "amen" from the crowd didn't persuade me to pursue singing in public.

I sincerely tried to listen to some of Reverend Frederick's fire from the pulpit, but his substantive messages rarely resonated with me. We prayed for people week after week, and nothing seemed to happen. Someone was always sick or just died, and I always wondered why God would let bad stuff happen to good people. This almighty and all-knowing being in the sky didn't quite connect with me, and I was never successful in finding a satisfying, valid answer to His existence. Relating it all back to me, I knew I was a sinner for stealing food, so I reasoned that was why God had my brothers and Mom split up. However, my brothers didn't know any better, so what in the hell did they do to deserve the same fate? Without having the option to stay home and just figure it out on my own, I struggled to connect with a deity that could only be described by faith. I was hurting deeply without a way to articulate it and realized early on that there were no angels coming to rescue me. While my prayers to return my family back together were never answered, Miriam's prayers finally returned results; Demarius was finally released from prison.

Miriam was on cloud nine when Demarius returned home. She was genuinely happy for the first time since she had taken us into her home. During the rest of that summer, she took us out to town more and even bought us more stuff for our back-to-school binge than she did last year. However, aside from a few dinners at the table, we didn't get to hang out with Demarius. Almost immediately, he returned to the streets to mess around with his boys. While it would have been nice to be part of his redemption process and have a big brother I desperately wanted at the time, it just wasn't meant to be. He was addicted to the street life, and I was being led astray by anyone I could find to resemble a consistent male role model. I decided to take my cues from any media outlet I could get my eyes and ears on. Although I was in search of direction that year, I entered my last year at Rappahannock County Elementary with a renewed sense of self. I wanted to be smart and successful like the men in the sitcom families. In September of 1993, I arrived in seventh grade with a flat top looking as fresh as the prince of Bel Air. I chose multicolor and swirl pattern shirts and MC Hammer style pants to brighten up my wardrobe and show that I was definitely in a class of my own. It felt great to see my friends again who looked the same, but were changing in ways I couldn't pinpoint at the time. I thought it could be new clothes or being reassigned to different classrooms or the new routine, but the world felt slightly out of order during those first few weeks. Looking back, that nostalgic feeling had to do with my academic chickens finally coming home to roost. All of those missed days during my earlier years and a dismal fifth-grade year when I learned next to nothing left me terribly behind the learning curve.

My classmates seemed to whiz through the new lessons while my brain simply couldn't compute the trove of unlinked information. Divisions and fractions might as well have been Chinese symbols. Reading through chapter books left me frustrated beyond belief since I would constantly come across words I didn't know, which distracted me from understanding the overall context. Within weeks, I just shut down and reverted back to what I knew best.

Ignoring all of my studies in another attempt to make money, I reverted back to drawing professional sports logos for all of the major pro teams and selling each one at fifty cents a pop. I was slyer this time but still managed to get caught within a month. At this point, I was angered because the system seemed to be working against me. I couldn't function within its confines and began expressing it by resenting my friends. Feeling as dumb as I did set off an inner struggle I couldn't even begin to articulate or contend with. I started looking for ways to get out of school, but Miriam wasn't having it. She ultimately became part of the system that I felt the need to reject.

The only outlet that managed to ease my self-doubt and anger was writing. Maybe it was a desperate attempt to reconnect with my mother since she was an aspiring songwriter. Maybe it was a way out of a world that no longer made sense to me, but I found solace in writing. I loathed required writing assignments for any subject, but creative writing liberated me from a seemingly oppressive world. The activity seemed to subdue my incubus by providing a way of expression that offered light to thoughts I couldn't otherwise express. I would get completely lost in my imagination writing scripts for Blacks Ninja's or Road Rash. After writing both screenplays, which I still have in a mint condition trapper keeper today, I ventured into designing a game system and urban planning for my ideal city. No doubt, I was an avid dreamer, but I wouldn't realize the value of the necessary education to accommodate those dreams until years later.

I got the idea from the motorcycle racing game I played on the Sega Genesis system. All of the characters had at least one of my flawed characteristics in some form or another. The Black Ninjas were kids on their own just waiting for an opportunity to kick some ass just like I wanted. I had a one-page list for other movie scripts I planned to write later, but they never came to fruition. I wrote a lot of curved letters to mimic Mom's penmanship, so it took a lot of time to generate the pages to complete a full script. I just carried the two screenplays in place of homework everywhere I went. I never showed them to anyone for fear of more rejection. I already knew from experience that the world wasn't kind to people who didn't conform to its societal expectations. I expressed that through my outsider characters in my Road Rash writings. Moreover, there were cuss words in almost every sentence of Road Rash, so I didn't want some grown up telling me how to write or even worse, taking it away completely. With both scripts being over twenty-five pages in length, they meant everything to me.

My misgivings with anger were an issue no one could identify after I settled in Miriam's home. All it took to ignite it was the flicker of one more betrayal. The one instance that finally exceeded my breaking point and solidified my decision to rebel against the school machine occurred during my seventh-grade science class. The wrath and intensity bottled up inside me for all of those years erupted when my science teacher, Mr. Rossini, overused his authority one day. He gave us an assignment to complete, and we were instructed to sit still when finished. Science was among the few subjects that I managed to take an interest in understanding, so I was among the first ones to complete assignments. I thought it would be a prime time to work on my sequel to Black Ninjas, so I pulled the script out of my book bag and began jotting down new lines. I didn't see any harm in it, but Mr. Rossini approached me from behind breathing like a mad bull.

When I turned around to make eye contact, he interrupted the class by loudly asking, "What exactly are you doing?"

I replied, "I'm writing a new movie script. I didn't disturb anyone, so it's not a big deal." He grabbed my twenty-page project I had been working on for months and ripped it into four sections as he was making his way across the room. Mr. Rossini turned around, looked right at me and dropped the shreds in the trash can like it had no value whatsoever. He looked satisfied with himself as my eyes widened and fists clenched. He went on teaching as I slipped into what I can only describe as a psychotic trance. I didn't know what to do. Afterward, I went to lunch but couldn't eat or talk.

About ten minutes into Mrs. Garland's English class, I exploded with a primal scream and flung my desk from the third row up against the wall in the front of the room. The shriek forced Mrs. Garland to momentarily freeze before fearfully turning around to ask me what the matter was. "NOBODY GETS TO FUCKING DISRESPECT ME!" She told the class to evacuate the room and followed quickly behind them as I continued to flip every desk in my path. She stood outside the door and asked, "Who disrespected you?"

I replied "That stupid mother fucker, Mr. Rossini tore up my movie script," as I kicked a chair up to the ceiling knocking out one of the tiles. I continued yelling every possible obscenity I could muster and hurled desks and chairs until our assistant principal Mr. Tanner arrived. "Adam, what is going on in here?" There was immediate silence. I stopped since there was nothing unturned and took a moment to witness my aftermath while heaving in an attempt to catch my breath. Ceiling tiles were knocked out, and every chair was toppled over. One chair even managed to sit atop an opened window. My blind rage finally abated, and Mr. Tanner escorted me to his office.

He sat me down in his office and repeated his question. "Adam, what could have possibly made you that mad? Do you realize what you've done here? It looks like a hurricane just tore through that room." After returning to a calm state, tears began welling again, and I explained how I'd worked so hard on that script and now it was all a waste of time thanks to Mr. Rossini. After hearing both sides, Mr. Tanner decided to keep me in the office for the last part of the day. He didn't even call Miriam. He finished by saying, "Adam, I never thought I'd see a kid in my lifetime exert that much strength." He shook his head as he left and went on about his business.

Ms. Garland was a sweet old lady who looked like she was picked up off of a shelf at a little off-the-wall country store. She didn't deserve the treatment she received throughout the course of that year. As an already tormented teacher by several of the other misfit students, I believe and regret to this day that my outburst was the final straw in her decision to retire before the school year ended.

Once the dust settled within, I was transformed for the worst. The incident with Mr. Rossini left me with my first case of writer's block, so I couldn't function without writing and grew even more frustrated with the world I lived in. There were almost no outlets for me, but sports and recess were safe havens. I still enjoyed play.

I loved kickball. Any sport, especially kickball, provided a much-needed outlet for my aggression. I was a lot more competitive than my friends. They played for fun, but I played to win. If my team didn't win, I left the field and entered the classroom with a crushed spirit for the rest of the afternoon. Letting go was a luxury that my soul wasn't afforded at the time. I played to win and tied it to my contentment. For me, it was all business. It's no surprise that my first fight occurred after a recess kickball game.

It happened shortly after the classroom hurricane incident, and it was over a boy on my team pushing me down into the dirt. Brandon had a crush on the girl up at the plate, and I got down in a set stance. He chuckled and asked why I was taking it so seriously. I ignored his question since the answer was obvious in my mind. The ball was coming my way, and just as I was about to catch it for the final out, Brandon shoved me sending my face forward into the earth. When I looked up, he laughed as she made her way to first base. Unknowingly, Brandon unleashed a series of flashbacks from my fifth-grade year of all of the kids who tormented me. I thought about the beatings and the inability to defend myself against four or five boys. Then, I suddenly realized that he was the only one. In an unusually controlled manner, I calmly got up, looked him the eye, and then told the kid standing beside me that I was going to whoop Brandon's ass after recess.

Mark, retorted, "Adam, you ain't gonna do shit."

"Watch me, mother fucker! No one gets to embarrass me like that anymore. He's going to fucking pay!"

The whistle blew indicating that it was time to return to class. Mark was still whispering in a taunting way suggesting that I wasn't going to do anything. I cut in line until I was lined up beside Brandon, and unleashed a clenched right hand across his unaware face. After the initial stun, Brandon charged toward me unknowingly into an epic whoopin'. Bloodsport was one of my favorite movies at the time, so I went into full Muay Thai mode by grabbing his head and landing a series of uppercuts and knees to his face. I continued to wail on him for at least a couple more minutes before teachers pulled me off and escorted us to the office. The demons within came across my face in the form of a sly grin. Watching Brandon cry uncontrollably as blood cascaded from behind his ears where I'd sunk my fingernails into his skull was tremendously satisfying. His mother, a teacher within the school, was called to the office to console her battered son. She burst through the doors and looked at me like I was Lucifer himself before she embraced Brandon's face to wipe his tears. I felt no remorse. I didn't care about her or her son's well-being. I didn't care about the imminent suspension. As far as I was concerned, my actions were justified. With the entire seventh-grade class as my witness, I was not one to be messed with.

Miriam had already received a call from school, so I couldn't deny it when I got home. She was surprisingly proud of me and even cracked a smile when we discussed it. Miriam always thought I was a bit of a sissy, so this newfound self-defense was a welcoming discovery for her. When she was telling people why I was out of school, she dubbed me as her little prize fighter.

To my surprise, she even brought up adoption. Noah wasn't too excited about it, since he was still holding out for getting back with Mom. I was in the phase of blaming Mom for all of my problems, so I welcomed the thought of having the security of a permanent home. She wanted us to choose a name that started with a D and a middle name that started with an A to match Demarius' and Damon's initials. I saw this as a chance to redeem myself from the Spikey misspeak, so I wanted to find a real good name. Daniel came to mind since it was a biblical name. I thought maybe Mom wouldn't be too upset if I kept it biblical, but I didn't look like a Daniel in the mirror. One Sunday, I was watching the Cowboys play the 49ers. I wasn't a fan of either team, but the flashy style and finesse of Deion Sanders caught my attention. The name "Deion" was an easy choice to make for an impressionable boy.

In school, we were learning about Alexander the Great. He was the only ruler to ever successfully conquer the world. I wanted part of my name to be that powerful. Plus, I was a legend in my own mind, so Alexander seemed to be a perfect fit. Miriam was very pleased with Deion Alexander, and I felt exonerated after being a complete cornball during the nickname process. Although I kept the name as an alias through tenth grade, the adoption talk was short lived. Demarius was in trouble with the law again, but not before getting some random woman pregnant. Miriam had to contend with his new legal troubles, a new granddaughter, and my swelling discontent with life. Afterward, adoption talk was more of a bargaining chip for good behavior than anything that would ever come to fruition. As a better attempt at positive reinforcement, Miriam decided to let Noah and I play baseball.

The mechanics of baseball require an artful motion from the body, which wasn't initially blessed upon me. Starting years behind the other kids as a ten-year-old on my minor league Orioles team; I spent a lot of my at bats striking out. However, I didn't have to sit on the bench as often. Once my minor league coach discovered my speed, I was pinch running for his catcher and others if needed. I'd had the opportunity to watch Rickey Henderson play on television while at the Resnick's house, so I mimicked his style. I learned to watch the pitcher and anticipate the perfect opportunity to run. I don't recall hitting the ball once during a game that year, but I was never tagged out stealing bases either. While my teammates were interested in their stats, my favorite pastime was going to the store afterward to buy up as many of those one cent candies as I could carry.

I moved up to the Babe Ruth League the next year, and my batting coordination was just as terrible. Pinch running wasn't an option as often, but when it happened, I didn't disappoint.

However, the submarine, sidearm, and curveball pitches were too much for my batting eye. My White Sox team had a lot of talent, but I was determined to be as good as or better than they were. Even taking a pitch to the head during practice didn't deter me from the batter's box.

The only instance that caused me to rethink my intensity level was Damon yelling at me during a game. It was late in the game toward the end of the season, and I was determined to get a hit. It was the first time I can recall being in the zone athletically, and I had two nice hits that went foul. The last strike was called well below my knees, and I went down looking. I turned around and shouted, "Are you kidding me?" I took my bat and slammed it into home plate and stomped over to the dugout to yell, "That is bullshit! We're not fucking playing golf here." I looked up, and Miriam looked completely ashamed and embarrassed. The umpire looked in my direction, and the whole dug out went completely silent. No one said anything and seemingly out of nowhere, Damon barged into the dugout with his finger pointed right in my face and a vain popping right through the middle of his forehead, "You are being disrespectful to everyone around you, and you're going to play like you have some sense if you want to stay in this game. I'll beat your tail right here in front of everyone if that's what it takes. Don't ever let me hear that language come out of your mouth again." Caught off guard, I immediately shut my mouth. He stormed out of the dugout, and the game resumed.

Without any sense of shame or recognizing my awful behavior, I was pissed that he humiliated me in front of my team. I managed to end that year with a highlight catch that no one expected since I'd been known to drop pop flies before. That catch gave me the spark of confidence I needed to continue the next season.

The following spring, I was struggling academically and psychologically through my eighth-grade year. I desperately needed some sort of outlet and baseball served that need. At the beginning of the season, I wasn't great, but I was starting to get hits into the outfield, and getting to base on my own accord. Stealing, sliding and diving for catches started to become second nature for me. After the regular season had ended, I was good enough to be invited onto the traveling All-Star team with a group of boys from the league. I was doing so well that I even started thinking baseball could be my way out. During that first game, I could envision the ball coming in contact with my bat, and made it so with little effort. I was even named the MVP of the second game, but all of that came to an end as I failed Math on my last eighth-grade report card. I'd struggled all year, but Miriam made good on her threat to pull me if I couldn't bring that grade up. I tried to explain to her that I just wasn't good at it and begged to finish the season, but she refused to give in because it wouldn't teach me anything. Without baseball and everything else I felt had been taken from me by that point, I had nothing holding me back from rebelling against society. Miriam inadvertently reinforced this notion with her complete disregard for my most anticipated birthday.

The morning of my thirteenth birthday was filled with anticipation. I imagined a big cookout with the coconut cake and black raspberry ice cream I had asked for. I also asked Miriam for the fizzy juice she made from frozen punch and ginger ale. I recall her asking if I thought I was deserving of a party just weeks before, but I didn't think anything of it until the day dragged on until she got home around six that evening.

Miriam had worked all day, and I spent the better part of the day at Damon and Lisa's house. Just before Miriam arrived, Lisa wished me a happy birthday with a six-pack of socks and a card with five dollars in it. As strange as the gift was, I should've been more appreciative since it was the only gift I received that day. When Miriam got off of work, we went home and had leftover meatloaf, mac and cheese, and peas and carrots. Noah and I were in bed shortly thereafter.

Maybe I didn't deserve anything since I had back talked a lot that summer, but Miriam's silence that day was a defining moment in our relationship. Through my interpretation, she made it very clear that I was nothing to her, and anything she did for me was a favor. I was nothing more than a ward of the state. My only thought going to bed that night was that this was unforgivable. Looking back, it seems petty, but my resentment toward her after that night triggered my self-destructive psychological and emotional states for the next eighteen months.

Chapter Five

Swift Awakening

The transition to high school further escalated my stress levels. There was no longer a burst of color here or there on the walls. When I entered the school, it was tantamount to walking in between two slices of wheat bread. Growing up was seemingly as boring as it was terrifying. The school itself was considerably smaller than the elementary school, but the older teens appeared so much larger than I was at the time. The level of vulnerability took me well out of my comfort zone, and I immediately felt the need to posture to ensure I wouldn't get trampled in the crowded hallways in between classes.

Although I was satisfied being around my friends again, there were just too many unknowns to feel comfortable in yet another foreign environment. I spent most of my eighth-grade year in a distant trance. Rappahannock County's school system clustered kindergarten through seventh grade in elementary school and eighth through twelfth grade into high school. That's the way it had to be in a rural county with such a small population of children. However, the transition forced me to grow up way faster than I'd anticipated. Now I was in school with all of my older, girl foster cousins, and I didn't get to see the Hillside boys until we were on the bus to and from school. Plus, I couldn't open a combination lock to save my life. After a week of this new frustration, I had a friend help me take it off and left it unlocked the rest of the year. I figured if someone wanted my books that bad; they could have them.

My class load was an in-my-face reminder that I was nowhere near ready for this level of higher understanding. The requirements were downright intimidating for me. I couldn't even begin to comprehend the math equations or the complex comprehension and critical thinking required in English; my F in Math and D in English for the year were near solid proof. The first part of that year, I made a genuine effort to understand the material, but there was a blockage I couldn't manage to overcome. There was no option for a tutor, and I didn't have an outlet for the pent up frustration. Before the end of the first semester, I stopped creatively writing altogether. I thought to myself, *why would a failure like me waste time writing if it won't take him anywhere?* By that point, I'd convinced myself that I was stupid and worthless.

When I decided to quit trying altogether, boredom set in almost instantly. Acting out by disrupting class was my middle finger to a system that didn't accept me. I'd crack jokes or poke fun at the teachers only to get sent to the office. I only managed to rack up two in-school suspensions, but that was only because the teachers chose to ignore my antics most of the time.

My insecurities began playing out in other ways as well, mainly by finding meek girls and verbally picking on their looks. The teasing wasn't relentless, but I'd become the exact bully I used to hate. I would do nonsensical things such as taking a pair of pliers to school to pinch my unsuspecting peers. The only thing that stopped me was turning the pliers on myself one day to get a feel for what I was doing to my friends. I quickly decided that it wasn't funny and put them back in Miriam's junk drawer. I also put tacks in people's seat, but was unsuccessful and surprised by how many people checked their seats before sitting down.

Most of the time, I just stared aimlessly at the blackboard. Every once in a while, a teacher would call on me to participate, and I'd reply, "I don't know."

"Don't you even want to take a guess?"

"No!" After trying to pry a response out of me, they would move on to another student and just leave it at that. I'd just revert to staring at the chalkboard completely devoid of thought until the bell rang. I'd sit in the next class and repeat. I can't fully explain the reason for my steady decline, but it was certainly worsening as time went by. Throughout the year, I'd managed to alienate most of my friends and family.

The only time I ever participated was during gym class. I received an A for the year, but did the absolute minimum to pass the rest of my courses. I would have been content just dropping school together and doing my own thing. I don't know what that would have consisted of, but sitting in a seat with recess and gym only every other day was for the birds.

Since outside recess wasn't an option, someone decided to bring a football to lunch one day and toss it with some of the boys in the baseball outfield and a routine football game broke out. Every day during lunchtime, a group of boys would gobble up their food and head out to the baseball-turned-football field to assign teams and kick off. We started out with tag, but decided it was too weak for us country boys and converted to tackle. After the lunch bell rang, we'd come in every day with new scrapes and bruises, grass stains, dirt in our hair and sweating while heading back to class. We didn't give a damn about looks. We just wanted to play football, and that was really all that mattered. Rappahannock was one of three schools in the state, including a school for the deaf and the blind, that didn't have a football team for most of my years there, so we made the best of it. Despite that setback, we still found a way to create our own sandlot legends.

After playing football with boys my size, I finally realized just how much bigger I was compared to the rest of the Hillside gang. I didn't care to do much during the summer of '94 since the boys were too small for the kind of games I wanted to play. We mostly hung out inside listening to the radio or playing video games until Miriam would kick us outside to go play. The boys would scatter back to their house, or we would ride bikes up and down the road. Mostly I'd wander around aimlessly dreaming up new schemes to become someone I wasn't.

Since I'd developed a closer relationship with my foster cousins throughout my eighth-grade school year, they would ask if I'd like to go to the store from time to time. I'd lost my will to play, so riding around seemed like a good alternative. I never had money to buy anything, so I started stealing what I wanted. Although I knew it was wrong, I didn't think anyone would miss a pack of bubble gum, so I grabbed it walked around for a bit to catch up with my cousins and slipped it into my jean pocket. I didn't tell anyone or even think about sharing. The gratification was almost euphoric. Some describe it as a high, and like any high, I had to steal more to reach the same level of ecstasy I experienced the first time. It wasn't satisfying enough to stuff a pack of candy or several packs into my pockets. It didn't take long before I reached for sweets, drinks, chips and even ice cream.

The mall was my favorite destination. Using the justification of lacking money and coveting the latest shirt, I graduated to theft of clothing. CDs and tapes were also ripe for the picking. Without cameras and sophisticated security measures used today, it wasn't difficult to become good at being a thief. My only strategy was overcoming my desire to be greedy since I could always return later. I would simply walk up to the merchandise, slip it off the hanger, and tuck it into my jeans and walk out. Miriam was working so much at her new job that she never noticed enough to inquire about my new wardrobe. I finally had to tell Noah since he caught on pretty quickly that I had accumulated so much stuff. Since we shared a room, it would've been too difficult to hide everything.

Fortunately, I had a close brush with a security guard at a large retailer before the thought of jail finally entered my mind. I already had a stick of deodorant, lotion, and candy when I went to grab a tube of toothpaste I'd wanted to try. The guard came by as I was slipping it toward my jacket pocket. He stopped and looked in my direction, and I started walking toward him with the toothpaste in hand trying to signal my intent to purchase. He looked directly into my eyes before moving on. I emptied my pockets and put the stolen goods back on random shelves and left empty handed. As I shuddered at the thought of going to jail, I took that moment as my cue and stopped stealing altogether that fall of '94. That decision was also partly due to what I initially considered a positive male role model who entered my life.

I can't recall how Doug and Miriam met, but she was head over heels for this man. He was a tall, slender, light-complexioned, always sporting a dress shirt equipped with a vest, black curly hair that was just so, and drove a great big Cadillac. He was an easy speaking, overall suave kind of gentleman. I liked him, but he arrived at a time when I'd shut out all outsiders. I didn't need anyone else telling me what to do, so I kept to myself when he came around.

Doug and Miriam's relationship was strained from the get go. The long distance between them meant that they couldn't visit as much as they wanted to. Miriam called him quite a bit at first, but I got the impression that Doug wasn't a fan of phone talk. The conversations never lasted long, and before I knew it, Miriam was packing us up and heading to Germantown, Maryland from our little neck of the woods in Amissville, Virginia. It was easily a two-hour drive depending on which way the Northern Virginia traffic was swaying. More often than not, we were heading his way every free chance Miriam had available. From that point on, Noah and I could kiss our weekends goodbye since we were regulated to stay indoors at all times. It didn't take long for us to miss the fresh air on the hillside.

The weekends were terribly boring in what can only be described as an asphalt jungle. Instead of exploring the countryside, we had to listen to cars zooming on the expressway behind the house or go to the front window and stare at the parking lot as far as our eyes could see. Typically, we passed time by watching cable television, which was nice because we were exposed to so many more channels. That magic box worked so much better than our temperamental antenna trying to get the four main channels to gleam without static across the screen.

Doug never told us there were channels we couldn't watch. One day while I was comfortably channel surfing, I came across the adult films. I was prompted to buy after a preview so naturally my curiosity was sparked as I followed the instructions. For the next few weekends, I managed to run Doug's cable bill up an extra seventy-five dollars. When confronted with the orders on the bill, I flat out denied knowing how to order anything from a remote control. I knew it was a long shot, but Doug just gave me the doubtful eye and let it go. From then on, we were monitored more closely but not closely enough.

For the most part, we ran around free range in the basement. We were bringing toys from home, but eventually Noah and I would get bored again. One time, I got the idea to go through some of the boxes in the basement closet to see what I could find. We hit the jackpot of what I imagined every pre-pubescent boy wished he could find; a secret collection of Playboy magazines. Shoe boxes, filled to the brim, were stacked as high as my head. He must have owned every issue from the past twenty years or more. As Noah and I stood there gawking at the pages, we quickly shut the door as we heard footsteps coming toward the basement door. We quickly closed the closet door and dived onto the couch before anyone could determine what we were up to. Thankfully, it was

Miriam who tended to walk slower than Doug down the steps. She looked at us and probably wondered why we were sitting on the couch without the television on but didn't say anything as she trekked back upstairs. I turned on the television to mask the noise while Noah and I plotted how we were going to get some of this treasure trove back to our forts. The Hillside Gang would've never believed us without proof, so it was necessary to deliver. For the rest of the time Miriam and Doug dated, I brought a new Playboy to our hideout every week. Page by page, the gang relished in what could only be viewed as a mini gentlemen's club in paper form, and that was our introduction to the full female physique in all of its glory.

I don't know if Doug ever found out, but he did begin to get agitated with us, me in particular, toward the end. I was still struggling in school, so Miriam had convinced Doug that maybe I needed a positive male figure in my life. He reluctantly went along with it and took me on long rides to discuss my future and other things I simply dismissed as bullshit. At the time, I didn't think there could possibly be a future for someone like me.

He would ask what I wanted to be, and I'd mumble, "I dunno," and look out the window daydreaming about playing, writing or listening to the local rap station.

"Well, is there anything that you like to do?" he would retort.

"I dunno."

His patience quickly wore thin with this type of behavior, but he still refused to yell or even raise his voice. He would just simply say that I needed to get my life together or I would end up on the street with the rest of these little hoodlums, and then we would ride onward in silence.

The final straw for Doug was one Saturday when Noah and I decided to waste an entire day recording mix tapes from the radio. Doug decided to come down that weekend to watch us while Miriam worked, but we didn't interact with him the entire day. We had a list of songs we wanted and each claimed one side of the dual tape stereo player. When his song came on, we would hit record on his side and vice versa for me.

When Miriam returned home that evening, Doug lectured her about taking a harder stance on us, but she shrugged it off and tried to switch the subject about what they were going to for the rest of the evening. I'll never forget overhearing Doug snap, "These little niggers are retarded, Miriam. Why don't you get rid of 'em? You've done all you can. They just don't have the basics. Adam is as dumb as a box of rocks, and there's not much hope for Noah either." After Miriam told him about our background, Doug always dismissed us as being slow since "we didn't have the basics" as he always put it. Rather than give into my instincts, I placed my newly recorded tape in my Walkman and slipped my headphones on to ignore the rest of their conversation and delved into my usual trance.

My ninth-grade year forced me to rethink my entire outlook on life. Up to that point, the world was against me, and it was my prerogative to reject their ways. My enlightenment didn't come instantly, but the mounting evidence against my belief system was too overwhelming to ignore. By that point, I had managed to alienate everyone who used to care about my well-being. My mistrust for authority descended into absolute paranoia and completely disrupted my ability to reason through any situation. In essence, I was alone because I chose to be alone. I came to accept that I wasn't the only one facing hardships, but I was the only one who could change my fate. If I didn't, I was going to end up depending on the very system I hated.

I started by trying to watch the news more to understand the world I was growing up in. The news media were flooded with the OJ Simpson trial, so I received my crash course in class privilege and race in our country. While I understood the effects of slavery and Jim Crow Era oppression from a historical standpoint, I couldn't comprehend how any of it mattered during my time. It was clear that whites and blacks were pitted against each other during that trial, but I didn't fully understand the magnitude of race relations in our country until my science teacher, Ms. Garrett, flipped on the radio in the middle of class to listen to the verdict.

The lead up to the decision was excruciating as the commentators repeatedly stated that this black Hall of Famer killed his white wife and partner and what this meant for race matters in America. I could feel the eyeballs gazing my way as the only black kid in the room. This was one of the lowest moments in my life. I've had moments when I didn't want to be black during my fifth-grade stint, but this feeling made me sink deep into my desk chair in a desperate attempt to just be invisible altogether. As the verdict was read and OJ was found not guilty, Ms. Garrett gasped and covered her mouth in shock. Then she stared right into my eyes like I'd killed those people. I didn't know what to do. I looked around the room to detract her piercing gaze, but everyone was staring at me by this point. That bell couldn't ring fast enough for me to get the hell out of there. My peers walked around calling me OJ for an entire week until I told one of them to shut the fuck up. I seriously thought about knocking some of their asses out, but couldn't afford any trouble that early in the school year.

After that episode, I was officially done with school and looking for any means to get out. They clearly didn't want me here, and my feelings were mutual. I started cutting up in class more, but the teachers ignored my attempts to get kicked out. My worst episode happened when my math teacher, Mr. Edgar, handed back our tests one afternoon. I had recognized the F before he laid it down on my desk.

I argued, "What is this nonsense? I studied for this test."

He replied, "Well, not hard enough. You deserve the grade you get."

I retorted, "Well you know what this F stands for? Fuck this class, that's what!" Nothing. He went on handing out the tests while I crumpled mine and tossed it on the floor. That's where it stayed as they went over the answers. I even put a whoopee cushion in his chair only to have it taken away and never returned. Mr. Edgar was good at beating me at my own game.

My shop teacher Mr. Shultz even let me go on too many occasions. I was always cutting up and cursing in his class. One day, he didn't let me take a few more minutes to finish a project, and I called him a fucking Pollack to mock his Polish descent. His face turned beet red, and he gave me two demerits by poking two holes in an index card with my name on it, which were his way of keeping record of our bad behavior. I later apologized and referred to myself as an asshole for saying it. I don't think it meant much at the time, but it sure came through when he rounded me up a quarter of a point to pass his class later that year.

Next, I picked a fight with a gang member who was picking on one of my friends. They were supposed to be a dangerous group associated with a national gang, but we always teased about them being nothing more than a goof troop behind their backs. "What are they running, the streets of 211? Where's their territory, that plot of trees over there? They ain't running shit." That boasting gave me the confidence to tap the leader on his jacket as his posse surrounded my friend,

Taj. "Leave him the fuck alone! He didn't do anything to you. You wanna pick on someone; then, you come after me." All of his clowns got wide-eyed waiting for his next move. He grabbed my jacket collar, and I returned the favor. Christine, my cousin, intervened by grasping my left arm and threw me on the bus while someone else held him back. She put her finger in my face and asked me if I was crazy. I had a feeling she already knew the answer since she went on telling me that they sell drugs and would kill me if they got the chance. He was at my window yelling with four people holding him back. I put my window down and yelled, "I ain't scared of you, boy," and spit in his direction. The bus took off toward the elementary school, and that was the end of our beef.

I tried to start fights with others on the field or at lunch, but no one wanted any part of it. I had no problem getting in someone's face over the slightest error within my personal space. Looking back, it was all senseless. The only thing I managed to do was alienate the few friends who still wanted anything to do with me.

Shortly after the Christmas break of '95, I decided there was no need to hold my anger in anymore. I decided that the next person who spoke to me was going to get hit in the face. My friend, Aaron, decided to greet me before entering science class. Without hesitation, I hit him dead in the eye right in front of Ms. Garrett. She looked directly into my eyes and pointed toward the principal's office. Principal Tanner got my side of the story, left to get Ms. Garrett's account, and I was suspended for five days. Miriam just shook her head and said that I was going to drive her to drankin', but I had to stay home the entire time. I listened to Miriam talk on the phone, telling people how far gone I was and why she didn't know what to do with me. I spent the entire week tuning her out, lying on my bed and listening to music.

When I returned to school, I was kicked out again two weeks later for fighting. Jared, a stocky hulk-child with dirty blond hair was easily twice my size, but I'd decided he needed to be taken down a notch for picking on Taj. Leading up to that fight, I ran down the hallway to drop kick him in the back and run off. That's when the talk about who was tougher kept exchanging between our friends, so we decided to settle it in the parking lot during lunch one day. When it was going down, our friends started the whisper chain, and we had a circle formation around us in no time. We circled around each other about five times before I realized his size and began thinking the whole ordeal was a huge mistake. Regardless of my fear, I threw a punch and landed it to the right-side of his jaw. It surprised me, so I failed to follow up, and we continued to circle each other as I dodged a couple of his punches. It was then I realized how powerful Jared's swings were coupled with the size of his fists. By this point, I was searching for a way out without looking like a punk. About that time, Wally yelled "Teacher!" and I foolishly looked up. When I began to turn around, Jared's fist connected with my right jaw, and I was down for the count face first into the pavement. When I finally came to, I had two friends and Principal Tanner peeling me off the ground to escort me to the office. I'll never forget the walk of shame as my peers pointed, laughed, and some shook their heads in disappointment. I was kicked out of school for another five days.

When I informed Miriam that I had been suspended yet again, she was at a loss for words. Driving her to drankin' just couldn't capture how disappointed she was in my actions. This time, she didn't just let me sit for five days. I had to go everywhere she went and listened to her talk about me like I wasn't even there. Maybe she wanted her disappointment to finally sink in. Instead, I was usually bored out of my mind.

Five days just wasn't long enough. I didn't want anything to do with school anymore. Just as I did throughout eighth grade and most of the ninth, I sat in my desk chair refusing to participate and allowed my mind to wander. My report cards that year showed F atop F grades, and I even stopped participating in gym. Miriam wondered how in the hell I got a C in gym class, but I could never bring myself to articulate what was going on in the locker room.

The thought of getting naked in front of other boys horrified me, and getting dressed into shorts was bad enough. The moment I finally braved the unknown to take a shower after a hot, sticky outside gym day, Evan, a kid I played baseball with, started going around pinching butts and snapping people with towels. The towel snapping was kind of funny until he hit me, but I drew the line at touching my behind. Next time, I wore shorts while taking a quick shower and was immediately targeted since I was the only one with shorts on. He approached me from behind and yelled, "Look! This nigga's got shorts on!" There were a couple of laughs before he tried to pull my shorts down. I pushed him off warning him not to fuck with me. At that point, I decided that he needed to be taught a lesson. Nobody got to call me a nigger. I hurried up to dry off, so I didn't have to endure his unwelcomed play. I contemplated punching him in the back of the head while he was sitting and laughing, then I realized I had a combination lock in my hand. Without any further thought, I drilled it into his lower back. Evan sprang up and knew immediately who had done it. He grabbed me by my shirt asking what the fuck was wrong with me, and I grabbed his throat letting him know that no one calls me a nigger and also warned if he ever touched me like that again, I'd kill him in his sleep. We were broken up before the gym teacher reentered the room. Nothing else had to happen after that. I think we were on the same terms even though we didn't respect each other.

After opening the report card for the next to last period to see more failing grades, Miriam was at her wits end with me. I was no longer her prizefighter. I was no longer her pet project.

I was just a boy too far gone for her to save. Staring at my report card in disbelief, she sat me down at the kitchen table after dinner for a "come to Jesus" talk that I can recall like any major life milestone.

"Adam, I don't know what to do with you. How many fights are you going to start? You're mad at the world and for no damn good reason. What the hell are you gonna do, fight everybody? You're failing every damn subject at school except gym. It's like you've completely given up on yourself. The least you could do is at least act like you give a damn. You haven't brought a single book home all year to study, and now you're about to fail the ninth grade. Well, I'm here to tell you that you're not staying here if you do. Nobody else gives a damn about you. Don't you understand that? Your next road is down to the juvenile detention center. I don't know what's going to happen to you, but I can't deal with this shit no more. You better make a decision about what you want in this life, and you had better make it quick! It's your decision. I'm done!"

She got up from the table and walked away. That was the most pivotal moment toward becoming the man I am today. I didn't know it at the time, but Miriam's heartfelt words were exactly what I needed to hear. It was a wake-up call that finally penetrated my hardened soul. Her melancholy tone suggested that she had genuinely given up on me. Miriam was my last refuge, and I'd at least realized that much.

All of this time, I stayed waiting for some angelic savant to swoop down and save me. I came to the realization that I was going to have to save myself. However, I had no idea how to go about this transformational change. I thought to myself, *"I wasn't good at anything except listening to music and writing, but only to keep it enclosed in my prized trapper keeper."* Dropping out and running away crossed my mind, but I'd already tried and epically failed at that once before. If I had a car to make it all the way back to California, I could just start anew. The notion was foolish and unrealistic, but it was always a source of hope I desperately hung onto in stressful times. Somehow, I believed, the southern California sunshine would whisk my angst away. I had difficulty accepting reality since I was only interested in a façade where the world catered to me. Applying myself meant living up to someone else's expectations, and as far as I was concerned, anyone who expected anything out of me could go to hell. Then I thought, *"Maybe this was my hell. No matter what I did, my life was going to be relegated to hell on Earth."*

Either way, I reverted back to my religion and decided to give prayer a chance. I wasn't a good person, so I didn't see the odds being in my favor of deserving another shot. However, I didn't know where else to turn. I'd pushed everyone out, so there was no one left to advise me. After everyone went to bed, I went into Miriam's off-limits living room to get on my knees and pray over the couch. Even in complete darkness, it took several moments to clear my distracted mind. After shaking off the doubt and self-interruption as to whether or not this exercise would work, I started by asking for forgiveness. I assured God that I didn't want to be this way. I admitted to being scared of the uncertainty and asked for the Lord's hand to guide the way. I finally asked for help to be a good person. I was tired of being terrible and feeling unaccepted. I paused as I had finally awakened from my reign of mischief. I flashed back through my worst moments, all of the bad grades and finally came full circle to hitting Aaron for no reason. I was ashamed of my transgressions and once again begged the Lord for forgiveness. I closed, "In Jesus' precious name, Amen."

I didn't know what to expect next, but I had tapped into something extremely powerful. It wasn't a voice that I could translate, but more akin to a reawakening of my soul. When the doors had all but closed on my life, I'm nearly certain that a greatness that can only be explained as God let itself in and convinced me to achieve something greater than myself.

The next morning, I awoke feeling liberated after that deep prayer. Without a doubt, I'd finally tapped into the depths of my stumbling faith. As I moved through my morning school routine, I felt empowered to rewrite my future. When the bell rang to signal the end of the day, I cleared my locker for the first time and filled my backpack with every provided textbook. I started my renewal by studying on the bus ride home and well into the night.

Everyone was skeptical about my overnight change. At best, most thought I would fizzle out at some point and just fail out of school. I was never shy about not wanting to be there and how much I hated sitting still. To go from a nonconformist to treating teachers with respect, raising my hand to answer questions, and turning in homework on time doesn't just happen in everyday life without some sort of explanation. Conversely, the thought of proving my teachers, peers and Miriam wrong motivated me that much more. After buckling down and studying every night for six straight weeks, I managed to pull off my great comeback and pass the ninth grade by the skin of my teeth. For my final report card the cumulative grades read:

English 9: C-

World History: D-

Math 8: D

Earth Science: C

Keyboard Applications: C-

Physical Education: B+

Energy and Power: D-

There were no celebratory gestures, but a few of my teachers told me that they knew I could do so much better. Miriam even managed to crack a smile and mentioned that she was happy that I finally decided to act like I had some sense.

That sigh of relief was short lived once I showed Doug my improved report card. Instead of words of encouragement, he did a double take, took a deep breath, and handed it back to me without saying a word. Crow is a tough bird to chew, but I never expected much after he referred to me as a dumbass.

For a number of reasons, Doug left Miriam shortly thereafter that and returned to his hometown in North Carolina. He didn't even give her the courtesy of breaking up face-to-face or even a phone call. He just disappeared for weeks and out of the blue he called one night from North Carolina. They talked for hours that night, and we were on our way to North Carolina early the next morning. We spent an entire day down there doing nothing while Miriam tried to convince him to come home. As Noah and I got situated in the car, they kissed one last time. I don't know what happened, and I didn't even dare to ask. I could only assume the worst since Miriam was silent the entire ride back. That was the longest trip of my entire life. There wasn't a damn thing to do except sit and hope to God she would stop and let us get a bite to eat at some point.

After months of anxiously waiting by the phone for his call, Miriam finally accepted that she had lost Doug. In return, she immediately became bitter toward me. Noah was smart enough to keep to himself, but I decided to rebel against her demands. She didn't want us inside at all, so we had to spend the better part of the day outside during that sweltering summer when she was home. If I went into Granny and

Granddaddy's house, she would call and tell us to get out. She claimed we were eating up too much food and drinking everything in sight. The real kicker for me was that she moved us to the back seat. Noah and I had always played shotgun, but now we were both relegated to the back of her Altima. If our cousins, Marcel and Dante were in tow, they got to sit up front, but somehow we weren't good enough. To this day, I think Miriam blamed us for her loss in the end. We certainly didn't do her any favors, but Miriam had other challenges going on her life, which included going on excursions throughout Northern Virginia looking for Demarius' daughter, J'nelle. She was actively working the system to gain custody of her, but that process took time. Sometimes Doug traveled with her, but with my ill-behaved actions and everything Miriam was taking on, it ultimately proved to be too much for him in the end.

When J'nelle was born, Demarius was in prison and would remain there until she was six years old. Miriam opened a reserved space in her heart for her first granddaughter. The few times I got to hold her, I could understand why. She was just as innocent and precious as any newborn infant and deserved to be loved. At the time, I didn't put any thought into how her coming into this world might have an effect on my life. Logically, it didn't make sense to be jealous of her in any way, but I would constantly be accused of that very charge in the coming years.

J'nelle's mother was a crack addict, but her newborn daughter didn't manage to slow her addiction. Instead, she went to great measures to track down a hit, snort, or bag leaving J'nelle in someone else's custody for days or even weeks at a time. When Miriam discovered this news, she went into a tailspin like any loving grandmother would do. Miriam would get on the phone immediately yelling at J'nelle's mother at the top of her lungs until she would come out of her drug-induced stupor to remember the last home she had left her granddaughter. Miriam would drop everything to go get her and bring her back to our house.

J'nelle's mom would show up out of nowhere and take her back, repeating the same, tired old habits from before. Miriam always worried about neglect, perverts getting a hold of her or worse yet, killing her. I didn't understand the magnitude of the situation at the time, but when Miriam finally gained custody of her after years of fighting, things seemed to go back to normal with an extra toddler in tow. She slept with Miriam at night, and it stayed that way for the rest of the years I lived with them. The only time the two were separated was when Miriam had to work. At that point, Granny took her in with all of the other kids during the day and sometimes into the late evening.

Nothing had really changed for us until Christmas time. Noah and I would receive eight to ten gifts, and J'nelle would have a pile as tall as I was at the time. I was satisfied with new clothes and music, but I noticed this as a turning point in the way things were going to be from that moment onward. Miriam made sure to let us know that we belonged in the back seat and J'nelle at three years of age was worthy enough to sit up front. I quickly grew tired of putting up with the subtleties of second-rate treatment. However, that was only the beginning. Miriam's hard line, unfair approach with us versus her laissez-faire approach with J'nelle caused me to resent both of them, and my only outlet was penning my frustrations to Mom:

"... She also has a granddaughter named J'nelle that everyone thinks I'm jealous of which is not true. She is 4 years old and she calls me stupid, tells me to shut up, cuts our lights and TV on and off, she pulls the sheets off Noah's bed, she spits on us, throws food at the table, stabs me with her fork, she licks me, bites me, and scratches me, screams in my ear and then she'll ask me for juice or to put a movie in and usually when I do something for her she says thanks stupid and runs and I can't do nothing about it. She manages all that with her room stuffed with toys and TV and VCR, and loads of movies, and she takes a big toll making my temper hard to control. I pray to God that this will end someday, but I'm starting to lose faith, not in Him, but myself."

I needed a solution, and driving my own car seemed like the best option. I'd earned my learner's permit during the spring of my ninth-grade year. When I approached Miriam about it that summer after my ninth-grade year, she stated that I wasn't mature enough, and I needed to prove it by getting good grades next year. I was disappointed that she couldn't see the new me, but I kept the back talk to myself. I figured it was fair since I'd given her so much trouble over the years. I was motivated to prove her wrong, so I suggested passing the time by working. She retorted that I wasn't mature enough to handle a job. I rejected her logic and gloated that she couldn't possibly know that unless I showed her how hard I could work. I knew I would be great if given the chance, but she dismissed it as back talk, and I wasted that summer doing next to nothing.

To prove to Miriam that I was a born-again child with good intentions, I made plans to clean her house once she left to visit Demarius at the state penitentiary. I peered out our window to ensure she had left for the day. The house was an absolute disaster since she had been working so much, and I hadn't noticed enough to pick up the slack. I knew I had at least six to seven hours before she returned, so I started with the dusting then moved to wiping down walls and baseboards. Then I moved to the bathrooms, which I still dislike doing to this very day. Nevertheless, the sinks, toilet, bathtub, mirror, and floors were scrubbed to perfection. I moved from making all of the beds to cleaning, drying and putting away the dishes. I didn't even bother to stop for lunch. Instead, I pressed onward to vacuum the floors and finished with sweeping and mopping. Finally, I mowed the yard and still had time to spare before she returned.

Her face lit up like she had received Christmas in July. When she told me her intent was to come in and start cleaning after being gone for nearly eight hours, I knew my decision to forego playing video games all day was the right move. It was the first time I can recall her hugging and directly praising me.

Shortly thereafter, along with my sulking and relentless pestering, Miriam finally wore down and coordinated with Nana to get my foot in the door with the Cartwrights. They were a couple in their late sixties enjoying retirement life out in the countryside of Flint Hill, Virginia. As I gazed through their luxury A-frame home overlooking a pond, I was convinced that they probably swam in piles of cash when no one was around. I knocked on the door, and Janet answered with a warming invite. I couldn't help but look around in one of the most beautiful homes I'd ever set foot in. Their furniture was so fancy I asked if I was allowed to sit on it. I'd only seen stuff this nice in magazines, and no one was ever sitting on the furniture. They didn't have show-only rooms like Miriam, so I was invited to sit down.

As I waited for Leonard, I kept turning my head like an owl to admire their floor to ceiling bookshelves. I'd never seen a house with a library in it. I was fascinated by the window architecture that allowed me to take in the mountains from their living room sofa. Leonard finally strolled downstairs after a few minutes. He looked somewhat regal coming down a staircase outlined with books and large bay windows. He was a tall man who walked with a hunch that signaled tiredness from a meaningfully accomplished life. His sweater vest was unusual attire in my experience, but he always wore one, even in the middle of summer. Although I could never see myself in such a get-up, I admired his book collection and wondered if he truly had that much knowledge stored in his head. I didn't see how it could be possible.

Leonard interrupted my sightseeing by asking me what I wanted in life. Without hesitation, I told him I wanted a house like his. Well, you need to be smart and work hard to earn a house like this. "Well, what do I need to do?" It didn't take long before I realized that was the wrong follow-up question to ask. After the grand tour, I started working at his home around 9AM and didn't stop until noon. I swept and dusted the entire downstairs, washed both of their cars, pulled weeds, mowed his yard and weed whacked his bank, which stretched the entire upper half of his lengthy, curved driveway.

I hustled hard and expected my first pay day to be big. I didn't have a set dollar amount, but I felt like I'd proven myself as a hard worker. Leonard calmly offered a seat at their kitchen barstool while his wife brought us sandwiches and water. We discussed my ambitions, which happened to be brief because I only made short-sighted references to making money. Leonard rolled his eyes and explained that I needed to find my passion for something and set my goals around that. His advice was solid, but I wasn't much of a futurist at the time. Instead, I had my sights set on what I was going to spend my money on if he ever decided to pay up!

We took the long way home through some dirt roads and talked a little bit more about my future and the importance of a good education. Finally, we were in Miriam's driveway. He stretched his hand into his pocket managing to pull a roll of bills while extending his opposite hand with my earned share. I unrolled the tightly curled bills to discover George Washington's face on both of them. While I didn't have a problem with our first president, I took issue with the "one" on each corner of the bills. I flipped both bills to make sure I didn't miss a twenty. I looked at him and gave him a chance to correct his mistake without saying something disrespectful. He gave me a crooked smile while nodding his head expecting a thank you. I shook my head in discontent and exited his car without looking back.

Miriam asked, "Well, how did it go?"

"Two dollars is how it went. My time and hard work was only worth two damn dollars!" Miriam asked if I was going back as I stomped off to my room. I turned around and screamed, "No, I ain't going back! I ain't interested in no damn sharecropper wages!" I thought to myself, *I couldn't even think about a car. All of that work, and I didn't even have enough money to buy the latest album."* I popped a mixed-tape into my Walkman, placed headphones on and drifted off into a better world.

Music provided a much-needed escape. Hip-hop and rap seemed to speak to me in a way no one else could. During my most turbulent years with Miriam, the only thing that could get through to me was a verse about hardship or struggle. When the Notorious B.I.G. or Biggie gave a shot out to all of the teachers who said he'd never amount to nothing or eating sardines for breakfast, I felt like we were one in the same. Finally, someone out there understood the shit I was dealing with. More importantly, I could accomplish something and be successful one day. While I couldn't relate to a lot of what he was rapping about since he survived in the projects, his verse in *One More Chance* was instrumental in rethinking the way I looked at myself. It would be several years before I'd regain my sense of self-worth after my fifth-grade year, but his line "Heart throb; never. Black and ugly as ever; however, I stay Gucci down to the socks. Rings and watch filled with rocks…" The relentless harassment during my fifth-grade year left me feeling too dark, unwanted, and ugly. I couldn't afford his style, but I internalized his bravado and accepted my "ugliness" with a renewed sense of pride. No doubt, the wounds were still raw inside, but that line convinced me that I would be okay in the end.

Tupac was and still is one of my favorite rappers of all time. His lyrical style was more versatile than Biggie's, and I could always find a track to fit my mood at the moment. Whether I needed inspiration or to release my toxic anger by rapping along, I could rely on Tupac to get me through my problems. However, toward the end of his life, he gave a lot of horrible life advice that I just couldn't get down with.

The aftermath of the east coast versus west coast garbage left me longing for another music genre. I no longer wanted to be associated with either one of them since I'd finally turned my life around for the better. However, that wasn't the way some of my black peers viewed the issue.

While at school, Devonte approached me about choosing a side. I retorted that I wasn't interested in being on either side since they were both being dumb as hell and went on to explain that rap is supposed to be about having a good time and hip hop was about the struggle. His reply suggested that none of my rant sunk in as he claimed to be on the west side. I explained to him that we were in Rappahannock, which is in Virginia and on the east coast. Again, his stupidity shone through as he informed me that he was on the west side of Rappahannock. I shook my head letting him know that his statement was the dumbest thing I'd ever heard anyone say. I also thought about just not being black anymore. I thought, *"If I had to be that ignorant then someone can go ahead and revoke my black card!"*

When both men were shot within months of each other, I gave up on rap and hip hop altogether. After Tupac had died that previous October, I wasn't trying to go that route. Besides, I couldn't pretend to be that hard even if I wanted to. My ears ventured out to alternative genres including Godsmack, Green Day, Korn, Nirvana, Sublime, Matchbox Twenty, Dave Matthews Band, Red Hot Chili Peppers, and System of a Down. The lyrics from these artists better related to what I was going through at the moment, and that they should've been in my rotation long before then. However, nothing could touch Rage Against the Machine and Linkin Park. I was never opposed to listening to other music, especially since I'd DJ'd several school dances during prior years, but I'd never paid close enough attention to the words. I found that I was able to relate better to the lyrics, and it helped mellow me out most of the time. Of course, that mellow feeling could also have been attributed to the weed circles I visited during field parties while taking in some music genres I wouldn't have considered otherwise. Marilyn Manson's music had to come with a toke from the circle to listen to. I even managed to take in some Garth Brooks, Alan Jackson, Reba McIntyre, and Tim McGraw at the time. The country reminded me of being home with Mom. She introduced me to country music when we were in California. Taking it all in provided the opening my mind needed to cope later in life.

Since I couldn't do without groups like Outkast, Goodie Mob, Lost Boyz, or Wu-Tang, I eventually returned from my rap hiatus. I decided to do away with the stuff that was too hardcore and decided to stick with the medium-grade stuff. Slick Rick, Will Smith, Salt N Peppa, Puffy, and Mase worked most of the time, but when I needed to feel down to earth, Queen Latifah, Bone Thugs, LL Cool J, and Nas would fit the bill. Anytime I felt anger pulsating through my body, DMX's flow got the job done. Although, I'd managed to straighten out, anger was still ingrained into my everyday life. It was just a matter of controlling it, and rap helped with the release. I was also a No Limit fanatic who had to have every tape or CD Master P's entourage released. At the time, it was just so different, and the beats were amazing to ride down the country roads; even in my busted up Mercury Lynx hatchback. As cool as I thought I was, listening to their lyrics on repeat contributed to my refocus on materialism.

I could reminisce about rap and hip hop all day, but R&B was where I truly wanted to be mentally. The only thing I obsessed about more than money was girls, and I was hoping Babyface or Boyz II Men could offer some advice in that department. However, that never occurred since I couldn't muster up the confidence to be that smooth on any given day.

I'd practice lines from some of the Soul 4 Real, Jodeci, or Tevin Campbell tracks in the mirror, but it all sounded so corny coming from me. I couldn't bring myself to say those words to tell my new flavor of the week. Somehow, I did manage to gather enough courage to ask two girls to be with me before giving up on them all together. Within a week of each other, I had been rejected without hesitation. I was livid, but my only reaction was venting on paper to Mom:

"...I am officially done with girls from Rappahannock County because they don't know what's good for them...."

I frequented that mentality throughout my early years of rejection from the opposite sex. I'd refocus my energy elsewhere in an attempt to conceal the hurt that inevitably followed. Yet, I always managed to come back with a new approach that was never quite "me." One of my most memorable instances was when I'd just turned 16. That late summer of 1996, I arrived at Jams, a dive night club in middle of nowhere Culpeper, VA, full of renewed confidence and self-convinced sex appeal. However, the end result proved to be catastrophic for my self-esteem. The evening started with my cousins taking me through the entrance line. The go-go music was bumping, and all of the boys were bopping their heads, so I tried to mimic their bravado. The array of perfumes the women had over-applied conflicted with one another, but smelled alright to me. I was confident that my Cool Water scent was going to be alluring enough to assist with the attraction. The excitement was building, so I took my money out way too early making the wait seem much longer. It was ladies night, so my cousins got in free with that set up. I thought this would definitely increase my chances of taking some numbers home and finding at least one female who would be feeling my vibe.

Instead, the four women I approached were certified ego crushers. As soon as I opened my mouth, it was like "articulate brothers need not apply!" I spent the rest of the night being one of the lames who tried to ease into one of the girls on the floor only to have their girl groups react with a synchronized scoot away from my all-to-familiar awkward approach. At one point, I would have preferred to drink this problem away, but I was underage. Just when I thought the night couldn't get any worse, the guy collecting the entrance fee shot a bullet into the floor right by my left foot and ran off with the money. My dejected state of mind quickly flipped into flight or fight mode, and I quantum leaped from a standing position to find cover under a pool table. After that nonsense, the night was officially over. My cousins found me since they promised to bring me home safely, and we headed home. I was grateful to still have my left pinkie toe attached, but I thought, *Man, you can't get a group of black peeps together, without someone messing it up for everybody.* I also remember coming to the conclusion that black women were never going to be interested in me.

After that night, I seriously considered changing who I was and thought maybe I was "acting white" as so many blacks had accused before that night. Maybe there was a "real black man" somewhere inside of me that was suppressed by my desire to succeed. To this day, that mentality seems to be illogical to any black person who isn't a rapper or baller. I could neither string two bars together, nor shoot a basketball, so both options were out of the question. That same night, I reasoned with myself and rejected the notion that I had to subject myself to blatant ignorance or some sort of unattainable athleticism to impress girls.

Searching for a girl in tenth grade did not prove any easier than when I was too young to be worried about girls five years earlier. I was on the honor roll for the first time and had a much better handle on my temper. Although I was still painfully shy, I decided to test my newfound confidence on Sylvia. My hesitant series of questions quickly led her to believe that I was clearly trying to ascertain her interest in me. She put an end to that real quick, by replying, "You ain't thug enough for me...I need a roughneck brotha to satisfy me!" while stereotypically rolling her head and sticking her hand in my face causing me to naturally blink. After she had walked away from her locker, I was only surprised by my unscathed reaction. Either I was subconsciously prepared for an abrupt rejection, or I realized that there would be other chances.

Whatever the case, I had Jackie interested in me at the same time. I didn't want to settle and hoped that she would eventually find a new flavor of the week. However, that never happened, and I had to let her down as gently as I could, since the chemistry just wasn't there for me. She finally cornered me in a room with three of her friends behind her after English class. I hated to embarrass her like that, but I had to say that I wasn't interested. I slid past her and exited as quickly as I could. I remember the tension melting away from my shoulders and going to lunch with a sense of relief that it was all over; except that it wasn't. The news made it around the cafeteria before I even had a chance to sit down. That was the unfortunate reality of attending a small school; my business was always out there in public regardless of my objection. Just like any other time girls became too much of a distraction, I renewed my focus on school.

Chapter Six

Trial by Fire

During the summer of '96 transformation, I was reading any magazine or books I could get my hands on. However, the most important reading I did that summer was thanks to the *Narrative of the Life of Frederick Douglass: An American Slave.* Mr. Douglass' sly tactics of tricking white children into teaching him how to read at a time when it was forbidden motivated my learning strategy. It wasn't a secret that I was severely behind the curve and needed make up ground if I had any intention of graduating high school. I figured the only way I was going to get any smarter and catch up with the rest of my class was by initiating conversations related to the material. While I knew it wasn't necessary to strive to be the smartest in my class, I wouldn't settle for anything less than A/B honor roll for the upcoming school year. First, I had to set out and regain respect and seek forgiveness from my peers.

My attitude to start the year was night and day compared to the prior year. The reformation was met with skepticism, but it didn't deter me from seeking redemption. Although my reputation was well known, starting the year with nearly all new teachers, made it much easier to begin with a clean slate. However, I realized my past actions were unforgettable to some, and it would just be a matter of time and patience to prove myself worthy of forgiveness. Thankfully, some of my friends were able to let bygones be bygones. They were willing to discuss subject matter and help me with questions I had related to homework that they easily understood. Once they saw me making the effort to help myself, my friends and teachers were willing to assist in any way they could. I allowed my teachers' words to absorb and expand my mind beyond anyone's expectations.

The depth of my intellectual journey began when my English teacher, Ms. Constance provided our reading assignment, *Anthem*, by Ayn Rand. The author's work was the fiction that opened my mind to understanding my place in the system. Immediately, I realized the similarities between the protagonist, Equality 7-2521 and me. The setting was exactly how I envisioned the world at that time. Instead of being satisfied with what authoritarians were feeding me, I always pondered about what other opportunities existed in the world for those who refused to conform. His desperation to defy the status quo in search of something greater reminded me of my insatiable curiosity. I thought, *"There had to be more than sitting in a seat and memorizing certain information for hours on end."* Despite the odds, no one could seem to crush his spirit, and that's what I admired most about him. I longed to discover a new world and a chance to start anew. Rand's book gave me the fortitude to reach my ambitions despite societal norms to grade and determine my future outlook on life. I was no longer a troubled boy destined for nothing but failure. I was a prospect with potential that had yet to be determined, and I could learn if allowed to express my gifts more freely. For me, the first thing I had to do was escape the confines of Rappahannock if any of my wild dreams were going to have a chance to come true.

As and Bs were coming out of the woodwork on my report card. Even I was surprised but more proud than anything else. That first report card with my principal's handwritten encouragement was the proof I needed to validate my transformational efforts. When I finally determined that I wasn't stupid and could accomplish whatever I wanted to, the self-limiting voice was silenced for most of my sophomore year. Miriam remained skeptical throughout this period but mostly due to my demanding attitude. Our relationship may have been beyond repair by that point. Compliments were hard to come by, so I just settled for food and shelter until I could graduate and get out with no intent to return.

However, Coach Van, the high school track coach, took an interest in my turnaround early in the year and was a source of encouragement. He recommended getting into sports and asked if I had ever considered college. I was definitely interested in getting back into some kind of sport, but I'd never heard of college before he put the thought in my head. Throughout the year, I was able to get my hands on a few magazines that listed colleges and what life was like on each campus. The possibilities began to swirl, and my first sense of hope for the future began to take hold.

The flickering dream of making it back to California excited me and by the spring of that tenth-grade year, I had my sights set on the University of Southern California (USC). Coach Van pointed me toward our guidance counselors for more information. Instead of meeting with Ms. Fixton, whom always had positive words for me, I had an ill-fated meeting with Mr. Farrell. I didn't have an affirmative opinion of him, but my unease around him was confirmed when I reiterated my college aspirations. Without hesitation, "College isn't for people with your background," he retorted. I was stunned. Without anything to say, I turned around and walked out of his office. I was incensed, but not in the way that I was known for with the impulse to physically hurt someone. I was pissed off in a defiant, self-motivational kind of way. His words certainly cut into my ambitious goal and caused me to doubt myself any time I was up against difficult subject matter. Regardless of anyone's opinion, I wanted to show Mr. Farrell and all of my naysayers that I was indeed college material. I could be smarter than the limitations they placed on me.

I started by finishing my tenth-grade year on a strong note. The feat wasn't easy, but I managed to defy everyone's outlook by maintaining an A/B honor the whole school year.

English 10: B

Pre-Algebra: B

Biology: A

French I: B+

Accounting: B

Physical Education: A+

Materials and Processing: B

I took a great deal of pride in that final report card since it was my first taste of academic accomplishment. Up to that point, I may not have been as smart as the rest of my class, but that report provided substance to the thought, *"I can."* However, my reaffirmed can-do attitude didn't come without consequences. With days of reckoning my past ahead of me, the pressure to be something different or better intensified. I didn't have a definitive understanding to articulate how I felt, but the level of stress was very real. It wasn't the stress of insecurity; instead, it was the stress of trying to succeed and meet my high expectations. Oftentimes, this felt worse since I didn't know how to cope this new form of pressure.

In high school, I walked around in what I can only refer to as a perpetual out-of-body experience. I attribute that elusive feeling to being around girls. The inability to control raging hormones is common among teenage boys, especially without the guidance of a positive male role model. I always wondered if there was a way to extract it and place it in a jar not to be released until age thirty-five. The awkwardness I was desperately trying to shed as I talked to girls always came back causing my tongue to trip on my words and let me make a complete fool of myself. I didn't think too much about any girl being out of my league, and my only rule was to refrain from messing with a girl who was dating someone else, no matter how much I liked her. Despite the influential rap lyrics suggesting otherwise, I afforded that level of respect to every boy in the school. Unfortunately, that same level of respect wasn't returned in favor. My first love affair ended in the worst possible way, and I wanted to forever alter the lives of the two who betrayed me.

The details are fuzzy regarding my decision to go steady with Aubrey, but I recall riding the bench during basketball season and admiring her full figure and brunette hair with blonde streaks curled just so while cheerleading. I remember her charming smile and twinkling eyes constantly focused on me. Although she'd recently broken up with one of my teammates, Devonte, she quickly turned her attention toward me. By that point, I had managed to turn my life around, but I was still struggling with my self-esteem. Nevertheless, she was persistent and sort of guided me through the phases of going steady. When Aubrey explained how all of this worked, all I remember thinking was *God, I really suck at this. How can the rest of the boys in my family get all of the girls they want, and yet I didn't get an ounce of game in the relationship department?*

Even though I was excited about the possibilities, I was at an immediate disadvantage without a car. Dating was difficult in Rappahannock because everything was a thirty to forty-five minute drive away from us. We managed to talk on the phone often, but it wasn't the same. Even though I bought her gifts and thought I was saying all of the right things, I could tell she was getting bored after a couple of months of the same monotonous routine. The other important thing I could not muster up enough willpower to do was kiss her. Other than holding hands or a peck on the cheek, I could not handle the embarrassing feeling that came with expressing public affection.

However, that all changed one night after a basketball game. I went in to give my robotic, standard issue peck on the cheek when she softly clutched my face, and we passionately connected for what felt like a dream spell. There were so many feelings going through my body. We stepped back, smiled and kissed one more time before heading to our parent's cars to take us home. Although my irremovable smile suggested my elation, I really wished I had a car at that moment. Oh, I wanted so much more.

Our relationship was going well after that moment, but I still couldn't shake off my shyness. Although I brought flowers to school and made other romantic courtship gestures, something did not feel right toward the end. I never felt like I was doing enough and often compared myself to her ex-boyfriend. Even though the insecurity was material, I felt inferior because I didn't have a car. My anxiety was not necessarily about the car as it was about taking Aubrey on dates or shopping. I began to obsess about my lack of material possessions instead of being such a lame boyfriend. One Friday, we held hands and kissed after basketball and cheerleading practice unknowingly for the last time. I called several times over that weekend, but they went unreturned.

The following Monday, my world seemed altered. I worried all weekend and the tightness in my chest signaled our relationship was about to change. I tried to remain cool as I stepped off the bus and headed toward homeroom. I received avoiding looks from some of our mutual friends, and then it happened: Aubrey burst through the double doors with an entourage comforting her as she covered her face crying uncontrollably. They immediately escorted her to the bathroom and encircled her, so I couldn't reach out. She didn't even have to look at me. I may have been socially awkward, but I wasn't a fool. I came to the immediate conclusion that she cheated on me; now I just needed to find out to what extent and with whom.

Since her friends were not talking, I turned to one of our mutual friends, Marjorie, who broke down and told me that she had slept with her ex-boyfriend Devonte at a party that weekend. Devonte was easily the largest boy in the school, so he was not hard to track down. When I approached him about it, he squared up and said, "You should've kept your bitch on a tighter leash." I was physically stunned by his words, but also emotionally exhausted by this point. Given that he was at least twice my size; the prior imagery of smashing his face into the lockers quickly seemed like fantasy revenge. The surrounding students were stunned. The teacher was just out of hearing range, or she was partially deaf toward his crude comment. With all eyes on me and mouths still wide open, I simply replied, "She's not mine anymore. She's yours now." With that retort, we stared at each other momentarily, and I numbly walked to homeroom. The rest of that day was a blur.

My vindictive anger consumed me over the next couple of weeks. I became obsessed with the notion that they needed to be punished for what they did. I was closing the shoe store where I worked when my anger finally divulged into a blind rage. Two of my friends, Liam and Jay, came in as I was completing my closing duties. We were making plans to go out afterward and somehow the conversation diverted to Aubrey and Devonte. Unbeknownst to me, they were at the same party. They decided to let me in on the rest of what happened that night. After closing the store, I had heard enough. I slid into the backseat of Jay's car and told him to give me his gun. I had heard him brag about having a Glock in his glove box and decided that this was a perfect use for it. Then I demanded that he drive me to the party Devonte and Aubrey were at that night. They spent the better part of that night trying to talk me out of my determination. I reluctantly went home and collapsed on my top bunk. I eventually came to my senses after a solid night's rest.

With complete disregard for my future and my friends being accomplices to murder of two people, I finally realized that my life was out of control over a damned girl. After some reflection, my obsession with revenge had led to mistakes at basketball practice, and my test scores had dropped. I had no choice but to turn to prayer to quell my rage. I can't explain the overwhelming sense of relief as I let go, but I refocused my efforts on getting out of Rappahannock and making something of myself. I quickly realized that a relationship with an ungrateful chick like Aubrey wasn't going to make that happen. After that epiphany, I quickly reassigned my focus to sports and school.

If I could have just focused on academics, my year would have turned out to be exceptional. Adversely, I took on more than I should have right from the onset. Extracurricular activities, work, relationships, and school nearly led me to my breaking point. I thought all of this would fill my persistent void, but the gap only managed to widen. The more I achieved, the heavier I felt and the more my sense of hope for the future diminished. However, I was determined to discover some self-esteem and would go to any lengths to achieve it. I just needed a taste of success, so I decided to give basketball a try.

With what I considered my second chance at life, I was trying my damnedest to change my ways. With the arguments between Miriam and me escalating over J'nelle, I needed another outlet. The job and school weren't enough, so I took it upon myself to discover a sport where I could release some tension and boost my self-confidence. The traveling football team, started on behalf of Rappahannock, had already fizzled out, so I decided that basketball was the best option. Miriam reluctantly agreed to give me permission under the conditions that I could find a ride home on her work nights and tell her when I would be gone.

As usual, Miriam was apprehensive at first. She expressed her concerns that she didn't know if I deserved to be on a team again since I hadn't proven myself. I didn't know what that meant and felt like she was doing it out of spite, so I walked away. Later that night, she came by my bedroom and told me that I could try out for the team. I happily thanked her and immediately started writing the stats I wanted to rack up during my first year of play.

My first year with basketball didn't live up to the stereotype. I was tall, and my skin was a dark chocolate hue as always, but it didn't translate into a natural ability to get the ball through the hoop as society seemed to depict. I could only assume that part of my genetic code must have been repressed to make room for my resilience. My inability to dribble in a rhythmic motion and absence of the natural aggression I was known for the prior year quickly got me tagged as a practice dummy and benchwarmer for future games. Rappahannock had a lot of basketball talent, so I can only imagine that it wasn't a hard decision for the coaches to make. I was likely going to be a high-risk low-reward project even if they had time to work with me.

The one area I excelled at was defense. I didn't necessarily understand all of the coach's schemes, but I could block anyone who dared to drive toward my lane. I earned the nickname Mutumbo and was encouraged to wave my finger in the no-no motion to taunt the player who got rejected. I did it to entertain the team, but I wasn't into taunting since every other aspect of my game was missing. I jumped high enough to have my elbows level with the rim and could do that from a standing position. I always made sure to finish each drill first, no matter how many times we repeated suicides, wall sits or other conditioning workouts. I never slowed, no matter how many times we repeated machine gun drills. I gave my absolute all, but it never translated into skill. I did it with the hopes of earning a meaningful position, but rarely felt like I would be considered for anything else other than a practice stand-in toward the end. My talents weren't enough to impress the coaches enough throughout the years to work personally with me on fundamentals or put me in a game for a meaningful length of time.

The excitement during my rookie year was short lived. A few months after being on the team, Miriam decided to pull me off for what I considered the smallest of reasons. I didn't come home after school and travel back up the long stretch of Route 211 to attend practice as she had wanted. I figured since it was a thirty-minute drive out of the way; I'd come home with a friend after practice to save her time and gas money. I thought it would go over as a gesture of consideration, but my assumptions couldn't have been more wrong. After a long school day and hard practice, I came home exhausted. I was planning on getting a bite to eat then starting my homework when her reaction took me by surprise. The yelling and cussing ignited a born-again anger I assumed was long gone. I finally snapped, when she commanded, "That's it, you're off the team!" Her overreaction was met by my overreaction, and I lashed words right back in her face.

With fists clenched and fear of taking a swing at her, I ran for the door instead and rushed down the street. By the last glimmer of light left by the evening dusk, she tracked and chased me down in her car and demanded that I come home. I told her I wasn't coming back, and there was no way she could make me. She wouldn't stop her pursuit, so I bolted back across the hillside and ran into my cousin's house next door. I began explaining, with tears running down my face, how

Miriam unfairly took me off the team, when she let herself into the home. I stood up behind the couch to keep my distance. I was terrified of myself by this point and felt like I'd lost all control of my emotions. I can't recall the exchange of words, but once I shouted "Fuck you! You will never control me!" my cousin intervened and told me that I should never talk to my mother that way. I snapped back, "She will never be my mother! She's just keeping us for the fucking paycheck anyway!" My cousin informed me that was enough of that kind of talk in her house and demanded that I go home. Miriam was strangely calm by this point and added that we could talk about it more at the house. I'd come down from my adrenaline surge and was worn down to nothing by this point. I reluctantly went home and face planted into my bed pillow. My inability to handle the pressure of performing in school, losing my first girlfriend, struggles at home and lacking control over any aspect of my life metastasized into an overwhelming sense of internal havoc. Although I was doing well in school, the lethal feeling ate away at my confidence to pull off any sort of successful transformation without feeling like someone was in my corner. Miriam's decision was the last straw.

My darkest moment came later that night. I laid in bed wide awake well past my bed time and waited to hear Miriam snoring to know she was out cold. Noah had been asleep for a while, so I slipped off of my top bunk and made my way to the kitchen. I opened the drawer and pulled out a random steak knife. *Any knife would do the deed*, I thought to myself. I traced my index finger across the serrated edge as I made my way to the foyer. I chose the foyer because it was the closest area to the door. I also didn't want to mess up the carpet in Miriam's show rooms, and didn't want the memory of my dead body to haunt any of the other rooms. The ambulance could step right in and wheel me out without too much effort. There I stood in the foyer only lit by the full moon outside. I checked to make sure it was only the moon since the light seemed so vibrant. I just hadn't noticed it before what I thought would be my last night. It was a nice image to end my life. I turned to the wall and sat with my back descending against the wallpaper. I concluded that it was time to go to a better place. Regardless of my preacher's teachings, I didn't believe in heaven or hell for my afterlife. My perception of life was a constant hell, and heaven was always too far out of my reach. I figured my soul would just dissipate or wander aimlessly in the dark just like it had throughout my lifetime.

Wetness began to flow from my face to my shirt. I hadn't noticed that I'd begun to cry until the tear splashed against my arm. It signaled a brief moment of reasoning and allowed doubt to surface as a self-negotiation ensued. Part of me pleaded to stay. The other side, unconvinced, determined that it was time to drive this knife right through my heart. My heart didn't want to bear the brunt of the wound as it began to beat to the point of feeling paralysis in my left arm. I ultimately sided with death as I clenched both hands around the knife handle, lifted both hands above my head, and held the position. One final plea in the form of water began to drench my shirt. My hands shook uncontrollably as my nerves inexplicably intervened. Against my better judgment, I thrust the knife intentionally toward my heart but haphazardly penetrated through the opposite side of my chest directly into a rib bone. The pain was indescribable, but I can only decipher what followed as a state of shock. I involuntarily let go of the knife and tried with the strength I had left to refrain from vomiting. My heart and nerves overpowered my body and rescinded my right to function. All I could do was hold my laceration and weep silently into the veneer floor for a good part of the night.

Somehow, I managed to regain my composure and went into the bathroom to inspect the self-inflicted damage. Luckily, I wasn't even bleeding very much. I left the dried blood around the wound for fear of the sight of wet blood and covered it with a normal band aid. A hole in the shirt was going to provide evidence that required an explanation I wasn't prepared to give had Miriam decided to inquire. I used the shirt to soak up the puddle of tears on the foyer floor and buried the shirt underneath some garbage in the trash can. I crawled into bed for a few hours before getting ready for school the following morning.

Miriam informed me at the breakfast table that morning that I would be allowed to stay on the team. She just wanted me to know how it felt to have everything taken away when I chose to disrespect rules. I didn't even bother with a reply. I continued with my routine and left to wait for the bus outside. I was through with her antics and began plotting ways to go to a college as far away as possible to show her that no one would be able to take anything away from me. Unfortunately, that ambitious plan was easier said than done.

Shortly after that incident, Miriam finally allowed me to work at her shoe store. Since this was my first real job, I wanted to prove to Miriam that I was becoming a responsible teenager despite my internal struggles. I also wanted to prove that I was grateful for the opportunity, so I followed every training guide along her direction to ensure that the store looked textbook perfect. No shoe was left unturned. I vacuumed floors and wiped mirrors when it was slow. And I was always respectful and helpful to the customers. Those manners Madeline and Miriam had drilled into my head all of those years had been recognized while working at that store.

Many of the people didn't expect such a high level of respect from a teenage boy. I was always surprised by how many people complimented me on my demeanor since I didn't think it was that far from the ordinary. Later that summer, Miriam even allowed me to check in the inventory and reorganize the stock area. I was determined to be her best employee, but I was always saddened by the amount of my paycheck considering my goal of purchasing my own car. Although I was thankful for the job, I quickly realized that $5.15 per hour wasn't going to cut it. At this part-time rate, I'd have a car by the time I was out of college. Later that summer, Miriam discussed the possibility of a raise with her district manager who determined that I needed to be there at least six months before I could earn a ten-cent per hour raise. I thought to myself that I'd need to work ten hours for an extra dollar, which was two and a half shifts for me unless I worked weekends.

When I crunched the numbers and included insurance, I would never be able to afford to drive. The thought of riding the bus for the rest of my high school years devastated me. Miriam suggested that I request assistance from social services, so I wrote my first professional request to my state ward to ask for the insurance down payment. Within a few weeks, I had a check in hand and my eyes on a beat up 1989 Mercury Lynx hatchback. It wasn't a convertible Mustang, but the pickings were slim for $500. By the spring of '96, Mercury had discontinued that model, so I just pretended that it was a collector's edition. By lowering my expectations, I was able to find a solution if for no other reason than I was tired of bumming a ride from track practice.

The challenge of finding a sport at this late stage of my schooling had less to do with what could hone in on my interest as it did with finding a sport that could highlight my natural athletic ability. Basketball proved to be a disappointment, but I didn't want to relive my struggle with baseball either. On multiple occasions, I was encouraged to join the wrestling or soccer team, but neither sport piqued my curiosity.

When Coach Van discussed track and field as a possibility, I wasn't immediately excited about the idea. Other than Carl Lewis and Flo Jo, I didn't know other prominent names in track and field. Plus, I had no idea what each sport entailed. The sport was so unpopular in our school that we didn't even have a track for practice or hosting meets. The thought of running around the field on nothing but cinders didn't initially excite me.

Without any other options or experience, I took the best risk of my life up to that point and joined Coach Van's makeshift track and field squad. I didn't come in with any set of expectations or set impossible goals after learning that hard lesson in basketball. Instead, I just ran with every bit of strength and energy I had and let the times and distances fall on the coach's clipboards. My natural affinity for competition was better suited toward individual performance rather than the team pressure I felt playing ball. Coach Van always told me that I was built for speed, so I stuck with the 100-meter and 200-meter sprints as well as both the 4x100 and 4x400 relays. Triple, high, and long jumps were also added to the list of events I engaged in at each meet. Every event Coach Van assumed I would shine didn't always pan out in my favor. I performed below average for my first year in the high and long jump, and never really mastered the triple jump during my three years; although, I placed well enough to earn medals or ribbons in most meets. I excelled in the relay races as an anchor leg, but still searched for an event that was solely mine. The sprints should have been ideal, but my amateur running form didn't allow me to maximize my speed.

Finally, I heeded to Coach Van's recommendation to try the hurdles. At first, I was apprehensive about the 110 highs since so many of the athletes were smashing through and tripping over the hurdles. I thought to myself, *who in their right frame of mind would run this crazy race?* My first attempt at the 300 intermediate hurdles was on an asphalt track with basketball shoes on. We didn't have hurdles at the school, so my crash course was during the warm-ups as they set up the ten rows at Page County High School. Although I managed to avoid hitting them during the warm ups, I noticed how heavy my basketball shoes were and wondered how I would make it over ten hurdles as fast as the rest of the pack. All I kept thinking was *if I fall on this asphalt, it's going to hurt like hell.*

After securing that initial 300-meter intermediate hurdles victory, there was no other event for me. It was time to put all of my fears aside and showcase my competitive skill set. I wanted this event to be my outlet – to prove to myself that I was good at something and prove to everyone else that I was more than just another bad kid with a chip on his shoulder.

My reaction to the starting gun was still somewhat slow since I didn't want to have to deal with the embarrassment of a false start. However, I nailed the reaction during this first race. While I realized my clear height advantage, it didn't click until I was out in front and heard the crashing of hurdles behind me while I sailed effortlessly over each one. By focusing on form first, mainly due to fear of falling, and adding speed as I grew more confident, I was cruising to victory race after race. I ended the season as the district champ in the 300 hurdles. From that point on, the fifteen seconds in 110 highs and forty-one seconds in the 300 intermediates were a sanctuary for me. I would always scan the length of the track with a self-confirming reminder that this was my moment.

To discover something I was good at that wouldn't be taken away freed me from a lifetime of feeling repressed. I managed to win nearly every race that year in my basketball shoes and didn't face stiff competition until the regional championship. It was at the University of Virginia (UVA) where I realized what was in store for me when I eventually attended college. The rubber track surface, comprised of recycled tires, felt like clouds floating beneath my spikes compared to the asphalt that punished my back, joints and feet throughout the season. Although Miriam finally let me get a pair of running flats for the occasion, I still fell short of qualifying for state competition. Surprisingly, even to myself, I wasn't overly disappointed but excited about the possibility of next season. I promised myself states next year.

Chapter Seven

Sporting Chance

I started my high school junior year full of promise. My classes were manageable, or so I thought at the time. I was in my second year of participating in two sports, so I knew what to expect. My reputation was largely restored since I'd proven myself the previous year. The only uncertain aspects of my life were my future with Miriam and whether or not I would be able to overcome my self-doubts I battled on a daily basis. I was always seeking ways to pull myself upward, but the stress from the need to be great without having the proper resources negated any good that could have come from just simply participating. In search of filling my elusive void, I added cross country running to my already packed schedule and continued to play basketball much to my detriment.

When Coach Van convinced me to run cross country, I didn't have a clear concept of what running 3.1 miles would entail. The distance appeared to be especially short after glancing at our course around a vineyard across the road from our high school. Our course was one of the more admired ones among the runners since it was relatively flat compared to the rest of the schools in the mountain region.

During my first practice, I compared my physique to the other boys on the team and immediately assumed that I would be a top contender. I had so much success running multiple events during track and field season the prior year that I brushed off the thought of running long distance as being any sort of challenge. As Coach Van lined us up and gave the go command, I dashed out into the front of the pack and never looked back. As I sprinted through the rolling vineyard hills, I took in the Blue Ridge Mountain backdrop while huffing and pumping my legs toward what I thought was the finish line. Coach Van was encouraging me to keep my form as I leaned across the finish line marker. I placed my arms above my head trying to expand my lungs to catch my breath while heading straight for the water table. As I thought to myself, *this wasn't so bad*, Coach Van interrupted my self-congratulatory mindset, "Adam, what are you doing? You only ran half the course. Keep going!" I couldn't feel my legs, and my motivation to take another step had vanished. I reluctantly jogged the straightaway until I was out of sight then dragged my feet sloth-like until the rest of the boy's team passed me. I was embarrassed as they cheered me on, "Come on Adam, You can do it! Keep up!" I had nothing left to give. Completely disoriented, I didn't realize that I was back in sight of the coach, "Adam what's taking so long? Let's go!" I made a conscience effort to pump my arms to propel my body forward since my legs were involuntarily flailing to the outside. With each step feeling like a hill climb and my head bobbing like I was being controlled by an amateur puppeteer, I finally collapsed over the finish line. The leg muscle spasms quickly turned into vice-gripping cramps, and Coach Van tried to convince me to do my cool-down run. "What?" I protested. "What the hell is a cool down run? Running makes me hot! I can't even breathe, man!" He walked me through some stretch techniques to release the cramps, and that was the end of the worst practice of my entire sports career. I didn't quit the sport, but the psychological damage after that day reverberated through every run during my two-year stint as a wannabe distance runner. My work ethic probably came into question when it came to cross country, but long distance running was never my gift. However, my commitment was never questioned during basketball season. To this day, I don't know why I put so much pressure on myself to succeed at basketball. Maybe I tied my dedication to society's expectations for black boys or just one of my many unattainable goals, but whatever the case, it crippled my playmaking ability in front of a crowd. The handful of other times I was placed in a game, I managed to score during a few instances, but I was probably better known for my cringeworthy foul shooting. The immense pressure of having every head in the gym turned in my direction caused me to shake with unprovoked panic to the point of my arms going numb. I had the form but lacked the range as I'd lob the ball a foot or two short from the rim. At home or away, the same self-terrorizing routine pitting me against myself would play out with our fans covering their eyes or mouths in disbelief. During an away game that year, I managed to throw up consecutive missed foul shots to the unison chant, "Air ball! Air ball! Air ball!" I stuck my middle finger in the air as I backed down the court to position in defense. The next day, the coach showed me the videotape and suspended me for the next game. By that point, I didn't care anymore. Basketball aggravated all of the insecurities I'd battled over the years, and that night was the beginning of the end for any hopes I had in making it as a respectable baller.

My game time during those years of play was unremarkable. Still, I'll never forget the first time the coach put me in against a local academy team. After hustling down the floor, I got in position to work the high post and lifted my hand to signal for the ball. Our point guard, David, passed it to me, and I used the opportunity to prove myself. I took two hard dribbles to the top of the foul line for a turnaround jumper. The ball had barely left my fingertips before being swatted back down to the floor. As a flash of orange whizzed by my face, I lost balance on the way down causing me to crash to the floor with my blocker standing atop me with a sterling glare. I was taken out of the game less than a minute later and relegated to the bench. It was hard to look up after that moment. I felt that I'd let the entire team down with my weak shot.

After I'd accepted my role as a pine rider, Liam and I grew closer as friends by cutting up and flirting with cheerleaders. To this day, he's still the coolest redneck I ever had a chance to meet. However, he was a hard one to figure out. He sported cowboy boots and a wide-brimmed hat to top off the wardrobe, drove his big boy truck, listened to rap music, played ball and had access to some of the best weed in high school. He even explained the heritage of the confederate flag when I was uncomfortable entering Stonewall Jackson's high school gym because of their over-sized tribute to Dixie country. We spent the better part of that game night on the bench cracking racist jokes at one another.

Later that Friday night, we went to a field party and toked up together for the first time. As much as I enjoyed alcohol, I had binged too much at the last party, so I made a personal vow to steer clear of anything unless it was water. After helping Liam roll blunts for several minutes, we went outside to light up. At first it was just the two of us, but it didn't take long to attract a needy crowd. We welcomed everyone who paid a visit to sit in the weed circle puffing and passing until it disappeared. It turned out that I was an overly friendly pothead giving out hugs to anyone who would accept them followed by an, "I love you, man!" Afterward, I got the bright idea to hang upside down in a tree and yell, "Look, I'm a mother fucking bat!" The outbreak of laughter turned into panic as people scattered in different directions. I heard someone yell, "Cops!" and I high-tailed it about fifty yards through a hayfield into the forest and ducked behind what smelled like pine trees. I could sense some people around me, so I whispered for names. I heard five or six names, and we waited cold and silent for about an hour until the commotion appeared to die down. Someone asked, "Starks, are you gonna go check the scene to see if we're in the clear?" I replied, "Hell no! I'm the only black dude at this party. What do you think they'll do to my black ass smelling like weed? Fuck that!" After a few laughs, one of the white boys went to check the situation and in a few minutes yelled that it was okay to come out. All of us headed for the nearest warm car and got out of dodge. I didn't get to reconnect with Liam until the following Monday, but I managed to get a ride home with a car full of girls who lived near Amissville.

As much as I enjoyed Liam's friendship, basketball proved to be a colossal waste of time. It added an element of stress I didn't need while trying to determine who I was and discover my self-worth. I was deeply ashamed of my inept skill and chalked the experience up to nothing but a personal failure. Although, I'd like to believe people are well-intentioned, I loathe when people start a conversation with the question, "Do you play basketball?" While I understand it as an attempt to break the ice, my heart sinks a little since I know they are going to be disappointed with the answer.

I was never one to comply with the external forces attempting to shape me. I eventually grew to become aware of my limitations whether it was in sports or study. More importantly, I was okay with those limitations. I learned how to move on, but I also knew I was capable of greater things than shooting a basketball.

My girlfriend that year, Joanna, also knew I was more capable and convinced me to believe it. Joanna was a happy-go-lucky, completely innocent, highly intelligent, small town girl. She had a rare, genuine smile that always made me feel like I was appreciated. Whether she was watching me during track practice or we were sitting beside one another in class, I always felt like I could be myself. I remember our first encounter being in French class. Our teacher partnered us together to start speaking French to each other. We had to pick French names, so I chose Jean Claude since it sounded sort of badass and she took the name, Jacqueline. French is considered one of the most romantic languages in the world, and it was true in our case. We were going steady soon thereafter, which shocked a lot of people.

Some of the teachers seemed appalled by the idea of an interracial couple while our peers didn't seem to care one way or the other. Although I had engineered a 360-degree life turn around by this point, I hadn't successfully shaken my bad boy image. I think some, especially from her circle, were shocked because she seemed too innocent to go against the grain. For me, I rightly didn't give a damn what people thought. For all of the judgment I faced, she could see the true person I was becoming and her encouragement lit my soul aflame. She was the perfect intervention between my awakening during the last period of ninth grade and self-doubt that crept in while I underwent my self-transformation. No matter what I did for her, I never felt pressured or obligated to do it. She appreciated the gifts, but more importantly she cherished the time we spent together. She was a great listener to my aspirations, but she was a better conversationalist when I ran out of things to talk about. I had just finished reading my first novel, *Anthem* by Ayn Rand last year, so I was not as primed for intellectual conversation as she was.

Joanna was easily one of, if not the smartest, student at Rappahannock High. Seeing straight A's on her report card gave me something to aim for. It wasn't a competition since I wasn't on her intellectual level yet. I also knew I didn't have the basic curriculum preparation that she had throughout her privileged life, but I refused to make excuses for my shortcomings. I accepted my behind the curve status and often asked Joanna to explain things to me from her perspective. She always happily obliged, and I think she was somewhat honored to play that role. I also gave credit to her with helping me pass French II and III and having the fortitude to work with me after I regretfully had to break it off with her. Beyond academics, we always seemed to be in sync with one another. This laid back approach was a nice change that allowed me to focus on something more than the opposite sex.

However, she would do things that were sweet-natured but completely caught me off guard. When I received balloons and candy in history class one Valentine's Day, I wanted to melt onto the floor and through the ceramic tile crevices to hide my embarrassment. How in the world was I supposed to maintain my swagger carrying a heart-shaped balloon down the hallway? I scanned over the card to make sure it was not a mistake amidst the girlish giggles coming from every angle of the classroom, and I'd be damned if it were not mine. So here I am sporting a balloon and a cup full of candy at my desk with every eye in the room piercing my self-conscious soul. Nonetheless, as the class bell rang, I decided to put up a front and strut out of the class with my delivered goods. Joanna had the biggest smile on her face as the balloon floated well above the crowd of students. It was contagious, so I smiled cordially and thanked her for the gifts.

Unfortunately, the quick dates in her car, hand holding and sneaking kisses in between class would come to an abrupt end. Her father forbade us from dating and threatened to disown her if it continued. Unbeknownst to me, the community was talking and "the phase" his daughter was going through was too much to withstand. I was not allowed to date a couple of other girls in the school for the exact same reason, and never understood why I was good enough to shake hands with the fathers, but never worthy enough to date their daughters. Reflecting on the way others dads had rules for their precious daughters dating outside of their shade of skin put me front and center with a decision I did not want to make.

Joanna's solution to rebel against her family was not feasible. She wanted to run away and get married. She was willing to allow her family to disown her for a lifetime together with me. I remember being overwhelmed after considering it for the longest two seconds of my life. I'd watched a couple of movies about hopeless romantics and happily ever after storylines, but I had no idea that I had this kind of effect on her. To be truthful, she had the same effect on me, which made the decision even harder. However, I reflected on growing up without parents and knew she would come to regret that decision. Although she was under the impression that she would be forgiven, it could have been years before she would see them again. I didn't even consider the other logistics (moving in together, jobs, giving up sports, effects on our academics, etc.) or the fact that my foster mother, Miriam would have whooped my ass for pulling a stunt like that. The only thought that kept coming to mind was the love her family had for her. Although her parents were trying to protect her, I assumed that I would never be able to overcome the uncertainty and fear of my dark skin that led to their misguided decision. Right then, I knew it was necessary to make one of the hardest and most mature decisions I would make as a teen. I unwillingly told her that we had to end our relationship. I adored her but wasn't ready for that level of commitment. I told her that her family was more important than what we had. In my heart, I didn't feel it was the truth, but my conscience was confident that it was the right thing to do. I went home that night and yelled, "FUCK RACISM!" into my pillow so Miriam wouldn't hear me. However, the mixture of anger and uncontrollable levels of testosterone mercilessly led me to punch a dent into the side of my dresser. After trying to shake the pain out of my hand, I decided that breaking up with girls was bad for my health, and I was going to handle the next one better, or so I thought.

Once again, it was time to focus on sports and school. My junior year track season had a more promising outlook. I was apprehensive about Mr. Rossini joining the team as an assistant coach given our history, but I didn't allow the move to affect my goals. I was going to perform regardless of who stood in as coach. Surprisingly, it was thanks to my reverend's sermon on forgiveness and redemption that I even considered letting bygones be bygones. If I could change my ways, maybe he could as well. When I decided to let go, it was the first time I had genuinely forgiven someone for past misdeeds and signaled a turning point in my life.

I managed to come across a pair of cheap spikes at the mall, which felt much lighter but didn't necessarily help with speed on asphalt. My team would always inform me of sparks flying from under my feet as I landed my lead leg and sprinted to the next hurdle. Grinding those spikes into the hard surfaces made my body aches intensify, so I switched back to my running flats since I anticipated being far enough ahead of the pack to win. At the beginning of the season, my coaches found some old hurdles in what seemed to be an abandoned closet in the back of the high school. Those old-school clunkers with rusted metal holding them together would get the better of me and end any potential I had at achieving greatness. Although I expressed my doubts, I went along with the coaches' direction to perform my new set of practice drills over each of the few hurdles. I ended up with splinters in my thighs among other poor technique-related ailments. The repetitiveness of landing on cinders in spikes made my knees constantly ache. By mid-season, I dreaded practice because of all the constant joint and back aches that would follow. All of my minor aches and pains would eventually go by the wayside, but it was due to a much more serious injury.

I was losing a lot of sleep due to the pain, so I resorted to energy sodas and candy to stay awake in class. All of the poor nutrition and lack of sleep caught up to me one day as I collapsed while going over a hurdle and entangled my legs on the way down. I woke up hyperventilating and completely disoriented. Finally coming to during the ambulance ride, I had the mind-shifting thought that I was doing everything wrong. I needed to slow down, and I needed to address everything that was stressing me out. The revelation left me feeling very alone; although, I was surrounded by two paramedics who couldn't perform the needle stick needed for my IV bag. The doctors diagnosed me with severe dehydration and ordered me a dinner since I hadn't eaten anything of substance in a couple of days. After I had taken in the second bag of IV fluids and ate, I was on my way home with Granny since Miriam was stuck at work.

Once I was finally mentally aware, I concentrated on my physical ailments from the fall. I dug some of the cinders out of my arm and peeled back the large band aids to see the extent of my scrapes. These injuries and my ego would eventually heal, but the one invisible injury that kept pressing was in my right hip. Nearly every time I extended my lead leg, the hip flexor would snap. Regardless of what stretch or exercise I performed throughout my years of follow-up therapy, the pain extended through my lower back throughout the rest of my track career. Nevertheless, I ran through the pain and managed to salvage a successful season with the highlight being a district champ in the 110 and 300 meter hurdle events. Track and field positively redirected a reserve of strength that ultimately helped subdue my silent madness. With my newfound confidence I gave my best effort to come of age, but containing my explosive behavior managed to get the better of me if tested beyond its limits.

Damien was a hurdler from Manassas Park but largely unknown as a rival until we met on his home track. I don't know what I did to this guy other than my mannerisms weren't black enough for him. I recall talking and laughing with a group of girls on my squad and turning around to this brother sneering in my direction. I brushed it off at first, but a few minutes later he had gathered around part of his team to start shooting off at the mouth about my mother within hearing distance. After laughing and pointing ensued, I walked off the bench seats looking for something to hit but didn't succeed. Although my first instinct was to beat his ass in front of his team and on his home turf, I let the anger serve as motivation to beat him on the track. I didn't realize he was a hurdler until we stepped into the same designated area to warm up. He had the nerve to ask, "What are you looking at?" I replied, "What the hell do you think I'm looking at?" "Man, ain't nobody worried about you." Trying to refrain from hitting him, "Oh' you're gonna be worried after I take this race on your home turf." Damien replied, "Whatever, man," as he went back around the bench to get closer to his team. I countered, "Yeah, I got your whatever. You keep talkin' shit. I'll see you at the starting line."

"Runners, take your mark." Without hesitation, I got set in my blocks. My face full of sweat from my warm-up routine on overdrive and my feet set back hard in the starting blocks and ready to spring to the sound of the starting gun. Damien's routine took too long as he went through a series of stretches and arms swings typically reserved for elite athletes. The rest of us had to freeze in our positions to avoid a false start penalty. "Get set!" I arose with an enraged tenseness flowing through my entire body. I lifted my head to look toward the finish line through the labyrinth of hurdle bars. I closed my eyes to dig…"Pow!" The starting pistol interrupted my zone and the rest of the heat got a half second jump ahead of me. I caught up with most of them by the first hurdle. Damien kept his lead, but his form fell apart over the fourth hurdle as he slapped me across the shoulder before I passed him for good. All of his mouth didn't have an answer for the mad version of me. I crossed the finish line and made a sudden stop to turn around and stare him down as I skipped backward in a "yeah-I'm-bad" kind of way. I didn't say a word since we still had one more race to go.

Typically, I socialized in between my jumping events and relays, but it was hard to ignore that I was going to a dark place internally as Damien kept taunting me from his end of the bleachers. From the onset of the 300-meter hurdles, I had no intention of letting him win. He was weak in the 110s, and I wanted to show his entire school just how pitiful he was. From the gun, I took off without reserve. During the last 100-meter stretch, I couldn't feel tiredness and refused to accept anything less than absolute domination. As I crossed the finish line, I extended my arms and expanded my chest to release an alpha male roar as he was still crossing over the last hurdle. Our eyes had connected before he crossed the finish line. Without any regard for sportsmanship, I yelled, "This is my turf now! You make sure you tell all your friends about me. I'm running this shit now, boy. You hear me? Don't you ever in your life talk about me or my momma, boy. Now go sit your ass down somewhere before I beat you again." At the time, I thought he received the lesson he deserved, but the consequences proved to be a learning opportunity for me as well. As my dark side subsided, I realized that I had embarrassed my coach who had to talk the staff out of disqualifying me and scared the hell out of some of my team. Instead of relishing in victory during the bus ride home, I reflected on my outburst and what I could have done better. I apologized to Coach Van and some of the girls on the team for having to see that side of me. It never happened again.

I remained hopeful throughout the rest the year thanks to a fundraising drive that reached its goal to construct a track around the soccer field. I was being touted as one of the success stories which elevated the donors to imagine to possibilities from adequate training amenities. The thought of having a track to host meets my senior year would've brought a sense of school pride to life for me. However, that idea was cut short due to the funds disappearing. The rumor at the time was the funds were used for a new school roof. It was believable since we had a new green tin roof the following school year.

One of the biggest disappointments of my junior year was taking the SATs. I'd stayed up several nights trying to convince myself that I was smart enough to earn a positive score and study long enough to comprehend years of what were essentially gaping holes in my intellectual base. Unfortunately, it wasn't nearly enough. While my friends were boasting about scores between 1200 and over 1500, I scored a 780 on my first attempt. *There must've been a mistake somewhere. Surely, I couldn't be this damn stupid*, I thought to myself. Well, it turns out that I was according to their standards. I walked around dejected for a few days after the results. Maybe Mr. Farrell was right. Maybe I was too dumb to succeed in college. I didn't think a single university would accept me with this score. Even the NCAA had a minimum requirement of an 820, so I had no choice but to be a nobody after high school. I didn't want to hang around the gas station leaning on my car like the lames did years after graduating. When that thought crossed my mind, I refused to settle. There had to be a better solution, and I would have to access it through some other method than some shortsighted test drummed up by privileged people. Coach Van told me not to sweat it and try again early next year.

Chapter Eight

Lord Willin'

In preparation for my second attempt at the SAT, I spent a better part of the summer trying to understand math I didn't know and words I'd likely never use just to pass a test so colleges would deem me acceptable. About midway through the summer, I had an epiphany. I'd worked hard for two years proving myself worthy of college. I wasn't the smartest kid in the class and not even in the top twenty. However, I could do the work. So what if I didn't know most of the hundreds of thousands of words that existed. People could still understand my English in conversation. That should account for something. So what if I didn't understand complex math. I didn't have anyone teaching me in the way I needed it broken down, but I understood the basic concepts good enough to do basic math in my head faster than I could pull out a calculator. That should account for something. With that reasoning in mind, I stopped sweating the need for a high score. I accepted that I wasn't going to reach their standards of excellence and realized I would have to work just a little harder to get to where I needed to go. I took the test a second time during the fall of my senior year and scored the 820 I needed to meet the NCAA standards at the time. I wasn't proud of the score, but I didn't care enough to let it get me down. I would eventually get the chance to prove myself, and I wasn't going to let an abstract test score get in my way.

I couldn't help but think about all of the school days missed and years spent disrupting class had finally caught up to me once I was finally on the right track. The grades I earned in Chemistry and Algebra would prove to be a struggle as I could only muster a C average in both courses for the year. I studied so hard for those two classes that it managed to bring down my grades in others. In addition, the battles in Miriam's home with J'nelle made it near impossible to do homework in peace. My inability to get away from what was becoming a toxic atmosphere ate away at any energy I had left for studying and homework at the end of the day.

The worst occurrence happened during my junior year when J'nelle got ahold of my assignment I'd left out during dinner. The English paper was a critical analysis and a major part of my grade for the year. I had been working on it for weeks and managed to accumulate at least eight pages. The little heifer saw me working on it that night, so she decided to pester me and ran before I could snatch her. The project was nearly complete, but I wanted to take a break so I could finish strong. I sat at the dinner table largely ignoring J'nelle when she just hopped up from the table without being excused. That was just another double standard I'd become accustomed to, but I didn't think twice about it once she disappeared. When I turned to go into my room after washing dishes, I found her dripping juice all over my papers strewn across the rug while laughing. It was the first time I'd aggressively put my hands on her, but I refrained from hitting her while dragging her body down the hallways cursing her as she flopped her weight to the floor. Miriam demanded that I take my hands off her that instant or get the hell out of her home. I had to yell over top of her to explain that J'nelle spilled juice all over my entire report and ripped it up. I stomped back into my room and picked up the paper still dripping with red punch and stormed back out, "Look at this shit! That little bitch ruined my fucking report. This is over half my damn grade this period. You keep letting her get away with this stuff. This is some bullshit. What am I supposed to do now?" With that outburst, I walked out before I did something I'd truly regret, but not before nearly slamming the glass out of the front door. Granny and Granddaddy's brood weren't home, so I went to Glenn's house to vent.

I stayed up all night rewriting the report. I almost fell asleep driving to school but managed to make it without driving into a ditch. I gladly turned in the paper but struggled to stay awake in my classes that day. I had to go to track practice then work at the gas station afterward. I went to bed that night too irritated to fall asleep. I did everything from reading a book to counting sheep, but J'nelle was deeply in my head now. I woke up the next Saturday morning to go right back to work at the gas station for an eight-hour shift. I still wasn't over how Miriam dismissed what had happened, so I decided to go to Manassas Mall to shop after completing my shift.

I'd never considered the dangers of driving exhausted, so I pressed forward without realizing how reckless it was to press through my tiredness. I was lucky to suffer minor repercussions from that poor choice. After shopping at the mall and grabbing a bite to eat, I decided to drive around to see some areas I hadn't visited yet and learn my way around. I often thought about moving to the area if I couldn't make it back to California, so this was as good a time as any to learn my way around.

Shortly after that decision, I fell asleep at a four-way red light. An antique car show was wrapping up nearby, so they were coming through in droves as I drifted into the center of the intersection. I woke up to someone yelling, "Noooooo!" but couldn't react before my busted up Lynx hatchback detached the chrome bumper off of a jet black 1936 Plymouth. I slammed my foot onto the brake pedal before crashing into an electric pole on the corner. The man got out of his car and became immediately hesitant due to what I can only assume was my height and black skin. I was still in my gas station uniform. Thankfully, I wasn't wearing one of my football jerseys or that may have given him a heart attack. I reassured the agitated little man by letting him know that I had insurance and gave him my phone number. The police arrived, and I took full responsibility. I was sitting on the sidewalk with my head cupped in my hands when they approached me. The officer was surprisingly calm toward me and ended up telling the Plymouth driver to shut up. Once the cops got there, he just went irate and didn't stop yelling the entire time the officer was investigating and filling out paperwork. With no visible damage to my car, I took my ticket from the officer and went home. That irate little man called me every day for two weeks until my insurance company came through with the claim payment. It was just one more stressor I didn't need at the time, but it was another hard lesson learned. The whole ordeal left me feeling even more directionless.

I was clearly in need of an intervention. The forces that be decided that I needed another counselor, and Kent was tapped to do the job. Miriam required convincing from social services but reluctantly went along with the plan. She was always uneasy about people coming around the house, and at first glance she was more skeptical than I was. Kent was the third counselor since I'd been in foster care and the second once since being under Miriam's roof.

The initial meeting was very short since I had to be pulled out of class. My first thought was that social services had sent another snitch. I was emotionally hardened to outsiders by that point, so I refrained from too much eye contact and kept my answers short. Toward the end, Kent briefly mentioned that he lived in Manassas. The fact that he traveled all that way for such a short meeting impressed me. Without thinking that he most likely had other clients, I thought maybe he would be the one who could really help me.

Activity Notes from Family Services:

- Serious problems between Adam and foster mother centering around controlling anger and high level of stress for both Adam and Miriam – she had requested his removal once school is out

- Kent worked on situation. Foster mother sees Kent siding with Adam and has no time to meet with him.

- Social Services wanted to set up a meeting between Adam, Miriam, Kent and Social Services. Miriam has no time.

- Adam continues to do very well at school and in sports…injured back in track.

During our second meeting, we established a game plan to effectively deal with my anger. The Dr. Jekyll and Mr. Hyde bit wasn't working for me. I was doing well in school, but verbally abusive toward Miriam and J'nelle. I was to the point when I would proactively tell J'nelle to get the hell out of my room and slam the door in her face. She would run tell Miriam and the cycle would ensue. Provoke. Yell. Repeat. I didn't want it to be this way and neither did Miriam, but I refused to put up with the ugly habits J'nelle managed to pick up from her birth mother's poor influences. I wanted to react more calmly, but she would hurl insults such as "stupid" or "dummy." I could brush it off once or twice, but she would continue until I reacted, often within Miriam's hearing distance. Miriam's inaction would piss me off by that point because she knew I was trying to do homework. I'd ask her to call J'nelle back to her room. She would dramatically huff and finally address the situation, but not before accusing me of trying to get rid of her. I'd usually mumble, "You damn right I'm trying to get rid of her" and go on about my studies. I was ashamed that I could not get a grip on this issue, so Kent came along just in time.

April 1998 - Memo from Kent Aronson to Rappahannock Department of Social Services:

The following goals have been developed by Adam and his counselor:

- To assist Adam in developing positive outlets to express his various feelings and emotions. Specifically, Adam has difficulty expressing his anger in an appropriate manner.

- To assist Adam in recognizing and accepting responsibility for both his positive and negative behavior.

- To assist Adam in better organizing the various activities he is involved with and set reasonable goals and expectations for those activities.

Adam has expressed the desire to remain with Miriam, his foster mother. He understands that his aggressive behavior toward her granddaughter is inappropriate and must stop. Adam appears not only willing to develop ways to handle this anger and frustration in a positive manner, but recently he has expressed an interest in exploring the possible causes of some of his anger. Adam has displayed a tendency to focus on his perception of how he is/has been treated unfairly by others to justify some of his inappropriate behavior.

Adam is involved with various school-sponsored activities, maintains an A/B academic average, and holds a part-time job. All of those appear to be positive for Adam, but at times his personal expectations in regard to these activities are a major area of stress for him.

In between our mentoring sessions, Kent invited me into his Manassas home. I jumped at the chance since it gave me another escape route from Miriam's home. His wife, Jessica, greeted us as I cautiously entered and offered a drink and a snack. I immediately noticed their blond haired blued-eyed, toddler tumbling around the house in his little imagination world and his bright-eyed older sister halfheartedly playing along but mostly skipping through the hallways. Kent gave me a tour around his house, and we ended up in his office space filled with sports memorabilia. I thought to myself, *I needed a space like this for homework*. It was peaceful, quiet, and away from all of the commotion. Being in his family's home allowed me to enjoy a sense of calmness I rarely experienced anywhere else.

After dinner, I was convinced that Kent had the sweet life I'd always dreamed of while watching sitcoms except the real version was much better. Kent and Jessica's genuine kindness toward one another was a trait I wanted to aim for with my future wife. If they ever had marital problems, it never showed during my somewhat regular visits. There was a sense of tranquility between the two. For a brief period of time, my tension released allowing me to gather my thoughts and make sense of the world I'd eventually have to reenter.

November 1998 - Memo from Kent Aronson to Rappahannock Department of Social Services:

Adam continues to express frustration with J'nelle. Adam has stated that it is his opinion that Miriam shows favoritism towards her and that he and his brother are often blamed for her inappropriate behavior. Adam has chosen to distance himself from situations in which he will have to deal with J'nelle for any extended period of time…

Adam continues to do well in school, participate in school-sponsored activities, as well as hold down a part-time job. Adam has an extremely busy and at times stressful schedule. With support, he has been able to organize his schedule to alleviate much of the negative stress. This counselor has been able to visit Adam at school, and will explore what role would be appropriate to assist Adam in pursuing his goal of attending college.

Although Kent was doing everything in his power to mentor me in the right direction, I was still stressed beyond my max and mishandling my attempt to meet societal and personal expectations of holding down a job, sports, school, and home life. I needed a break from this balancing act.

My friend, Mark, was throwing a party since his parents were out of town one weekend. I'd been invited by several other friends, but I remained hesitant due to my chronic tiredness. When I heard Alexis was going to be there, I couldn't turn it down. Even though I was trying to stay focused and ride out of Rappahannock with a clean slate, I still had problems with the temptation of alcohol. Even knowing it had destroyed my family, I didn't see that it was slowly happening to me as well. Nevertheless, with all of the accolades from sports awards to getting accepted to college, I was feeling invincible; especially on this particular night.

At some point before the party, I was determined to ask Alexis out on a date. To work up the courage, I decided to drink to calm my nerves, but by the end of the night, I had downed nearly a half bottle of Jim Beam and a 6 pack of Jack Daniel spiked wine coolers. I remember laughing and joking with the guys and teasing some of the girls, then someone handed me something in an unmarked bottle and said, "Try this shit!"

I replied "What the hell is this fruity shit?" and tipped it up. My tongue went numb about half way through the guzzle. At that point, the room spun as I tried to find Alexis. As soon as I found her, I gazed into her eyes from across the room and threw up in a corner. Embarrassed and knowing more was on the way, I stumbled outside to release the rest over the edge of the porch. When I turned around, I saw her staring at me with a mix of disdain and disgust. The moment was ruined. I would never have a chance with her. Ever. Suddenly, I felt hot and could smell the alcohol seeping from my pores. I laid face down on the cold, wooden porch slats to get relief.

The next morning, I woke up on the porch in the same position and struggled to get to my feet. I was kind of hazy and noticed that the place was completely trashed. It was still early and foggy, but I had to get home. I'd promised Miriam I would be home that night, and there I was on a stranger's porch. I looked for my keys and eventually found them in a bowl. Thankfully, someone had taken them from me during the course of the night...so I stepped over a couple of people, accidentally waking up my friend Dean. Before I could say "my bad", he asked for a ride home. I waved him toward the car in approval, and we hopped in my hatchback. He lived just minutes from me, and we were at least 45 minutes out, so I didn't mind.

We turned out of Mark's driveway and was lost almost immediately as I'd forgotten that I followed someone else there. We were on a stretch of gravel road as I was going too fast around a turn and ran up a dirt embankment right into a tree. The car slid back down, and I put it in reverse to do a K-turn and head back the other way. Although I was going much slower, less than two minutes later, the steering wheel started doing a 360-degree turn throwing my hands off. We hit a thick patch of gravel, and the car flipped over luckily only once. My left shoulder hurt something awful, but I immediately asked Dean if he was okay. He looked shocked but assured me he was fine. I replied with, "My mom is going to pimp slap me!" We hand rolled our windows and climbed out to survey the damage. We arose to our feet and scanned the exposed engine in wonderment. After a quick discussion, we agreed that Dean would walk back to the house to see if he could get a group of guys to come flip the hatchback back onto its wheels. I stayed with the wreckage, but before Dean could get back, a farmer rolled up and got out of his truck to make sure I was okay. "Boy, what in the hell...how did you manage to do this?"

Ashamed, I shook my head and muttered, "I don't know."

"Well hang on and stay right there, I'm gonna go call for help?" I'd never felt more lost and vulnerable in my life than at that moment. Clearly, the invincibility had worn off. Plus, I could have killed my friend. I would have never forgiven myself had he been hurt or killed. I looked up toward the sky, asking God for help. My final thought had to do with Miriam killing me.

During the excruciating wait, I wondered where Dean was by this point. As soon as that thought crossed my mind, a Culpeper County officer showed up. In response, I tried to straighten up as much as possible. As he got out of the squad car, I said, "Good morning, officer."

He replied, "Only for one of us. What happened here?" I told him how I ran into a bank up the road and hit a tree and when I turned back to go up the road; the steering wheel started spinning, and the car flipped. He asked me to get in the passenger seat of his patrol car to take a Breathalyzer test, and I complied. I didn't understand how they worked, but I could smell the alcohol and vomit real clear by that point. Officer Mitchell looked at the reading, his eyes widened as he looked over to ask how much I had to drink.

As I sat there in silence trying to count the types of liquor and other drinks I'd consumed, he interrupted my thoughts, "Don't lie to me, son."

I assured him, "Sir, I'm not going to lie to you. I had a lot of drink, and I'm just trying to make a list in my head. It was a half-bottle of Jim Beam, six Jack Daniel wine coolers, a few beers, and I think some moonshine.

After a brief silence, he asked, "Where do you go to school?"

"Rappahannock, sir."

"What year are you?"

"I'm a senior, sir."

"What are your plans for next year?"

Well, I plan to go to college if I don't go to jail today, sir." I realized at that moment that I had ruined my life over some damn alcohol.

"Which college?"

"Eastern Mennonite University, sir."

He took a deep breath and reluctantly said, "Well, I tell you what; I'm going to take it easy on you since you were honest and respectful. I'm going to give you a reckless driving ticket, and you make absolutely sure this never happens again."

"Yes, sir and thank you, sir. I promise, no more drinking."

By that time, a tow truck arrived, and Dean and Wally were right behind him. The officer made sure I had a ride home and left the scene. I thanked Officer Mitchell one last time and gave the tow truck man my insurance information, grabbed all of my belongings and loaded into Wally's truck. I never saw the Lynx again. Wally gave us a ride back to the party house to let Mark know that everything was going to be okay. Mark agreed to take Dean home and Wally took me to face Miriam's consequences.

As I gathered my stuff out of Wally's car, I only remember being numb from the thought of what Miriam might do to me. I tried to think up some lies but always fell in the same trap. Plus, lying in a small town, she was going to get the truth from someone else, which I knew would be worse. I'd figured the news probably already made it to her before I had the chance to get home. By the time I arrived, I decided no more lying. I returned home and told her the truth right away. I just told her everything and then held my breath awaiting her response. She looked me in the eye and said okay. "Okay. Really, that's it? "Adam, I'm so happy you finally told the truth about something, I don't know what to do. Besides, you have to ride the bus again as a senior, and that, by itself, is punishment enough."

Man, I hadn't even considered that yet! *Oh, how embarrassing!* My shoulders slumped, and we made plans for the court date and getting me to and from work. I told her that I would get a ride from track practice.

After about two months of anxiously waiting, I showed up to court dressed in my best suit. My case followed a scraggly-looking, middle-aged man donning a teal blue tank top and orange booty shorts and couldn't string together two sentences that resembled anything close to American English. I looked real good after him, but I was nervous; so nervous I forgot to say whether I was guilty or not guilty. When I mixed up the two, the judge jokingly asked, "Are you sure?" After a brief lecture about staying safe on the road, replying "yes, your honor" during the pauses, and nodding my head in agreement, the charge was reduced to a misdemeanor.

February 5th 1999 - Memo from Kent Aronson to Rappahannock Department of Social Services:

- Adam is in the process of applying to colleges. The college application process was at first very overwhelming for Adam. By breaking down the process, he has been able to face this task and has already been accepted by one college.

- Adam faces many financial-related obligations. He maintains a part-time job, which provides the resources to pay for his car expenses, graduation expenses and other various obligations. The challenge of budgeting his income to meet those obligations is ongoing.

- Adam continues to exhibit some feelings of frustration towards J'nelle, but this mentor has not been informed of Adam acting on his frustration in a negative manner.

- Adam has begun to express a variety of feelings in regard to leaving and going to college. In addition, he has expressed concern over his younger brothers, in particular, Noah who he feels that his behavior he exhibits will cause some difficulty in the future.

Life went back to my depiction of normal after my court appearance. I wasn't sure if she was proud of me or not, but for whatever reason Miriam stood behind me from the accident up to the day Demarius came home. She even surprised me with a gold class ring, which I didn't expect since we weren't on the best of terms. I didn't necessarily deserve one since I never kept my mouth shut and preferred arguing over obeying. As I was becoming more educated, my headstrong arguments began questioning her logic and way of thinking. Even when I knew I was overstepping my boundaries, my brain never managed to engage the shut up valve. There was no doubt that I was a certified smart ass, but Miriam finally managed to control my behavior with the threat of taking away my permission to attend my last prom.

My senior prom turned out to be a night of unexpected outcomes. I was dressed to the nines in my black tuxedo and escorted by my friend's limo. Although I was still somewhat of an outcast trying to make a mark my senior year in high school, I was fortunately popular. I'd like to think it was because I associated with all groups and was finally comfortable in my own skin. I was an All-State track and field athlete without a track, my grades were stellar, and I'd just been accepted to Eastern Mennonite University. I was on top of my game, and no one was going to bring me down. Then Kacie came into my life.

Although I had known Kacie throughout high school, I didn't spend a lot of time with her inner circle. Other than partaking in weed circles at field parties and one of them likely falling victim to one of my friendly high hugs, I didn't relate to them very well when I was in a sober state. The way we hooked up was somewhat stupid thanks to my boyish ways. I had to make the seemingly impossible choice of deciding between two girls, Kacie and Andrea, to take to the prom. Usually, this would've a guy's ideal situation. However, I was not that kind of guy. To let fate decide and avoid feeling like an ass, I flipped a coin. I called heads for Kacie and tails for Andrea. The coin hit the floor, and it landed heads up. I told Kacie in the morning and let Andrea down before lunch. I still felt like an ass, but I didn't have the heart to tell her I decided fate with a coin toss. I ended up making some lame excuse.

She reluctantly accepted my decision, and I incompatibly went with Kacie.

For some reason, this wasn't just a prom date. Kacie asked if I wanted to go to her parent's house. I was always down for free food, so I accepted. We traveled up a gorgeous countryside road and down a gravel driveway to her McMansion. I wasn't as surprised by the Southern Living magazine cutout home and Ethan Allen-like furniture that I was afraid to sit on, as I was by her parent's age. Although they were vibrant and energetic, they must have been pushing 65 or 70. I never had a chance to meet the parents before in any of my previous relationships, so I took this opportunity quite seriously. I wanted to make sure I looked presentable and respectful, which meant ditching the huge chain and football jersey. I had already been accused of "talking like a white boy," so I had no reason to fake the rest of my persona or dialect. I recall her parents being very hospitable and saying that I was a delightful young man. I told them an abbreviated version of my life and the obstacles I had overcome to reach my senior year, which impressed them. The visit was very enjoyable, and I left feeling vindicated of my troublesome past. I had never presented my entire story to anyone, and I couldn't have found a better pair of genuine listeners than Kacie's parents.

Prom night proved to be very special, but very uncomfortable for Kacie and me. When Andrea suggested that we dance and I happily accommodated, I didn't realize that the competitive aspects were still looming between the two women. Worrying about the magnitude of that night, I was completely oblivious to being in the middle of their rivalry. Kacie was kind of stand offish after the dance took place, but I never linked the two until I began reflecting in an effort to write this story.

Nevertheless, I was having a good time mingling with anyone who wanted to talk or dance and much to my surprise, I was voted prom king. I had the honor of dancing with Jaycee, whom I had a lot of respect for. Other than secretly comparing my grades with her in tenth grade, I never had the opportunity to talk to her on a close friend basis. Jaycee was definitely one of the more popular girls, but she was among the few who didn't let it go to her head. She was always approachable, always kind and just an all-around phenomenal human being. Jaycee was also one of the women my friends drooled over, but never had the courage to bother asking if she was interested in any of them. After dancing with her, my boys considered me amongst the gods. After the popularity contest put me on top, Kacie finally came around and acted like she liked me again.

Although I uneventfully went home late that night, I'll remember it if for no other reason than the stark reminder that I wasn't everyone's favorite that following Monday. I embarrassingly got off the bus and arrived normally like every other school morning and approached my locker. A folded note bleeding through from a pressed black permanent marker fell out from the bottom. Hoping for a girl's phone number, I picked it up and unfolded it only to read: "WE DON'T WANT NO NIGGER PROM KING." I immediately looked around and down the hallways, but people were just talking and moving about. I looked at it one more time to verify, then crumpled it up and tossed it into the bin as I walked into class.

I thought about telling Miriam, but she seemed to have enough stress on her plate. Demarius just returned home, and she was trying to get him to a place where he could take care of his daughter. I didn't have time to be angry and what little bit of anger that managed to bubble up disappeared after track practices and meets that week.

From prom night on, my relationship with Kacie got increasingly stranger. One day she drove me to her house, and I wanted to talk. Her responses were short and direct. For some reason, I realized that we had never kissed. Although the timing couldn't have been worse, I leaned in and connected with her lips to see if any true feelings linked us together. Nothing. That's when I realized it was over. We continued into her house and had dinner with her parents while pretending everything was okay. We discussed my aspirations and possible college majors.

However, by the time Kacie drove me home, she decided to tell me that it was over. Looking back, it was inevitable. I didn't seem to connect with her circle no matter how hard I tried. My sense of humor didn't amuse her in the least. We did not connect on an intellectual or physical level. To be more direct, she was too petite for me. Sometimes, I got the feeling my towering stature intimidated Kacie, which made me as uncomfortable as it did her.

The next night I had to work after track practice. I was coming back from my job at Sheetz gas station and started thinking about all of the women who had broken my heart over the years. When Jesse Powell's *You* belted across the radio waves, I finally lost it. My uncontrollable tears forced me to turn off the radio and pull over to the side of the road. When I regained control of myself, I drove home and started crying again. Miriam thought I was hurt, but I tried to explain through my chest upheavals that Kacie broke up with me. She held me trying to console me and eventually succeeded. I told Miriam that I had no idea why I just started crying like that. She made sure I was calm, and suggested that I rest. That night I thought through every aspect of my dating experience trying to search for lessons. Lesson One: I vowed never to sweat over another girl like that. Ever! Lesson two: This was not my fault. I was a good guy, and I was going to continue to treat my women like queens until I found the right one. At this point, there was no need to rethink anything else. The next day, her parents called me to apologize and invited me back to their house a few weeks later! While in college, they even sent me a care package with books, food, and money from their new Florida home. I must have really had a positive impression on them, but I had to have my jaw lifted off the floor once I realized who it was from. I remained in touch as I felt comfortable doing so. Once I lost touch with Kacie, I fell out of contact with her parents as well. By that point, I was truly done with women from Rappahannock County.

Regardless of yet another year without a track or field, I managed to become the district champion and place well in regionals and states. I was in the top eight, which earned me a medal at the state level. I was proud of that accomplishment. Coach Van was very supportive of my efforts and congratulated me often. At times, I felt he was the only one who appreciated how hard I was working. While Rappahannock's administration didn't seem to care about the track program itself, I would be very well rewarded with recognition my senior year.

The most surprising award during that spring ceremony in the gym was the Marine Corps Distinguished Athlete Award. I remember coveting the award the prior year, but had no idea what it would take to get it. After gratefully accepting with a handshake, I just sat down and ran my finger across the seal to make sure all of this was real. I didn't have expectations for any other awards, but once again my name was called for Most Improved. I moved toward the front a little slower this time. As team captain of the track and field squad, I wanted to finally do something else to show some appreciation to my team. Once I reached our assistant principal, Mr. Tanner, who was handing out the awards, I signaled for the mic. I expressed my gratitude for the honor but asked our shot putter Byron to come up and accept the award. Bryon was one of the more talented teammates on the basketball team, and I always respected the amount of work he put in to better himself as a track athlete. Mr. Tanner was beside himself and asked me if I was sure I wanted to do that. "Absolutely!" I responded. Byron had asked me the same thing before we exchanged a guy hug to the applause of the student body. Without realizing the magnitude of what I had just done, I went back to the bleachers to a row of high fives.

I listened to the rest of the presentations very pleased with myself. I was feeling somewhat righteous as my name was called for Male Most Valuable Player. Completely stunned, I walked to the middle of the gym floor numbed by the amount of love and respect that resonated throughout the room. I didn't know what to say, so I informed Mr. Tanner that, "I was keeping this one!" before hugging him. I'd never been so overwhelmed by sheer joy. That was all the motivation I needed to make Rappahannock proud of what I would accomplish on the track during my last year.

I fully expected to float through track season my senior year. The cocky attitude derived from my inability to see any formidable competition until I reached regional-level competition. Coasting and winning were my strategies to get to states, and I'd give my everything to place in the top three. With my sights set on college, all I had to do was work on beating my personal records in both hurdle races.

I started the season winning as expected, but our team traveled for an invitational meet to Manassas Park where I'd just made an unwanted name for myself the prior year. I competed and placed well against the high caliber athletes, but I'll never forget my humbling 300-meter hurdle experience. Without knowing the competitors, I blasted out of the blocks with the intent of turning it up on the backstretch. I had a poor assignment out in lane six, but that was no excuse for allowing a guy to pass me from behind, before I extended my lead leg over the first hurdle. As I looked up in disbelief of his uncanny speed and grace, I managed to trip over the next two hurdles trying to recover my step pattern, which only placed me further behind. When it was all said and done, he finished in a remarkable 37.6 seconds, and I set my personal record of 40.2. It was by far the most humiliating second place finish during my entire track career. The crestfallen experience let me know just how much farther I had to go if I was ever going to reach my goal of becoming an Olympic-pedigree hurdler.

The rest of my season went as planned until I reached state level. I was ranked 5th going into the championship meet, but I had higher aspirations. My future coach, Pete, was there scouting, and I had every intention of showcasing my ability. I knew I couldn't win the 110 high hurdles due to the returning champion who went on to play running back in the NFL. My only goal was to place in the top three. I placed well enough through two heats to land in the middle of the pack in the final heat, but I snapped my lead leg down too quickly causing my trail leg to drag over the fifth hurdle and the stumble landed me in eighth place at the finish line. I was disappointed, but I didn't let that deter my attempt to become the surprise 300 champion. I felt it was within my reach and the disappointing 110 performance made me that much more determined to do it.

Lane five was not an ideal lane assignment, but it wasn't as detrimental as lanes one or eight. I felt great getting set in the blocks and had the confidence of a champion. There was no reason for me to hold back during my last race as a high school hurdler, so I exploded out of the blocks and glided over each hurdle with a forceful grace. The defending champion passed me at the 200 mark, but I refused to show any quit whatsoever. I dug deep to give whatever I had left and the reigning silver medalist caught me on the last stretch with two hurdles to go. I didn't feel tired or worn as I summoned my last reserves to glide over the second-to-last hurdle tied for second. I wasn't going to pull off a gold medal, but it was going to be a huge upset if this Podunk country boy without a track managed to place better than the boys with top-notch facilities at their disposal. Over the last hurdle, I may never know exactly what happened but my body gave way to the weight of the hurdle, and I smashed face first into the ground. With complete disregard for the pain, I bounced upright from the track, which no longer felt like a *cloud* and placed eighth for the last medal. I limped off the track completely disheartened with my performance. Both Coach Pete and Coach Van tried to lift my spirits, but I was in disbelief that my high school career ended in such dismal fashion.

It's easy to look back and think I should have just run my race. However, the stakes were never higher for me. If I had to do it all over again, I would've still given it my all. The only change I would have made would have been to make it about me and not focusing on all of the other talent around me. I wasn't intimidated as much as I was distracted. Nonetheless, I was grateful to use my talents to lead me to a more prosperous road to college and maintain my physical work ethic, which translated over to my schooling.

My ultra-competitive spirit rarely had the opportunity to showcase its talents early on. It's hard to reminisce about what could've been had I stayed in California, or attended the high school in the next county with far superior facilities or hadn't started so late in my childhood and so on. For whatever reason, reaching my full potential in sports was never in the cards. While it's a regret I'll always carry with me, the sports I was fortunate enough to participate in served as my lifeline.

The lessons learned during my athletic participation were crucial to my overall success. Without it, I would've never discovered my self-confidence, which I believe would have led to my eventual dropout as school became more challenging. I couldn't get the much-needed self-esteem boost from sitting in a classroom for the better part of the day. I needed an outlet and a path toward achieving something great. I was never a great student in the classroom. Although average was much better than the hellraiser I was known to be throughout the years, I didn't want to settle for being unremembered. The self-worth that came with success in track and field allowed me to focus on class when it was time.

I struggled to finish out the year academically. Although I pulled As and Bs in Public Speaking, English, French III, and Finance, I only earned Cs in Advanced Placement Government and Biology II and a D in Geometry. Being overcommitted without a solid strategy to manage my time and lacking the foundation to succeed in advanced math led to a lackluster end to my high school career. Conversely, I'd overcome a lot to get to that point. For me, it was time to start anew. It was enough to graduate, so I ultimately had to be satisfied since I couldn't change the end result. It was time to choose a suit and try on my cap and gown.

A graduating class of fifty-four stood in a bleacher sect of navy blue with yellow tassels. Although my 2.6 G.P.A. ranked twenty-seventh out of the fifty-four students, I felt as triumphant as the valedictorian. I was okay with that comeback average and grateful to be amongst my peers when six others fell short of that extraordinary day. I could've easily been left out if it hadn't been for the right people being in the right place at exactly the right time. I fully understood the magnitude of that day, and for a brief moment I relished in the confirmation of what I'd accomplished.

As I heard my name called to accept my evidence, I stood on that stage beaming with pride knowing some people didn't expect me to be there; however, the better community knew otherwise and expected more from me. The consequences of my circumstances nearly destroyed me at times. However, through a series of victories amid the struggle, I was able to overcome the inner storm that ensued throughout my years in foster care. By no means was the internal war over, but at that moment there was no longer a struggle between the two choices, victim or victor. Albeit emotionally-scarred and somewhat unprepared for what lay ahead, I managed to overcome every hardship and improbability to accept that diploma. There would never be a time when I needed to retreat back to that uncertain child with no hope. Although the path ahead was unmarked, I finally had the confidence to blaze my own trail.

I wanted to venture off to college the very next day. The summer of '99 was agonizingly long. I worked as much as possible to stay away from Miriam, Demarius, and especially

J'nelle, but the gas station was only giving me part time hours along with the hours at the shoe store. I took it upon myself to seek another job at a supermarket in Manassas, VA. The 45-minute commute was hectic, but I went from making $5.15/hour with Miriam's shoe store three years ago to $11.50/hour with this supermarket. Coupled with the weekly pay, I was finally able to afford my bills and think about the lifestyle I wanted.

During the summer of '99, I was just starting to get into hot cars and convinced myself that I was working hard and deserved something new. The plastic rims, seat and steering wheel cushions just couldn't manage to help with the aesthetics of a rusted blue '91 Ford Escort hatchback. On impulse, instead of turning left on Route 211 after a full day working at the gas station, I veered right down to the nearest car dealership and applied for credit to purchase a new car. I didn't have a long enough credit history, so I had to call and persuade Granddaddy to co-sign on the loan. After convincing him of my plan to make the payments, he agreed to drive down to the dealership and sign off on the paperwork. Three hours from the time I walked in, I was the proud owner of a 1999 Dodge Neon.

A few weeks prior to that, I'd walked into a car tech and rim shop in Woodbridge, VA with my cousin Christine who was having new rims installed on her boyfriend's ride. Cars were lined up in the parking lot already souped up with spoilers, rims, hood kits, and subwoofers. When I flipped through some of their magazines and saw a completely tricked out Dodge Neon, I just had to have it. Initially, I was intimidated by the prices, but the desires quickly became an obsession that was too coveted to let go. The list of items I wanted in my new car came to $18,000, which happened to be more than my car was worth. For whatever, reason, most likely naiveté, I wasn't the least bit fazed by that price tag. I planned to buy piece by piece to construct the dream car I suddenly wanted.

Of course, I never factored in responsibilities such as paying higher insurance for full coverage or basic maintenance. Nevertheless, I managed to have a new stereo system and tail lights installed that summer. Thanks to my reckless spending habits, I'd amassed a heap of credit card debt. Every free moment, I was driving around Northern Virginia flashy and dead broke. I didn't know it at the time, but I was inadvertently creating an uncertain future.

Before I ventured off to college, the Cartwrights requested one last visit. I'd visited on and off throughout the years, so I hesitantly agreed and hoped to God they didn't have more indentured servitude in mind. It was way too hot that August day, and I already had two jobs.

Thankfully, my worries were put to rest when Mr. Cartwright wanted to ensure that my self-vision was on the right track. He was relieved when I told him my dreams of owning my own business one day and handed me a copy of *Black Enterprise* magazine. He lectured me over lunch by urging focus and developing keen instincts, which I can only imagine was due to the lack of specific direction I wanted to take my life. That was going to be more difficult for me since I didn't have a solid example, but I assured him that I'd figure it out along the way. I thanked him for the lesson and the magazine.

When I returned home, I laid in bed and skimming through the magazine pages. Nothing really caught my interest until I came across an article outlining the lack of access to supermarkets in inner cities. I was immediately drawn to it since it evoked memories from my struggle with hunger during my childhood. I thought this was an area where I could do some good and make a living at the same time. Everything about it felt right, so I did something that I hadn't done in over three years by that time; I pulled my trapper keeper of dreams out of my closet and designed the ideal supermarket.

The design took several weeks of research. I started by visiting the variety of grocery stores and supermarkets throughout Northern Virginia and listed every aisle label they had posted to perfect my store design. I also asked the supervisors at my workplace if I could have the pile of grocery magazines piled on the management office floor. Once I got my hands on them, I studied long into the nights reading every word from front to back. Although the vision was a long way off, my outlook was clear; I wanted to be the founder and CEO of Urban Light; turning food deserts into food oases in inner cities throughout America. I spent a good part of that summer entrenched in jotting down ideas for the store, but the month of August had other plans in mind.

In early August, our graduating class found out David was killed in a car accident. The Class of '99 rallied around each other one last time to pay our respects and mourn the death of a good friend. It was my first funeral, so I didn't know how to feel. Miriam told me to dress in black and wear a tie. As I arrived at his wake, family and friends were grieving. I wondered if I was even supposed to be there. We were friends but not close. We drank together at field parties. We traveled forever and a day to get to basketball games. Then I reflected on our practices together. It was evident early on that I was never going to get to be a starter. I gave my all every practice, but always came up short when it was time to shoot. Nonetheless, I'd work in the low post and put my hand up for the ball. David was the only point guard who would bother to pass to me. As team captain, I always thought he took it upon himself to help everyone on the team become better athletes. When he was in, I didn't feel invisible in the post. He gave me what I wanted more than anything else on that court; respect.

If I didn't know how to feel, the least I could do was tell his mother and father how good David was as a person. This was a time to repay that same respect back to my friend. As we were walking out, everyone relayed their condolences to his parents. I didn't know what to say other than David was a good person. What was I supposed to say to a mother and father trying to make sense of their son's destiny being cut short? My turn came, and I recall saying, "I'm very sorry for your loss. If there's anything I can do for you, please let me know."

David's father grabbed me by the shoulders and looked me right in the eye and pleaded, "Promise me you will never do anything this stupid. Don't waste your life on unnecessary things. Just promise me that."

I was stunned, and my mind instantly blanked. I forced up an "okay" and nodded my head in agreement. I left there feeling strangely connected to their pain.

After returning home, I wanted things to go better from that moment. I was leaving for college in a couple of weeks, but fate intervened for one more drama production. That particular summer was full of praiseworthy comments from the community. My mentor, Kent, people in church, my workplaces and all over Rappahannock County expressed how proud they were of my accomplishments. After all, it wasn't every day that a foster kid actually turned out to be a success story. I did my best to stay in the straight and narrow that summer and maintain peace in Miriam's home by avoiding J'nelle and Demarius by any means necessary. I couldn't put my finger on it, but there was a definite tension between me and Demarius. There just didn't seem to be enough room in Miriam's all-of-sudden-small home for both of our alpha egos. My move to college couldn't arrive fast enough, but my ill-tempered nature ended up getting the best of me before I could leave in undramatic fashion.

J'nelle entered our room with a devilish grin. Whatever intent she had, I didn't want any part of it. Before she could get a word out, I interrupted, "Get out J'nelle!" I was finalizing plans for college, and I didn't need her shit that morning. I didn't think any more of it until Miriam came banging on my door. I opened up and knew immediately that I was once again in more trouble than I deserved. She asked if I had hit J'nelle. With an exhausted facial expression, I answered, "No, I didn't hit her. She came into my room to start trouble, and I told her to get out then shut the door. I'm busy."

Miriam interrupted, "Adam, she is a child, and you are getting ready to be an adult. I'm sick and tired of your attitude toward her.

I interrupted, "She is a lying child. You know it, and I know it, but you refuse to do anything about it. I'm tired of the unfairness."

About that time, the commotion interrupted Demarius' sleep, so he opened the back room door to investigate. I'm sure he heard everything because he stepped right in to tell me what he really thought of me. He got in my face to demand an explanation as to what I was arguing about. I reiterated what I said to Miriam, but my response and tone was unacceptable to him. He retorted, "I'm tired of your bullshit. You've been disrespecting my mother and daughter from day one. You need to get the fuck out. Pack up your shit and go off to your damn fancy college. Get out now!"

I looked him in the eye, and several thoughts crossed my mind. I wanted to remind him that he was the disrespectful one by being in prison all of these years. I wanted to tell him that this whole ordeal was his damn fault since he never bothered to raise his daughter. Instead, I looked over at Miriam to intervene, but she looked away. I needed my head attached to get through college, so I kept my mouth shut and started packing. I already had all of my stuff in trash bags in anticipation of getting the hell out of there, so it was just a matter of loading up.

Noah managed to escape and avoid a confrontation. After I had loaded up my stuff, I embraced Noah and told him not to worry about me. I reassured him that I would return soon and took off without looking back. I couldn't go off to my damn fancy college as Demarius suggested since the doors didn't open for another two weeks. Instead, I drove throughout northern Virginia and back through only to end up behind the gas station where I was employed in Bealeton, Virginia. I told my managers what had happened and asked if I could sleep out back in my car. They agreed to it and even made sure I had enough to eat during the five-night stint in my crowded hatchback.

I worried about Noah throughout those days and wondered about his safety. Demarius seemed unstable at best, but he got along well with Noah. Over time, Noah had learned to keep his mouth shut, and that was an area I regressed as I became more bookish. Nevertheless, I took the risk to go check on him one last time before going to Harrisonburg to live out my homelessness a few days before school. Mercifully, he was at Granny and Granddaddy's home. We embraced once more and talked for a while alongside the other Hillside boys. It briefly felt like the old times I'd left behind to chase grown-up aspirations. For a moment, I regretted leaving those boys to their own devices during the last of my teenage years. I didn't mentor them enough. I didn't encourage them to make a way for themselves or venture out into a new area that had some opportunity. In the end, they were young men capable of making their own decisions. The only action I could take was to lead by example. All of them, even Noah, managed to graduate high school, but all opted out of college to join the workforce.

As I was getting ready to leave and go prove myself to the world without anyone in my corner, Granddaddy pulled me aside and asked how many more days I had until I started college. When I told him three days, he expressed that he didn't mind if I stayed there and even offered me a room. It didn't take much convincing since I couldn't stand the stench coming from my body after five days in the sweltering heat. I gratefully accepted and jumped right in the shower, so I'd no longer offend anyone in the house.

Miriam didn't know it at the time, but she saved me from a lifetime of self-contempt by accepting me into her home. Even with all of the heartaches I caused, I needed to witness and experience what model black culture could be. Without the examples throughout the hillside, I would have never managed to meaningfully engage in society.

Ultimately, it came down to the impossible choice of blood over some kid that she spent a few years raising. I have to thank her for refusing to give up on me in ninth grade. She was my last refuge and without her, there would've been little hope for my outlook. She had to be convinced to keep me after my eleventh-grade year, so she had given up on me long before my graduation. On the outside, I was winning awards, doing well in school, and getting set for new beginnings in college. No one knew about the constant yelling matches between me and her over J'nelle meddling in my room and annoying the living hell out of me.

Overall, I think Miriam did the best she could with the support she had. She had the unfortunate dealings of an irrepressibly angry child trying to make sense of a world that seemingly kept taking everything away. In a way, the valuable lessons she instilled throughout those years taught me how to be a man in an unforgiving world. "The world is not going to feel sorry for you or give you a god-damned thing." "Don't you dare go out of this house acting like a nigger." As harsh as those lessons were, she was ultimately right. As hard as it was to live under her roof during my later years, life may have been very different if she would have just given up on me the day I brought that last failing report card home in ninth grade. While she unknowingly played a part in my downward spiral, she also stood by my side when it counted. Looking back, I confidently realize that every aspect of my hardships were a destined moment in preparation for the next phase of my journey. It was necessary to leave that life behind to fully embrace the freedom and responsibility I would be granted in college. The mending process was just beginning to take heed, and it would take Granny and Granddaddy to see me through the process of self-actualization.

Section Three

College IS For People with My Type of Background

The function of education is to teach one to think intensively and think critically. Intelligence plus character; that is the goal of true education.

Martin Luther King, Jr.

The beautiful thing about learning is that no one can take it away from you.

B.B. King

Education is a progressive discovery of our own ignorance.

Will Durant

I have learned that success is to be measured not so much by the position that one has reached in life as by the obstacles which he has had to overcome while trying to succeed.

Booker T. Washington

To cheat oneself out of love is the most terrible deception; it is an eternal loss for which there is no reparation, either in time or eternity.

Kierkegaard

Unless you love someone, nothing else makes sense.

E.E. Cummings

To love without knowing how to love wounds the person we love.

Thich Nhat Hahn

Chapter Nine

Lessons in Gripping

My decision to go to Eastern Mennonite University (EMU) came down to two things; a track and field coach who could recognize my potential and finding a college that felt like home. Coach Van escorted me to George Mason and Eastern Mennonite University with the thought that I would excel at either level once I had athletic resources dedicated to my success. I also visited Virginia Tech and James Madison University, but the more big-time college campuses I visited, the more I felt like I would get lost in the mix. Plus, neither university was impressed with my accomplishments nor did they want to take me on as a project. I weighed the benefits of attending George Mason and Eastern Mennonite, but the decision didn't immediately become any clearer. I needed a place where I could stand out in a crowd. The layout of each of the large college campuses and the anticipated intensity of the coursework intimidated me. When the thought crossed my mind, I wasn't exactly thrilled with the amount of effort I would take to continue school for four more years, but it was my only way out.

In addition to in-state choices, I was feeling pressured to seriously consider my ideal choice, the University of Southern California (USC), to move as far away as possible and finally return to California like I had always dreamed. I also had to consider Miriam's recommendation of a historically black college (HBCU). In reality, USC wasn't a feasible option since I didn't have the resources to move across the country. I wasn't an elite athlete, my overall G.P.A. was unimpressive, and the SAT scores were too low to attract academic scholarships. With those negatives weighing in, I reluctantly gave up on that option.

Given my inept relationship with blacks outside of my family, I didn't have the wherewithal to sustain a "black attitude" for four years at an HBCU. It always seemed to be the same issue, no matter where I went. As soon as I opened my mouth in Manassas or any part of Northern Virginia, I was immediately dismissed as "trying to act white" or referred to as a "corny ass nigga," mainly due to my mannerisms. I knew being around that type of black negativity would contribute nothing toward my pursuit of a successful life. By that point, I'd already accepted my role as an outcast and didn't see a need to revisit a person I was never going to be. I had already accepted myself and didn't see a further need to prove my blackness to anyone.

My sister, Eve, was living in North Carolina at the time. We reconnected with each other through letters and phone conversations during my senior year. She suggested Duke since she was attending for her master's program. The thought of being near her again was appealing, but I told her they would laugh hysterically at my 820 SAT score. I imagined a group of pompous pricks smoking cigars and drinking scotch, poking fun at my application in a professor's lounge. I ended up telling her that applying wasn't worth my time. Plus, I had to know my limitations even when others didn't. I was intelligent and had the potential to be a collegiate-level intellectual, but my lack of understanding complex math and certain elements of English left me playing catch-up well into my college sophomore year.

Although I needed to make my decision as soon as possible, I was fretful about making the wrong choice. In the end, I didn't want to go somewhere to prove myself once again. I needed to be somewhere where I could be accepted as a person, but stand out in a crowd. I had a fear of being forgotten, which I can only imagine stemmed from feeling disconnected over the years. I was leaning toward EMU because of Pete's relentless interest in my athleticism; however, after the second campus visit, my decision was final. EMU and Harrisonburg, Virginia reminded me of Rappahannock in so many ways – the friendly atmosphere, Blue Ridge scenery and slow pace of life. This was the place where I felt most like a home away from home. I knew it was my decision to make, but, I only felt like I disappointed everyone involved in helping me. My counselor, Kent was the only person who was openly proud of my decision. Although he expressed his concern about the amount of debt I would accumulate, a sense of worry never arose since I didn't have a clear understand of how debt worked at the time. However, Kent realized the magnitude of that moment for me and the reason behind my choice.

My freshmen year was an experience I'll never forget. The possibilities were infinite, and my life had never felt more invigorated before stepping on EMU's grounds as a college student. I gazed at students from all walks of life and the proud parents who accompanied them. I immediately recognized the genuine excitement in my new peers' faces as they began on the same journey. It was unsettling and sensational to see so many unfamiliar faces. Nobody knew me or my past, and I would finally get to start anew. To describe it; I can only guess it's somewhat similar to the freedom a man feels when he finds his way out of the wilderness and on a road that might lead him home. That zest for campus life led to a newborn confidence in the beginning.

Move-in day was memorable since Granny and Granddaddy were so supportive. Granny's face glowed like she was sending her son to college. I knew they were the only reason this transition was going so smoothly. Without them taking me in during that last week, I don't know what would have become of me. I may have arrived during orientation week, but uncertainty would have loomed over one of the most important milestones in my life. I realized at that moment how fortunate I was to have yet another person step up and support me in a time of need. This was vital to my confidence and ability to pull through my freshman year.

The most beneficial aspect of attending a conservative campus such as EMU was the lack of distractions. The girls were attractive and approachable, the parties were right across town at JMU, but I managed to keep my eyes on the prize that year. Without a model for study habits, I spent about half of my weekends in the library, studying in the dorms with a group of friends, or pulling all-nighters at the local Waffle House. Steak, egg and cheese omelet, coffee and a stack of books were my routine for as long as I could stand it. Early into my first semester, I had to go to the library to do research for an upcoming paper and came across the African-American section. I selected a random book, and my brain started to come alive. The basics: Crispus Attucks, MLK, Rosa Parks, and Harriet Tubman didn't even begin to touch the epicenter of Black History. To Rappahannock's credit, their school system covered more than most, but so much of my cultural history was left unexplored. The past was coming to life, so rich and vibrant; I felt like my mind was beginning to unlock. Reading about Dr. Charles Drew, who pioneered techniques for blood typing and transfusion let me know that I could set out and accomplish anything, regardless of my circumstances. I also came across controversial topics like interracial marriage in the Loving v. Virginia case and affirmative action. I received a much deeper perspective on a range of issues that would ultimately affect me in a positively reinforcing manner. Brown v. Board of Education, LBJ's role in the endorsement of the civil rights campaign, Buffalo Soldiers, Tuskegee Airmen, Freedom Riders, and Malcolm X all fascinated me.

After growing up my entire life without a hero, Jesse Owens quickly filled that gap. He was real, and his evidence of such heroism was tangible in the form of biopics and books. Every effort he gave during the 1936 Olympic Games was nothing short of valiant. I wondered why he wasn't revered in our history books. I knew we, the black race, were capable of more, but it had never been presented to me with such significance before. I was in awe of everything I came across.

This was my saving grace during the first year since I wasn't very interested in the required courses. I spent most of freshman year lost in transition mainly due to being ill-prepared for collegiate-level expectations. The discovery of my rich heritage kept me motivated to do my best and never abandon my goals. The greatest blacks knew life wasn't about taking pride in obtaining materialistic possessions to define themselves on the outside. Their pursuit of happiness was at a much deeper level than I could comprehend before arriving at EMU. They contributed more to our country's foundation under the most oppressive conditions, and it was all due to their relentless pursuit of knowledge. They didn't put other blacks down by referring to each other as niggers. They didn't put down other blacks by calling them lame if they didn't sport the latest designer wardrobe. All of a sudden my FUBU jersey and big sterling silver chain lost their personal value. At that moment, I realized the blackest thing I could do was to graduate from EMU. So many had fought and died to give me this opportunity; one I initially took for granted. However, if I was going to survive my college years, I was going to have to relieve myself of the anger and resentment that was continually destroying me from the inside.

As much as I studied, I spent a lot of weekends alone. My roommate, Spence went home often, so I was left with an eerie silence only interrupted by random patterns of footsteps in the hallways. In retrospect, I should've engaged my new friends, but I'd usually wake up early and let my negative thoughts take over. This self-destructive routine left me consumed by pent-up anger.

I had to get this weight off my shoulders, and it started with writing separate letters to Miriam and Demarius. I can't recall what I wrote verbatim, but I let Miriam know that I was disappointed in her inability to discipline J'nelle. I felt euphoric after releasing all of my grievances in the three-page letter. Now, it was Demarius' turn. The gist of my letter voiced my disappointment with him as a man, and how I expected more. He had talent that he wasn't using, and I felt he needed to prepare himself to accomplish something within his lifetime. I folded and pressed both letters, sealed them in separate envelopes and marched up to the Campus Center mailroom to send my heartache on its way. After watching both letters slide down the chute, I noticed an instant release of the weighted and unnecessary anger I was hanging onto. As soon as I left the Campus Center mailing area, my spirits were re-energized to take on the challenges facing me.

Looking back, the letters were arrogant in nature. My original intent was to express forgiveness, but I also wanted to convey that I deserved better. When I returned home for winter break, Granny and Granddaddy vocally expressed their disappointment. They were mostly dissatisfied because I accused Miriam of constantly lying. It was blatant disrespect on my part and regardless of whether it was true or not; it wasn't my place to point it out. I had disrespected my elders, and I was supposed to have known better. For me, it was about holding two people accountable and moving on with my life.

The other important issue I addressed that weekend was researching about forgiveness. I could no longer hold onto the resentment I had for my mother and father. I knew it was starting to eat my consciousness alive, and unless I learned to let it go, it was going to consume me and ruin my potential. Equipped with a new and more holistic perspective on forgiving, I began to write. Once the letter was finished, I begged God to take this anger from me and release the rest of the poisoning bitterness consuming me. Then I cried with as much control as possible to refrain from drawing attention from outside my hollow door. I smothered my face into a pillow and just let the waterworks exhaust me to the point of sleep.

A few hours later I awoke to footsteps running through the hallways. I figured it was the streakers again, so I waited until the commotion died down to take a peek out the door. Sure enough, these buck naked boys were running back down the hallway, so I refastened my door. I never understood why a group of guys would want to run around all over campus exposed, but everyone had their ways of getting through the boredom that sometimes ensued. After the commotion subsided, I went out to see what was going on around campus that night and overheard some of my boys talking about heading over to a party at JMU. After everything I'd been through that day, I needed a drink!

There weren't too many people who were into partying at EMU. The housing layout consisted of the all-female dorm above the cafeteria, the off-centered co-ed dorm, and the woods, which were a mixture of two co-ed dorms and one all-male dorm where I resided. Elmwood, the quiet dorm comprised mostly of girls, was where I'd go if I needed a moment of peace with some of the mellower crowd. Several of my closer friends resided in the other co-ed Maplewood, and they were fun to be around if I needed a reminder of life back in Rappahannock.

If I wanted access to off-campus parties, it was necessary to get in good with the juniors and seniors in Oakwood. The only time I ever mustered the courage to get off campus and learn my way around Harrisonburg was thanks to those guys.

While it was a good thing I chose a conservative campus, I often longed for one more Rappahannock field party. If I wasn't studying or being addicted to the latest computer game, I was generally bored. However, that didn't always last long.

Likely provoked by someone within our dorm; a couple of Maplewood boys placed sardines in our air ducts. The smell nearly made me evacuate the campus with no hopes of coming back. The boys of Oakwood couldn't let them get away with that nonsense, so a good-natured rivalry began. Harrisonburg probably had more roadkill than anywhere else in Virginia, so it wasn't long before some of our entourage returned with a dead opossum. It was officially on. We gathered in the main room and devised a plan that included, Icy Hot for the toilet seats, Jolly Ranchers candy for inside the shower heads, dirty athletic socks and underwear for the heat vents and the opossum for the ceiling vents. Our message was clear: Oakwood was not to be messed with on this night or any other night. One of the boys had the door code from his girlfriend, so we were able to enter without a scene. My mission was to find the bathrooms and insert the hard candies into the showerheads. Amidst the chaos, I frantically ran toward anything that looked like the restroom and started unscrewing shower heads. Fumbling Jolly Ranchers everywhere, I only succeeded on one floor before Oakwood started retreating. It didn't matter though; the night was epic.

We took pride in being the only all-male dorm primarily comprised of athletes. However, it was not a pride that equated to taking care of our property, but one largely hyper-driven by testosterone and a manly overconfidence. I admired them for it, but ultimately fell short of ever achieving that level of self-esteem. My initial bravado was waning as the reality of my trial-by-error life began to strike another blow to my efforts.

The big baller lifestyle I was trying to attain on credit came back to haunt me early in my freshman year. I had no idea how to handle money other than spending it as quick as I earned it. Saving and living within my means were foreign concepts to me. Regardless of my ignorance, the creditors wanted their past due payments, and they were relentless with phone calls and overflowing my campus mailbox with notices. The same semester I was trying to discover my path, I ended up having to work night shift at a local supermarket as well as work study to get the creditors to give me a little breathing room. I hadn't faced that kind of pressure beforehand, so had no idea how to make it stop. They refused to let up, so I shut down and ignored them completely until I returned home. I also had indoor track practice and classes that made me feel out of my element. Quitting school in order to work came across my mind but was not a viable option. I would've disappointed Coach Pete, Granny and Granddaddy and proven that worthless guidance counselor right. I'd never doubted myself more at any other time in college than that first year. Sadly, most of the uncertainty was self-inflicted.

Once I realized that I would make it through the first semester with tolerable grades for someone still trying to find their way, I began planning my next steps. First, I called Granny to ask if I still had a place to stay. Next, I called my supermarket manager in Manassas, VA. I asked for as many hours as they could give me, and they gladly accepted me. I was relieved to think that I might be able to pay down enough to get the creditors off of my back. I didn't waste any time. I left EMU early Saturday and went straight to work the following Sunday. Coach Pete gave me a workout schedule to stick to, but I figured I could depend on my talents to get me through track season. I had no choice but to work since there was no one to bail me out of this predicament.

Unfortunately the money I earned was barely enough to cover the past due amounts of the five or so credit cards I had acquired. I added up what I owed which came out to nearly ten thousand dollars, and I stared another hard decision right in the face. I finally had to give up my new car and ask Granny and Granddaddy to make payments with the promise that I would pick it up as soon as possible. I knew I had disappointed them, but didn't know what else to do. I kept working that last week but never brought in enough to make a dent due to the high interest and late fees.

After sending off as much money as I could to the various creditors, I finally had to walk upstairs and shamefully ask for a ride back to school. I was embarrassed and disappointed in myself. When the day came to go back, strangely enough all that kept repeating through my head was there will be no dating girls this semester.

The spring session started off rough as I began to lose sleep, which negatively affected every aspect of my life. This wasn't the experience I had dreamed about after all. I'd lost complete control of my life. Instead of feeling like a free-spirited eagle taking flight from its nest, I felt like a fledgling freefalling toward the ground. In addition to this self-induced headache, my course load was too heavy, and I immediately began to question the religious course requirements.

The professor in my second faith course started off with, "If my wife was raped, I'd go into the next room to pray." I never bothered to research or even ask what tenets of the Mennonite faith were, but it centered on pacifism - a belief that any issue can be resolved through nonviolent means. This man took the view to the extreme, and I was certain his wife wouldn't appreciate being married to such a cowardly man. In my opinionated thought, I'd figured, *If God blessed you with the strength to attack the rapist, then you had better utilize that strength by any means necessary.* I wasn't going to disrespect the man in front of the class, but thought to myself, *"It's your wife for God's sake!"* After that, I struggled through this class mainly because I had absolutely no respect for the man from day one. I had flashbacks to my mother being beaten senseless and how helpless I felt being unable to defend her when I was less than eight years old. In my mind, he was no better than the loser who hypothetically raped his wife. I didn't think much of the Mennonite faith after that and wondered if I had made the wrong choice since I couldn't drop the course; it was a requirement along with three more before I could graduate. *What the heck was I thinking?* I needed an outlet from the stress of a course load I just wasn't mature enough to handle but didn't even know where to begin.

Finally, outdoor track and field provided an escape. It was my initial reason for being in school and made the rest of the semester tolerable. At last, I was able to showcase my potential. I was getting used to the physical changes after working out regularly and having a real track for practice. Even though I ate like a horse and worked out in the gym as often as time allowed, I only weighed about 145 pounds. Luckily, standing at 6'4" the 3" height adjustments to the 110 high hurdles didn't prove to be such a problem. The 400 intermediate hurdles (400IH) on the other hand, were a bigger transition that I had anticipated. Those extra hundred yards might as well have been another lap. Practice days for the

400IH hurt; there's just no other way to put it. There was practice hurt that felt good and made me feel accomplished and rejuvenated. Then there was take-you-out-behind-the-woodshed hurt; that's how I would explain prepping for the 400IH. Determined, I muscled through it only managing to fall during one meet that year.

My first outdoor track meet was at the University of Mary Washington. Again, feeling the track give beneath my spikes was tantamount to floating on a cloud. I could barely contain my excitement as I warmed up and eventually wore myself out before the events even started. I wasn't required to be in the field events which was a nice change of pace. Although my focus would be hurdles, I was glad Pete had me on the relay squad. He managed to recruit a talented team, but we didn't have the numbers to cover a solely focused relay squad. Plus, I loved getting that baton. The beast within would get revved up and take off with a determined hustle once I felt that aluminum engage with my eager hand. I don't remember much about that first meet, but I'll never forget that 400IH race.

When that starting gun went off, I burst out of the blocks like a greyhound out of the gates. This was my time to shine, and I was ready to make it big. After all, I had naïve Olympic aspirations and wanted to prove that I belonged with the elite pedigree. All of that came tumbling down as my lead at the 300-meter mark quickly dissipated into not one, but two Mary Washington hurdlers passing me on the back stretch. The last three hurdles appeared to ascend higher and higher, and the last one felt like it was up to my navel, and I had cinder blocks tied to my spikes. I closed my eyes, lifted my lead leg with everything I had left and by the grace of God, I cleared it and propelled my cramped legs across the finish line. I patted the two guys on their back and told them good job. Trying to regain control of my breathing, I just walked off of the track shaking my head in disgust. It was a very humbling experience that caused me to rethink my level of commitment on the bus ride home. I had to do better next time. Even with an embarrassing time of just under a minute, my Olympic dreams didn't fade away. *I just have to work harder*, I thought.

With continuous improvement, I was able to end my freshman year on a positive note by placing well at the Old Dominion Athletic Conference (ODAC) Championships. The camaraderie on the long bus trips provided me with enough laughter to keep my mind from wandering off to the stresses that ate away at me throughout the course of any other day.

I finished the school year with semi-decent grades, but the credit card debt at the forefront of my mind had ballooned with over limit fees and compounding interest rates. I quit working spring semester to focus on school and track while I still had my work study job. While I paid the minimum or skipped some months altogether, the pressure was too much for me to handle. My life was quickly unraveling, but I had no idea how to overcome the odds I had clearly stacked against myself. I accepted blame, but that wasn't going to pay the bills. It was time to take the necessary action.

I kept this burden a secret throughout the year, which turned out to be the worst thing I could've done. I was pretty much emotionally shut down by the end of the semester. While my friends were preparing to go home to alleviate their homesickness and anticipating family vacations, I was planning to overcome a mountain of credit card debt. I relied on myself for the tough love advice I needed, *"You're going to have to work your way out of this one."* I immediately made a call to my former supervisors at the gas station and supermarket to ask if I could work for the summer. From May through August of 2000, I moved in with my cousin, Christine, in Manassas and plugged away at the 7-3 shift at the gas station and 4-12 at the supermarket with an additional eight hours Sunday earning time-and-a-half. I was proud that I never missed a single shift and received so much praise for my work ethic, which never slowed. However, I was more proud of the fact that I resisted the latest trends and car gadgets to pay off my debts.

Seeing all of the balances at zero, I breathed a sigh of relief and canceled most of my credit cards. Of course, this was another decision where I should've sought advice, but I was too embarrassed to tell anyone. I had some money left over, but once again, the concept of saving was foreign to me, so I treated myself to a dragon tattoo covering the right side of my back with the intent of having a lion cover the left side. The lion is still missing, but the dragon remains just as fiery as ever. After the tattooist had completed the artwork in one 5 ½ hour sitting, it was officially time to head back for my sophomore year.

Chapter Ten

Coming of Age

I was still a fledgling man desperately trying to come of age during my sophomore year. While I had somewhat matured, it wasn't enough to feel comfortable with understanding my sense of being and my place in the world. I was grateful to reconnect with the friends I met the year before and listened to their summer stories. I mentioned that I worked two jobs and showed off my tattoo since everyone made a point to pat me on the back as hard as possible. I understood that it was just a friendly gesture, but my back was on fire that first week. A back slap felt like a cattle prod being shoved into my skin. Still, it was good to be back on campus.

With creditors off my back, I set my sails with a renewed sense of purpose. The brand new University Commons that Pete touted before I committed to EMU was completed over the summer and equipped with a state-of the-art gym that allowed us to work out earlier than my freshman year. The new indoor track was a nice addition since I disliked running outside during the late fall and winter months.

However, new challenges and fresh doubts awaited me. My Probability and Statistics course would prove to be the bane of my existence. As I flipped through the textbook, it might as well have been Advanced Astrophysics. Doubt began to overwhelm my thoughts. I immediately made plans to spend as much study time as it would take to pass this course. However, distractions in the form of women once again took hold as I had to get to know Ginette.

Ginette was new on campus and had this *Something About Mary* quality to her. She didn't exactly wear form fitting clothes, so it forced girl chasers like me to focus on her dark curly hair and mysterious eyes, which both were illuminated by her constant smile. The first time our eyes connected, I just had to meet her. I asked my confidant, Niko, if she knew anything about her. After listening to how I had to be with her and the rest of my nonsense about Ginette maybe being the one, she laughed and we began talking about her disappointing relationship.

After leaving Niko's room, I went downstairs to grab dinner. I hadn't seen some of the guys, so after exchanging guy hugs and handshakes, we began talking about class loads. Somehow the conversation quickly turned to girls and Ginette's name came up almost immediately. I kept silent to hear their opinions, and while I can't recall what was said, I knew competition was on the horizon. When I headed down to my dorm, her name came up again in passing. Pressing my code to enter the building, I shook my head in disbelief. In my room, I regrouped before deciding to head over to her dorm across the main yard. I called my friend Walden to let me in and confidently marched up to her room only to find a guy and one of her close friends laughing. I looked in, waved and quickly made my smooth escape to hang out on the third floor. After arriving, I overheard my friends Rex and Sydney groveling over one of the new girls.

I interjected," Hey fellas, who are you talking about? Both replied in sync,

"Ginette!"

This was my last straw, "Aw c'mon man! You guys too? Damn, every guy on campus has a thing for her." I waited for two hours before checking again only to find three other guys talking to her. Short of stalking her, I knew that night wasn't meant to be. I had to study, so it was off to another all-nighter with my study group at the Waffle House.

Other than friendly hellos and waving, I never really got a chance to sit down with Ginette until the semester was halfway over. By that point, I'd given up on her. I couldn't bring myself to disappoint so many of my friends. However, I couldn't deny it when talking about her with Niko. When Niko suggested I just be friends with her, I took her advice and released the tension that came with mastering the art of the chase. Talking to Ginette like I talked to Niko allowed me to reveal my true self. When we finally had a chance to be alone together, I didn't stumble throughout the entire night. We slipped into a deep, intellectual conversation that started with exchanging our life stories then covered everything from race relations to philosophy.

The early morning light peered in, and one of the Oakwood boys came through the lobby. He looked at me and asked if I was ready for the big meet that day. I assured him that I was always ready.

Ginette, replied with surprise, "You have a meet today?"

Smiling, I said, "Yeah, I have to get ready in 15 minutes and get on the bus to go to VMI (*Virginia Military Institute*)." She felt guilty, but I reassured her that it was worth it and that I'd see her again soon. I hugged her and headed upstairs thinking the rest of that day was going to hurt badly.

VMI's track wasn't like other indoor tracks. The asphalt-like surface and the unusual rounded square shape didn't allow my tall frame to bend around the corners without aggravating my chronic back pain. This particular day, I won the 55M hurdles and gave my all in the relays. To better prepare for the 400IH during outdoor season, Coach Pete added the 800-meter race to my agenda. I was already too tired to stand, but I had to get it in. Afterward, I was looking forward to sleeping on the way home, but the pain was too intense. I knew something was wrong. The ice packs and ibuprofen didn't do anything to help it subside during the ride back to campus.

After the injury had ached all day Sunday, I scheduled an appointment to see a local physician. Before I arrived, I knew this injury was going to be a major setback. *What if I couldn't recover in time for next season?* Doubt once again overwhelmed me. At the appointment, I was diagnosed with a left inguinal hernia that could only be repaired by surgery. I decided to call Granny to help me set it up and took it easy the rest of the semester to ensure I didn't do further damage before the surgery. Fortunately, this gave me time to focus on my lagging statistics grade.

Although I committed 12-18 hours per week to studying with study groups, doing extra practice problems and tutoring with the professor himself, it didn't seem to help. For many reasons, I was grossly unprepared for this level of complex math. Nonetheless, spending time with the professor proved to be my biggest waste of time. When I told him that I still didn't understand how he made the logical jump from one step to the next, he conceitedly retorted, "I don't know how you don't get this." I always left his office more confused and frustrated than when I entered.

My inability to understand the material came down to exam day. I needed a B+ on the exam to pass the course. It was a long shot, but I gave one more all-nighter at the Waffle House in a last ditch desperation attempt hoping something would suddenly click. It didn't happen. The best thing about that night was my steak and cheese omelet.

Entering the classroom, I immediately sensed hopelessness. It was akin to going into a fight knowing I was going to lose. My hands trembled at the fear of failure. I didn't have a plan B. I needed this course to complete my Business Administration major. *How was I going to tell Granny and Granddaddy I failed? Would I be placed on academic probation? Would I lose my scholarships?* Scanning through each page, I quickly realized that I couldn't confidently work through more than two problems on the entire exam. I'd never felt more dumb and inept than in that moment. After answering the two that I knew and linking guesses together, I realized that I was just wasting my time. Instead of completing the exam, I left a paragraph-long note at the end explaining that the exam was a waste of both of our time. I also let him know that he didn't do a good job explaining in a way that I could understand and apologized for wasting his time. I put the exam on his desk and left feeling dejected. A third of us ended up failing the course. While it didn't make me feel any better, I was somewhat relieved to know it wasn't just my fault. I still maintained that I was not a stupid person, but I needed a good professor who could teach to all levels of understanding.

I'd failed before because I didn't apply myself, but never failed in this manner. I couldn't comprehend how I put my heart and soul into this effort only to come away with nothing. This encounter with failure numbed me to the point of giving up college. After discussing it with Niko, who also failed the course, she said it didn't affect her Liberal Arts majors and plans for graduating on time. If that major was good enough for her, then it was good enough for me. At that point, I just wanted to graduate and avoid statistics by any means necessary.

I passed the rest of my exams, but my GPA was drastically pulled down. I was convinced that the time spent focusing on statistics brought my other grades down. The only thing I would have done differently was to divide my time evenly between the courses. There was nothing I could do about it since the opportunity had already passed. It was time to go home and have my surgery. I was just glad the semester was over.

I worked at the supermarket through the first part of the break but tried to take it easy to refrain from causing any more damage. Finally, operation day had arrived in early January, 2001. Surprisingly, I wasn't nervous about the whole ordeal. I decided beforehand that there was no need to fear situations beyond my control and still maintained my trust in God providing a way forward. Granny and Granddaddy took me to the hospital that morning. The lead up and surgery prep went off without a hitch. That was until my gown slipped off and exposed my tattoo. Granny interrupted her sentence, "When did you get that great big old' tattoo on your back?" I hurried to cover it, but ultimately had to reveal that I got it at the end of summer just across the road from the hospital. It was a light moment before the surgeon walked in the room.

I didn't make up my mind whether I was comfortable with a woman doing the operation since I was completely exposed. I guessed either way, it was going to be a weird situation. She went over the surgical plan, and the last thing I remember was Granny saying that she was proud of me and loved me.

The surgery went as planned, and I was on the outpatient path to recovery. Shortly thereafter, Granny and Granddaddy took me home to rest. Initially, I struggled up the steps in a painful, drug-induced stupor. Granny kept the Jell-O and water coming for a few days before graduating to applesauce. She took great care of me while I tried not to be too much of a burden. Most of the time, I was left alone with my thoughts. I tortured myself about past mistakes, failing to have a girlfriend and my future.

I truly wanted to be an Olympic hurdler, but my performance times for both the 110 and 400 were embarrassing in comparison to world-class hurdlers. In high school, I couldn't comprehend the magnitude of the time lapse. I won a lot, but I never had serious competition until regional and state level, but it still didn't set in. When I watched both events during the 2000 Olympics in Greece that prior August, reality finally began to puncture my Olympic dreamscape. In addition, I had recently learned that only one out of every hundred thousand college athletes went pro. If I couldn't dedicate my all to this dream, then it simply wasn't going to happen. I made decisions to do just that, but life always seemed to get in the way. I was never a person who relied on excuses, but I also maintained a certain level of awareness of my limitations. After this semester, college life and my track career would be halfway over. It was time to decide what I wanted in life.

I wanted a degree and a family. I had no idea what to be other than a world-class hurdler. I could be a politician or an entrepreneur, but where? My aspirations for Urban Light supermarket and screenplays were buried in a box somewhere. The possibilities were endless, but I had to cut ties with my Olympic dreams. Even if I recovered in time to salvage my sophomore outdoor season, I still hadn't dealt with my chronic back pain that was radiating down my right lead leg during practice and meet days. I had already tried physical therapy twice to no avail and by medical standards was addicted to ibuprofen. All of the years of hurdling on cinders and asphalt had taken its toll on my young frame. It was time to accept the fact that I didn't have a legit shot of competing at an elite level. I needed to get back to school. It was time to redefine myself. As the tears welled up, Granny came in to encourage me to walk around.

Although I arrived at EMU a week late, I was grateful to be back on campus. Guy hugs greeted me throughout the dorm, and it was great to see my desktop computer again. I was ready to put it to work. My roommate Spence was in, so we caught up with each other's break stories. He explained to me that he might not be able to afford to stay.

Two weeks later, he was moving out. I immediately started worrying about who would be assigned as my new roommate. All I could do was hope that the next guy wouldn't be a prude. Spence was a cool cat. His random guitar playing and conversations about anything were missed almost immediately. I was disappointed to watch him leave over the inability to afford tuition, but I wished him the best. Missing him was short-lived, since I took advantage of the quiet space to get familiar with my new courses.

My second of four bible courses started out with the same rape scenario. I thought to myself, *are you kidding me?" Are Mennonite women really okay with this mentality?* I didn't pose any of the questions. Instead, I just decided to let the professor lead his course and tucked my beliefs away. After all, it was a religious college, and I wasn't in a place to challenge his religious authority. Being lost within my own Southern Baptist upbringing, it would've just compounded the confusion already taking place in my thought processes. Transferring briefly crossed my mind, but I quickly reminded myself that most of my Mennonite friends were cool and didn't share this extreme view. After that day, I never managed to maintain focus in my bible course. The lectures never held my interest and the students that did speak up were so far beyond anything I could comprehend. I couldn't intelligently engage even if I wanted to. Instead, I just decided to read for the required essays and final exam to pass the course. Thankfully, I passed with a C+.

Since the pressure was off to complete a degree in business, I decided to venture into a History of Africa course. The enlightenment received during this course completely altered my viewpoint on a seemingly lost and distant heritage. We always learned about Africans coming over on the slave ships in grade school, but the rich history throughout the motherland continent was never considered. Learning about this helped me fully realize the complexities of slavery and how it affected so many generations of my race. I wasn't upset over a past I had no involvement in; just grateful for a more holistic understanding of an ancestry I would never have an opportunity to discover. This course was the closest I would ever come to finding out how great my distant ancestry were and gave me a sense of purpose to continue my journey.

A few weeks later, my track roommate, Reese, moved in with me. His roommate had left around the same time Spence did, so it worked out in our favor. Reese and I had similar discussions about our aspirations and deeper philosophical issues. We watched movies, talked track and field, and hung out in the lounge with other Oakwood heads. On the other hand, as good as we got along; our quirks began to rub each other some days. Specifically, I recall having Black Rob's

Whoa on heavy rotation while studying or playing computer games. He'd constantly ask how many times I was going to play the song in a row. The room temperature was the other big problem. I was cold natured, so I preferred the temperature around 75 degrees or hotter. He was more of a 68 or below kind of guy. We eventually found compromise, but he probably felt like he was a Pop Tart in a toaster having to live with me. Our disputes were short lived as I finally connected with a girl.

My Leadership course required me to go to a forum one Saturday morning. While I can't recall the main theme, the report and attendance associated with it was a third of our grade, so I couldn't skip as I'd originally considered. I awoke earlier than I wanted to on a weekend day and headed into the brisk January air. I arrived and sat in the very back hoping this thing would be over as soon as possible.

During the first break, I thought about heading back to the dorm, but my class would have noticed and someone would have most likely turned me in. I dragged myself down the hallway to reenter the forum when I noticed a candy dish placed just outside the door. I shifted further right to grab a piece when I heard a sweet voice tease me about taking candy from the bowl that may have belonged to someone else. Gullibly, I doubted myself for a split second before smiling at her witticism.

There I stood, dressed in a navy blue ball cap covering my eyebrows, a heavy brown leather jacket, a football jersey, baggy jeans, and boots. I peered upward to match the face with that pretty voice and discovered a set of mesmerizing green eyes, long, curled strawberry blond hair pulled back away from her face, snowy skin tone and a warm smile that was directed toward me. She was wearing a green and white sweater and an amazing pair of jeans that perfectly complemented her curvy frame. She asked for my name and my response requested hers in return; Emily. My memory is kind of sketchy after that, but we exchanged a few pleasant words and went back into the forum.

Shortly thereafter, I ended up having to go up to the front of the crowd and tell a synopsis of my life story. I was proud of my perseverance over hardships and the man I was becoming. I'd forgiven my mother, my father, and everyone else who I felt betrayed me in the past. I was resilient, battle-ready, and prepared for whatever life was going to throw at me next. I was a warrior in my own right, so I was proud to share my story. I thought I would be able to sit down after the applause, but that was not enough for the presenter. This persistent man who called me up front to tell my story wanted me to vent my anger! Being a black male himself, I did not think he had much self-awareness when it came to refraining from the angry black man stereotype in public places. I froze; all I could think about was this guy ruining the only chance I had to make a first impression on this girl I wanted to get to know after this dreadful meeting. I thought to myself, *What kind of bullshit exercise is this!?!* There was a refusal and awkward silence from my end. He had an annoying grin accompanied by a set bulging and encouraging eyes. He kept pressing even though I gave him the slanted eye, but I finally gave in. I let something completely corny fly out of my mouth and assumed my life was over.

I was completely sprung on this girl I don't even know, and this fool just messed it up for me. Afterward, I walked back to my seat dejected while everyone gave me a forced applause. I was devastated. Once the forum ended, I gathered my pride off the floor and made a beeline out the door to wait for her by the candy dish. It was probably only two minutes, but it felt like time had stopped. This was a huge step forward for me since I usually succumbed to embarrassment and reluctantly accepted rejection when it came to girls. Once I started walking toward the doors thinking she must have slipped out of a side door, she approached me from behind. When I heard her angelic voice behind me, I was so relieved. Our eyes linked and smiles beamed with joy as we were able to reconnect. I walked her back to her dorm, actually got her number and went back to my dorm room. Reese was there, so I immediately told him about her.

Although she told me to call her later that night, I had to play it cool. The minutes passed slowly and time I'd usually spent at the gym was curtailed by my need to heal from my surgery a few weeks prior. Computer games and internet surfing filled the time until dinner. I headed toward the cafeteria for a quick bite to eat before visiting Niko to tell her about Emily.

She interrupted, "Wait, what about Ginette?"

"Forget about Ginette!" I replied. "Besides, every dude on campus has a thing for her." I went on to tell her how we met, and spent a couple of hours before heading down to my room to make the call I'd been jonesing to make since she'd given me her number.

I called and became gleeful as she picked up on the second ring. Afterward, Emily invited me to her room, and we spent that entire night talking about any and everything. The words just seemed to flow until daylight. I was in her all-female dorm room well after hours, but I knew there was one thing left to do. As I leaned in to kiss her, nothing ran through my head. No shyness. No awkwardness. No doubt. This was the moment. Our lips fit so perfectly together; so much that we were entranced by it. Everything about it seemed perfect. Once we pulled back to take one more look at each other, she said, "I guess it's time to see how to get you out of here."

Luckily, her dorm room was near an exit, so she peered out her door to ensure my safe departure. Once she gave me the all-clear hand gesture, I snuck in one more kiss and let her know that I would see her soon. After tip-toeing past a few doors, I slipped out the exit to meet the cold fog of that morning; however, it didn't faze me in the least. I envisioned sunshine without a single cloud in my sky. I don't think I'd ever skipped along on a sidewalk a day in my life, but for some reason I decided to give it a try that morning.

Emily and I went back and forth for a couple of weeks, but I could tell she wasn't ready to commit. I tried to sympathize since she had just broken off an engagement six months earlier, but at the same time I didn't want to play games or worse yet, get played again. I badly wanted to be in a relationship, not out of desperation, but out of aspiration. I wanted to share my dreams and most intimate thoughts with someone and still have the security of knowing that person would still want to love me. I wanted someone to understand my complex emotions and struggles in only a way a woman could. Sometimes I thought it was too much to hope for, but I never lost the ambition of my inner hopeless romantic.

Coupled with my impatience, the potential for this relationship was already heading downhill. The biggest doubt indicator letting me know that this wasn't the real thing was when she went out on a date with another guy. Although she had already committed to a date with a local radio host weeks before meeting me, I'd never had to deal with a situation similar to this one. To further complicate things, I kissed her as she was leaving the building only to turn my head up and see this guy. As he walked away with her, I immediately recalled my experience with Aubrey. I thought to myself, *"I'm not going through this shit again, and I deserve better treatment than that."* Before making that decision, I ran upstairs to ask Niko for her advice. Of course, she confirmed my doubts saying that I shouldn't be dating someone so indecisive. And she reminded me about Ginette. I have no idea why, but I can only guess that it was to prove her earlier point. I left Niko's room that night even more confused and crestfallen. Emily returned somewhat early and called me. She alleviated my insecurity by telling me that it was just a one-time deal, and the date was awkward.

Another week or so passed, and we were still feeling each other out. As much as I was trying to find myself, Emily was doing the same thing. Looking back, I wasn't very sensitive to her process, and things would have gone a lot smoother in the beginning had I been more aware.

For the reasons explained above, I coveted commitment. Emily wasn't at that point in her life, so being the persistent person I was, I needed her answer the night of our friend's birthday party.

Our mutual friend, Nina, was having a birthday bash at a brand new night club. Emily and I talked about going throughout the week, but she hadn't decided on whether she would go or not. She felt some of the black women on campus had shunned her since she had taken an interest in me, so she didn't want to deal with any potential controversy. I told her my intent, which was to go and have a good time. Once I told her that, I figured she would show up. I hitched a ride with a few friends since I still didn't have a car. There's not much to do in a club when you're not old enough to drink, so I slid right out onto the dance floor. It was nice to see familiar faces and actually have girls on the floor that wanted to party. I looked around for Emily a few times but didn't want to make it too obvious.

When Emily finally walked in, she was absolutely glamorous. She had guy's heads turning from every corner, but if I were going to convince her to be with me, I couldn't be like the rest of the dogs in the room. I pretended to not notice her at first, but I had every intention of making her take notice of me before that night was over. Two girls took an interest in me on the dance floor and stayed close for a few songs before the DJ put a song on that no one was feeling. As I was moving away from the floor, Emily grabbed my hand and brought me over to the table. For the rest of the night, she was my only dance partner.

As we were leaving the club, I grew tired of waiting for that spark that was going to join us together as a couple. I assertively asked, "Look, I'm not going to play these games with you. That's not who I am. I need to know, are we a couple or not because I have other things to do."

My Mr. Nice Guy approach always led to a rejection. I think she was taken aback by my approach, but she shot back with, "Well I guess we're a couple, now get in the car!" Our courtship was about as cold as that February night, but we would eventually warm each other up. I recall having an irremovable smile during that short trip back to campus.

A few weekends later, I introduced Emily to my version of a family. Granny and Granddaddy welcomed her with open arms. The rest of the family was more intrigued than anything, but willingly accepted her since she was good enough for me. Shortly after we arrived that Saturday morning, Granny offered Emily a cup of coffee, which she happily accepted. When Emily mentioned that she took her coffee black, Granny jokingly compared her preference to the way she liked her men. It conjured up a nervous laugh from Emily and a wide-eyed facial expression from me before we both burst out into laughter.

We trekked through the forest where I used to build forts and I drove her around in what was supposed to be my car. I had to keep it running smoothly by starting and revving it up during school breaks in hopes of getting it back in the mint condition I remembered when life seemed a touch easier. Plus, having Emily in the passenger seat served as motivation to get it back as soon as possible. Finally we attended church the following morning, and that Southern Baptist flare proved to be a new experience for Emily. Nonetheless, we returned to school after the sermon. The uneventfulness of that weekend signified success and a wave of relief. Granny and Granddaddy acceptance weighed heavier on me than I'd originally anticipated.

Emily was my muse during the rest of that semester. Right before registering for my classes, we had a discussion about how I'd given up my business major after failing statistics. Without hesitation, she told me to give it another try. Using the oddest form of motivation I'd ever received, she asked me if I knew Matthew. I recalled a dude who always walked around with a slump and didn't seem too terribly bright. When I answered, she informed me that he passed statistics. "If he can do it, then I know you can." I thought to myself, *Damn, she's right!* I decided to take the course again if a different professor came to teach at EMU. I also switched my major back to Business Administration after a semester of flirting with Liberal Arts. It was like adjusting my sails after rediscovering a compass that had been lost for months.

She also did things that went above and beyond later that spring. Noah was having trouble in Chemistry when I called to check in. Worried and looking for a way to help him, Emily offered to make the nearly two-hour long trip to tutor him for as long as it took to pass. I coordinated a time with Noah and told him to make sure he was there in time to study. I was worried about Emily being in Miriam's house without me, but I took comfort in knowing that my family had accepted her when I introduced them during a previous Easter weekend. I had track practice that evening, so I couldn't attend.

I was livid when she told me how her evening went. I expected Miriam to be standoffish and rude making the situation as uncomfortable as possible, but I was furious at Noah for being over two hours late because he decided to hang with friends after baseball practice. I reluctantly apologized for Miriam, but Noah had some damn explaining to do. I called to let him know that it was unacceptable to blow people off when they're committing their time. I also reminded him that she drove almost two hours to help him. He apologized, and Emily even went to help him two more times after that. He managed to pass the course with a solid C.

About three months after Emily and I met, she decided that it was time to introduce me to her parents. The plan was to meet them at their annual Mennonite church retreat after my track meet. It was a local meet at Bridgewater College, so we were only minutes from her normal route home. After a first-place performance in the 110 high hurdles, I decided to see what I had gained in the 400 hurdles by going all out from the start. Struggling more than I ever had by the 200 meter mark, I realized my all-out approach was a big mistake. Mentally, each hurdle looked higher than the previous, and by the time I reached the last one, it might as well have been a wall. I closed my eyes and lifted my leg up and hoped for another Mary Washington, but fate had other plans. The hurdle clipped my foot, and I went shoulder first into the ground. Disoriented, I got up and finished the race. I couldn't believe I had fallen on that day of all days. I pressed on through the relay races, but something was seriously wrong with my right shoulder. Emily suggested that I go to the hospital after the meet. It wasn't as much of a suggestion as it was her telling that's where we were going before we met her parents.

After hours in the hospital's emergency department, I was given some ibuprofen and a sling. While we were on the road, I contemplated how much I loathed sympathy, but thought it might work out in my favor in this case. I checked once again to make sure Emily told them I was black. Just as much as I disliked surprises, I couldn't imagine being in Podunk, West Virginia with a bunch of surprised stares and everyone inquiring, "Well, who's the black fella?"

We arrived at the retreat around dusk, and Emily's mother greeted me with a hug. The rest of their church members gathered around in the friendly way Mennonites are known for and greeted me one by one. Emily's father went around doing his business, so I decided to walk up and introduce myself. It was important for me to connect with him. In my mind, this wasn't going to work if I couldn't win over the parents. There was no way I could live with myself causing strife between Emily and her immediate family if they didn't approve. As the night went along, he was eventually okay with me. I didn't expect him to be ecstatic since I was dating his beloved daughter, but his subtle acceptance allowed me to take my guard down and loosen up a bit. The sling turned out to be a big hit throughout the night, and people joked about me planning it all along. I could only wish I were that manipulative.

As the semester dwindled down, the inevitable was coming, and Emily had to accept our distance apart. The trip from Granny's was at least four hours away, so I had plans to get my car back and visit as much as possible. I could tell Emily wasn't taking it as well, so I planned a candlelit dinner atop the campus to express my commitment to our relationship. I burned an R&B CD and took my portable stereo on the hill. I was trying to woo her on a budget, so the Chinese takeout, sparkling cider and flowers spread out on a table allowed the setting to feel reserved just for the two of us. The clear sky with shades of purple and orange allowed us to hold hands, gaze at the stars, and express our dreams to one another. I didn't have time during the semester to provide her with what she deserved, so it was crucial to get this moment right.

Although I had clearly fallen for Emily, most of my efforts that semester had been spent focused on reviving my G.P.A. and fully recovering from surgery. No matter how remarkable she was, I was determined to stay concentrated on the reason I came to EMU. Surprisingly, having her in my life made me more determined to succeed. When I was in the library, she was right beside me doing her work. It kept me focused since I didn't feel the need to choose between her and my studies. I was able to raise my G.P.A. back to a respectable level. and restore my confidence; thanks in large part to having Emily's support throughout that time. Our in-depth conversations were also a large part of the inspiration for the club I founded during that time.

Now that I had accepted the fact that I'd never be Olympic caliber, it was time to hone in on some of my other visions and talents. I thought about the alluring diversity on campus, and how everyone was sort of doing their own thing. *How beautiful would it be to bring all of these people together and get their ideas on solving the challenges facing us?* I consulted with EMU's multicultural director, and she mentored me through the process of beginning a new club. I considered several names, but eventually settled on Future Leaders of Diversity and Equality, or FLDE. I wasn't ecstatic about it until I discussed it with Reese, and he suggested that I flip Equality and Diversity. FLED; now that was an acronym I could live with. For me, everything was in the name. It seemed simple enough, but it made a world of difference for me.

I presented my idea in front of the student committee, which was comprised of several peers I'd never had the opportunity to meet. I donned my best suit, since I considered this a big deal, but everyone else seemed to be in what I referred to as Mennonite casual: earth-tone pants, Birkenstock sandals and a wool-looking jacket over a button-down shirt. I volunteered to go first so my nerves wouldn't have a chance to build up. I went with my beacon-on-a-hill grandiose speech and even garnered some applause afterward. I was confident that my club would be approved but felt bad for the guy who followed my spiel. He wore a white t-shirt and gym shorts to present his proposal for a ping pong club. He affably joked about the matter and proceeded with his pitch.

FLED was approved shortly thereafter. Reese and I hit the ground running with implementing our ideas. I wanted to put FLED on the map, so I decided to host the first religious forum on EMU's campus. I set the date, reserved the auditorium and grabbed a phone book to contact several local pastors from every major religion I could think of. I hadn't heard of the Muslim faith by that point in my life. Otherwise, they would have been up in the mix of the ten or so religious leaders who committed to the event. Branded as an interfaith open dialogue session, the meeting quickly gained attention from my peers and professors alike. One of my professors even asked why I was doing this. I explained that I was advocating for more open discussion, but it really came down to satisfying my own curiosity. My Southern Baptist preachers all told me the same thing; our way was the only and right way to our lord and savior Jesus Christ. It was a notion that I rejected almost immediately since I saw so many different churches during my backseat travels. I always thought to myself, "*What if the Presbyterians, Lutherans, or Episcopalians are right?*" *Would people really waste their Sundays and Wednesday nights on the wrong religion?* Unfortunately, I wasn't permitted to get answers to such questions because it was considered back talk instead of simple inquiry.

Finally, the day arrived. I was so elated that this event was truly happening and wanted the night to go off without a hitch. I double confirmed and ensured everyone I came in contact with knew about the meeting. I wanted the auditorium packed. We began the meeting allowing each preacher to give a five-minute spiel about their religion. While some had thousands of years to cover and others hundreds, it was about as uneventful as I had anticipated. Of course, there's always that one who drones on way too long and veers way off topic. Out of respect, I didn't moderate assertively as I probably should have. When he finally finished going down the extensive list of people he knew in the religious community, I was able to engage the audience with a question and answer period. That process was going as peaceful as I could have hoped until the fire-breathing southern Baptist interrupted the Jehovah's Witness by blurting out that it was his God-given right to go to war. I had no idea how to diffuse the situation, but Emily assisted by asking the Catholic priest about the meaning behind the rosary. That subtle interjection proved to be my saving grace.

Afterward, the religious leaders shook my hand and thanked me for the opportunity. It was definitely a success, and I continued to receive praise throughout campus for my efforts.

Then I had to mess it all up by deciding to host the first gay community forum.

When FLED put the word out about the gay and lesbian forum, it immediately ruffled the establishment's feathers. First, I had to rely on my network to get the gay and lesbian community to attend. While I expected the forum to cause a little controversy, I didn't expect the university president to inquire into the matter and direct the multicultural director to watch me. When she broke the news to me, I immediately started to rethink the whole thing. I wondered if I would be targeted or blacklisted if I moved forward with my idea. I felt that I'd put the multicultural office, my club, and myself at risk. To think all this happened because Emily convinced me to go to a gay club in Roanoke with her friends. I spent the whole night trying to figure out how two seemingly heterosexual couples ended up in a gay joint. As the night progressed, I decided that Emily's friend was gay and pretending to be engaged to his fiancée. He was just way too damn happy to be there. I was about as uncomfortable as any straight man could be without the experience of having any openly gay friends growing up in a tight-knit, rural community, and the number of guys that hit on me only made that situation worse. However, I wondered how this community struggled in the real world, so I used FLED to give them a voice. That's what helped me forge ahead amidst the controversy.

The five-member panel bravely shared their struggles and by the end of the forum, FLED had managed to open the minds of the fully-packed venue. The campus and the larger community left with wonder and a direct challenge to their preconceived notions. I left thinking that I had done my part to make the world a better place and deflected any sense of controversy that worried the establishment. EMU hosted a much larger gay community forum the following year, and I'd like to think FLED had a part in opening that elusive window of opportunity. Going back to the dorm that night, Reese and I talked about various things on the way back. When we reached the room, he said something that I didn't necessarily agree with, and I responded with, "That's gay!" Reese, shot back, "What's wrong with that?" I thought to myself, "*I still have a lot of growing up to do.*" Unfortunately, I couldn't continue with the large-scale meetings. The class load was intensifying with more tests on the horizon and projects coming due. Also, it was time to prepare for track and field season.

Before track season started, recovery from my operation required me to sit around and refrain from doing anything that involved strain or stress. Emily encouraged me to go to the gym when I had clearly fallen into an idle routine. She was studying to become a nurse, so I trusted her judgment even though I had grown content with lounging. While I was at peace with my decision to pursue another dream, I still wanted to win. I wasn't the type of person to give up on anything, so I pressed on for the team and for Coach Pete, who believed in me more than I did myself.

While I gave my all throughout the year, my back injury came back with a vengeance and another misdiagnosis further hindered my potential. I managed to pull off some wins and do my part as the anchor for both relays, but it bruised my pride to place a distant second behind the reigning champ in the hurdle races at the ODAC championship. Always optimistic, Coach Pete assured next year was my turn.

Just like that, half of my college life was history. I was returning for another summer to work at the supermarket and finally save some money. During those couple of months, I missed Emily terribly. I thought, *if this is what life was like without her, I needed her back as soon as possible.* I daydreamed about her often. And the more I thought about the way she inspired my being, I decided that she was definitely the wife type. On impulse, I strode into a jewelry store one evening after work and bought an engagement ring. I decided on a princess cut diamond with baguette side stones at a store where I frequently window shopped during my breaks while working at Miriam's shoe store. I couldn't determine why that ring was the one other than it looked so much different than the collection they were offering. After turning back to gaze at it a third time, I knew this had to be the one. As strange as it appeared, I always had my mind set on starting a family. That whimsical decision served up more complication than I could've ever comprehended in one lifetime.

Chapter Eleven

Out-of-Body Experiment

During the middle of spring semester, I was encouraged by our multicultural director to start thinking about my required cross-cultural trip. The options seemed endless; countries throughout South America or Africa seemed exciting, but each location required me to dedicate a full semester. Although I'd receive a semester's worth of credit, the decision would have put me back one semester against achieving my business major. I had already committed to so much debt, so there was no way I could stay an extra semester. I was initially disappointed with this dilemma since the states didn't seem as exciting as the chance to go international. I came across some three-week summer options, and London was the obvious choice. Each U.S. option would've provided an unforgettable experience, but I wanted to be bold. It was time to venture out of the country.

At that moment, it was time to devise a plan. I had to express my interest to Professor Landers, who was arguably the most popular figure on campus. I loved this guy but couldn't give a valid reason other than his zest for life and the passion he exuded behind his lessons. Nevertheless, I sat down and made my case for why I should be placed on the list alongside my plan to pay and to make an initial deposit. Unfortunately, summer trips weren't covered by tuition. Next, I had to call Granny and ask for her help. We had a few months since the trip wasn't until May, but I wanted to see what I could do to help pull that money together. As always, Granny came through, and all I had to do was wait for the big day.

I was completely stoked about the opportunity to leave the country for the first time. The possibilities in London claimed half of my daydreams throughout the rest of that semester. Of course, I didn't have luggage or a camera, so my cousin lent her camera and Granny and Granddaddy let me borrow their luggage set. Since I usually packed everything in a few trash bags, this was a huge upgrade for me. Professor Landers told us that the weather was fifteen to twenty degrees colder, so I only packed jeans and long sleeves. With all of my details finally situated, I was ready to face a new world.

The long, early morning car ride to the airport gave me one more chance to daydream about the possibilities. When I saw our British Airways terminal, my daydreaming turned into reality. Even though we had Professor Landers' leadership, I was nervous about the thought of going over there without knowing too many people within the group. However, my track teammate Maurice was on the flight near me. I was relieved to see a familiar face since I didn't initially connect with anyone in the group. Feeling the plane rise into the air was nearly euphoric. Soon afterward, the flight attendant introduced me to tea with milk and honey. With the first taste, I asked myself, "Where has this been my entire life?" I glanced at Maurice to say, "Cheerio ol' chap and tipped the cup with my pinkie sticking out. Everyone around me got a good chuckle out of it. A few hours later, I grew impatient due to overwhelming excitement. The eight-hour flight over the Atlantic seemed to take us into eternity.

When I stepped off the plane, the chaos ensued. People just seemed to be running around directionless like ants scattering from a little boy's foot. We eventually retrieved our luggage and made it to the cash exchange counter. At this time, the exchange rate was nearly two-to-one. I didn't have as much money as I'd hoped, but I never adjusted my spending plan since it didn't exist to begin with. At this point, it was just about going with the flow and keeping up with the group.

We made it out together and began looking for restaurants. Our timing was right in the middle of the mad cow disease outbreak, so the group was leery of eating anything with beef ingredients. I was only determined to avoid kidney pie, so my first international meal consisted of a Whopper, fries, and a flat Coke from Burger King. No one warned me that the sodas were flat in England until after the fact. While I was initially disappointed, I quickly adjusted since the alternative was water.

Our vans took us out of London and up north to a village in Ely. We arrived late afternoon, so we were somewhat on our own to stay in or explore the town. Most of the group decided to stay in, but I had no intention of being a hermit crab, as Miriam would always say. Instead, I ventured out with Maurice completely oblivious to our black male status in a quaint little village outside of London. Other than a few people out and about, Ely looked deserted. It was just after five England time, so I couldn't understand why everything was closing up. It wasn't until much later in the trip that I realized many within the British culture didn't place work above their livelihoods as we did back in the states. Finally, we came across a tavern and noticed that some of our group members had beat us to it. We grabbed a table, placed an order, and shared our hopes for the rest of the trip being more exciting than the first night.

By the time we arrived in York; I was in full exploration mode. Again, most of the group decided to stay in after touring all day, but I was just getting warmed up. I wanted to know more about the town and people, and the night scene provided the perfect opportunity. It didn't take much to convince Maurice and my new friend, Craig to go club hoppin' with me. We grabbed a taxi and asked our driver to lead us to the hottest club in town.

We ended up at Club Ikon. Looking on the outside, I thought to myself, *You have got to be kidding me.* I'd never seen anything like it. Ikon was a three-story club with a different music genre on each floor. The lights, beats, and girls were a far cry from the dive full of stuck up chicks at Jams. I was just awestruck by the entire concept. Every floor was crowded with people having a good time and not even being bothered with the competition and mean glares that most men gave off in my American club experiences. We definitely weren't on the countryside anymore, and I was ready do some serious partying on all three levels before the night was over.

I was completely naïve to the British attitudes toward Americans, so little did I know my American status would be considered an exotic commodity. As soon as we stepped in the club and bought a drink, the women seemed to come in droves. I was awestruck by the number of women that asked me to dance that night. They didn't require me to buy drinks for them first, and once I hit the dance floor, the girls just started circling around me. I don't know what happened to Maurice and Craig, and didn't exactly care. I'll never be able to fully explain the sense of confidence this gave me and how quickly I became entranced by it.

Maurice, Craig, and I were toasting shots to England and any girls that were at the table with us. However, I didn't stay there long. I grabbed the hands of the three or four girls sitting on or beside me and headed back onto the dance floor. There was no need to go anywhere else that night. This was obviously the place to be, and every girl I approached accepted my offer to dance. My confidence level was officially in overdrive. That shy boy with constant doubts about himself was buried by my newfound bravado.

I was immediately introduced to the downside of my playful ways, when one of the girls grabbed my shirt and kissed me. The kiss lasted a lot longer than it should have, but I eventually backed away telling her I had a girlfriend back in the states. She shied away and held her hand up displaying her wedding band. I looked over at Maurice and said, "Wow, I need another drink after that one." He was fist pumping and patting me on the back in support, but I knew I was in trouble back home. We continued to dance the night away and returned home to sleep a few hours before touring again. I sat up those few hours sweating off the five shots of whiskey and thinking of what I would tell Emily.

I did manage to fall asleep, but I had to skip breakfast in exchange for a shower. I didn't want to embarrass Professor Landers or explain why I reeked of alcohol and cigarettes. On the bus, I caught up with my required journal and Maurice set the plans in motion for going out again that night. I thought about staying in, but I didn't really care to get along with anyone else in the group. Besides, I was there to explore and couldn't do that from a hotel room. So that night, we were off to see what New Castle nightlife had to offer.

My seemingly reckless behavior quickly spilled into other aspects of the trip. After the amazing nights in York and New Castle, we stopped at a mega mall. It wasn't much different from the malls in the states, but the same temptations were there. It wasn't enough to blow my limited funds on shots and club entrance fees; I had to look stylish in London. Instead of coming from the logical standpoint of already having plenty of clothes for the trip, I bought an entire outfit and shoes! Looking back, it's a wonder how I was able to afford the basic necessities to survive the trip. I also wanted to bring back something for Emily, so I saw a bikini in a window display and purchased it. At the time, I didn't put much thought into it other than saying that she would look great in it. I eyeballed the size, and turned out to be spot on. It was a risky buy given that I couldn't return it, but I was confident that she would like it.

As we voyaged through England visiting cathedrals, castles, museums, and even the southernmost tip of Scotland, I became more fascinated with the rich history throughout the country. However, one thing that particularly bothered me was the number of artifacts confiscated during the colonial times. I wondered how other nations felt about this country holding onto its most prized tangible pieces of history. Then I came to the conclusion that it didn't matter since losers don't get to write the history books, and apparently they don't get to keep their art. But surely they had to be disappointed knowing that their ancestors' work is sitting encased in a foreign museum like a trophy.

One thing that impressed me the most was the easygoingness of the British culture. Nothing seemed to be a big deal here like it was in the states. Beyond the night life, the people in general seemed to be hospitable; especially toward Americans. I wanted to get to know them on a deeper level.

Shortly after we toured northern England, I had the opportunity to visit with a host family. Craig and I were paired together for a one night stay. I remember a mother and two daughters, ages nine and eleven, who were very comfortable with us in their home. At dinner, we exchanged questions and answers about each other's cultures and personal lives. The mother asked if we wanted wine with our meal. Of course, being somewhat uncultured, I inquired about wine. When she said that there was alcohol in it, Craig and I happily replied with an enthusiastic, "Yes!" She introduced us to pinot noir, and life as I knew it had greatly expanded in that one moment. Luckily, I watched her drinking while making dinner to see how to properly hold a wine glass and enjoyed it.

Afterward, the mother invited us into the living room and turned the channel to a football match as she called it. Other than being on the sidelines as an athletic trainer, I wasn't very familiar with soccer. While it was popular at Rappahannock and EMU, I never got into it.

I watched with appreciation as she insisted that I prop my feet up and returned with my wine glass refilled. The concept of drinking and relaxing was foreign to me. In every instance I could recall; I was partying hard anytime drinking was involved. Instead of guzzling, I savored every sip allowing the tension to slip through me and into the chair. I noticed the second glass was a sip or two away from being empty, but I was completely satisfied and dozing off when I heard the pouring of a third glass! Craig slurred, "Man, if I finished this glass, I'm gonna be completely sloshed."

With a big grin on my face, I raised my glass for a toast, "To the British!" After the clink of glasses, I can't recall much from the rest of that night.

The days leading toward London seemed infinitely long after that host stay. The rumor mill was running full steam as the hotel dwellers had nothing better to talk about on the bus rides. I guess they were incapable of whispering because I heard my name come up a few times. That kiss at Ikon revisited my thoughts constantly, and I racked my brain during the long bus rides trying to determine the best way to explain myself. If I told the truth, I'd be stuck with a ring as a constant reminder. Emily and I kept in touch through collect calls and e-mails at internet cafes. But anytime I thought about it throughout our conversations, I failed to gather the courage to just tell her.

I needed to deflect any attention the gossip twins were aiming my way, so I planned to lay low until we arrived in London. However, Maurice insisted that I come out. When he offered to pay, I just couldn't resist. Before that night took place, I managed to lose my wallet. I'd asked Craig if I could borrow a five pound note to get a bite to eat. When I turned around, the gossip twins were right behind us, and I had apparently asked Craig within earshot. They immediately started whispering while looking at me without a hint of shame. Against my will, I ignored them and went back to the room to look for my wallet.

Right before dinner, I had begun to look for Maurice to see if he wanted to join Craig and me for dinner. I knocked on the door on our floor and overheard my name once again from the gossip headquarters. I listened as they complained about me being too showy, whatever the hell that meant, always asking for money and didn't trust me at all. My first instinct was to kick in the door and tell them what I really thought of them. Instead, I knocked on the door and let myself in. "Have you seen Maurice?" When they replied no in unison, I headed out then turned around to ask if either one had a few pounds to spare just to see what they would do. The looks on their faces were priceless. Interrupting their thought process, I interjected, "Just kidding!"

All of us were required to eat within the same vicinity so we could catch an evening play. I was uneasy with the decision because of the cat-sized pigeons hanging around the area. I'd had some bad experiences with birds in the past, so I spent the entire dinner contemplating how I was going to evade them. I was on edge when we left, so I dashed across the street into the park to avoid the mutant birds. As I turned back to take in the crowded scene, the gossip twins stepped out in front of the restaurant to smoke. Just as they lit up two pigeons perched on an awning just above them unleashed the largest pile of dung right on top of both of their heads. The wait staff rushed out with towels to wipe them down. I went over to get a closer look as someone tried to console them by telling them that it was a sign of good luck. I busted out with laughter and told Maurice, "If that was good luck, then I hope every pigeon in this yard pays them a visit. That's what I call poetic justice!" I snickered through the entire play trying to contain myself.

When we finally regained our composure, Maurice, Craig, and I got ready for the night. This night was different because some of the group finally decided to come out of their shells and hang out with us. I was mesmerized by the personality changes after one or two drinks. Everyone was letting out their inner freak. The night was entertaining, but I had to curtail my drinking since I was running low on funds. I spent most of the night chilling at a table thinking about Emily.

The next morning, I had a chance to call Emily and the conversation quickly turned to my lack of calls and not hearing from me in a few days. I reassured her by revealing the gifts I bought for her. For some reason, I went into detail about people cheating on each other. Of course, the follow-up question was, "Adam, are you cheating on me?" With hesitation, I did what everyone else planned to do; I lied.

That lie ate me up for the rest of the trip outside of London. Everything seemed to be a mirage, and I was just going through the motions. Alongside that worry was the glaring reality that I had run out of money 12 days before we were due to come home. I had no choice but to call Granny and ask for money to be wired.

Finally, London. The Ferris Wheel. Big Ben. The Tower Bridge and Western Union! I was never so happy in my life. Granny had come through for me once again. I repaid Maurice and Craig then sat in my room kissing the remaining money. Failing to take away any lesson, Maurice and I went to the concierge for the best night life London had to offer. He suggested Oxford Circus and Piccadilly Circus. The guilt-ridden stress was eating me alive, and I needed to be reintroduced to my reliable friend, Jack Daniels.

That night we settled for Oxford Circus. I immediately noticed that everything in London was more expensive. If I was going to survive the next eleven days, I was going to have to control my spending, but not on that night. We hopped on the Underground, London's version of the subway, and got right back to our close interaction with everyday British. As soon as we stepped up from the Underground, a random guy in a trench coat tried to sell us heroine. We declined and continued toward the lights and crowded lines. Once the women heard our American accents, it was York and New Castle all over again. Before we got into our first club, we had an entourage of women escorting us to the hottest clubs around Oxford Circus. With a woman under each arm, I felt like a celebrity.

I splurged on shots at six pounds apiece like I was drinking for three. By the end of the night and three clubs later, I downed twelve shots of Jack. Although, I'd fallen right back into old habits, the alcohol alleviated the stress I couldn't seem to handle alone. I was feeling untouchable until Maurice interrupted our 2a.m. flow pointing out that the Underground and trolleys had stopped running. The clubs were closing, and none of us had change for a phone or had the wherewithal to locate a taxi cab. The fog was setting in, and the cold started seeping through my clothes. We had no idea where we were, so we walked around for at least two hours before making it back to the hotel.

I was so grateful to see my bed, but as soon as I embraced my pillow, the Earth started spinning out of control. I'd been there before. If I stayed put, the vomit was coming. All of a sudden I couldn't remember where I was at or find my way up. I lifted my hands into the air while holding my breath in an attempt to force everything to stay in my stomach. My muscles began to cramp, and feet bent without prompting like someone had them lengthwise in a vise grip. With one of my flailing arms, I grabbed a wall lamp or headboard to pull my 145-pound frame upright while gasping for air. I felt my stomach crawl downward and back off of its attempt to reject all of my contents from that night. Sweat dripped from my face onto my already soaked shirt. I stayed wide awake for the next couple of hours and embraced the sun's rays piercing through the window. It took me a couple of days to fully recover from that night.

The second day, we visited a Roman Catholic Church, and I recall thinking how this massive structure put my church to shame. I wondered if God really wanted this type of competition between us instead of using that money to help others. Did He really need buildings like this in his honor? We were encouraged to donate to the unattended container to contribute to the $9000 daily operating cost. I just couldn't determine the logic behind all of it and didn't even bother to pose the question. After going down and up from my knees multiple times, I just wondered what was next. The grandiose nature of the church made me uncomfortable.

One of my favorite moments had to be when I was touring through one of the many botanical gardens, and a group of German high school students approached me. One of the boys informed me that it was their first encounter with a black person and wanted to know if they could take a picture with me. I was somewhat taken aback and amused at the same time;

however, this wasn't an opportunity I couldn't pass up. To this day, there's a picture of me with a group of German kids floating around somewhere in the world. For some reason, it just reminded me that I needed to get back to the nightlife.

Fully recovered, it was time to hit the scene at Piccadilly Circus. With a better game plan of sticking to one club to avoid paying multiple entry fees and leaving at a decent hour, I was back to my confident self. As Maurice, Craig, and I stepped out of the Underground, I immediately noticed the lights were bigger, brighter, and more plentiful than at Oxford Circus. If the outside was an indication, the clubs were going to be the best in all of England. We didn't walk ten steps down the street before two girls snuck under my arms, and one even asked if I was an American basketball star. Typically I hated that question since I knew I was terrible at it, but that night I just went with it and replied, "Yeah baby, so is my friend Maurice!" I wanted to help Craig too, but no one would have believed his scrawny frame was suited for balling. It turned out that the girls just wanted entry into the club and some drinks, but in exchange for that, I had dance partners all night long, and they even brought more of their friends to encircle me. This was the essence of the high life I thought only happened to rock and rap stars.

No doubt, I enjoyed life to the fullest extent during my time there. It was a life that would indeed be short lived as I continued to spend well beyond my means. One stark reminder of the potential consequences was the number of homeless people I encountered in London. I wasn't prepared for that part of London. With my false sense of extravagance, I couldn't seem to shake the images of the men, women and children sleeping on concrete or begging for change in or around the Underground. I wondered what led to society's rejection of them. Although I had a selfish agenda, I couldn't ignore their plight like so many other people. When my eyes connected with theirs, I was reminded of my own hunger pains and feelings of hopelessness as a child. Somehow, I felt an emotional attachment to the ones I interacted with. Although the exchanges usually involved money and gratitude, I felt a calling toward a higher purpose in life. It was the moment when I finally realized that everything didn't necessarily revolve around me. My journey toward understanding my purpose on this Earth came to light as I'd finally done something to alleviate my conscience without the assistance of a stiff drink. My discovery of this intangible urge to do something bigger than myself empowered me to go above and beyond throughout the rest of my college days. However, I just had to make it out of London with the shirt on my back.

The rest of my days in London were fairly low key. One of the last great memories was getting to see King Lear at the world-renowned Globe Theatre. We had tickets in the standing yard, which I thought were the best seats in the house since we were so close. History informed us that it was where the poor stood if they wanted to be entertained, and I soon figured out why that was the case. It was something extraordinary to witness the raw passion of each actor and actress performing on stage. I didn't have much knowledge about stage acting, so their ability to remember and recite so many lines left me awestruck. After about an hour and a half of standing, I knew firsthand why the poor got to stand. My feet started burning with needle-like sensations, and there was nothing I could do about it.

Intermission finally gave me an opportunity to rub my feet and curse my new dress shoes. My feet were just numb by that point, but I took most of that time to walk around barefoot in the grass. By the time intermission had ended, I had devised a plan to take the concentration off of my feet and refocus on the play. For the next couple of hours, I did calf raises and rolled my ankles clockwise to distribute the pain. It seemed to work, and I was able to enjoy the rest of the play. I thought to myself, *Next time I come here, I don't need to be rich, but I have to be well off enough to get a seat.* After this experience, I was ready to go home.

We had a couple more days left before heading back to the states, so I spent time catching up in my journal and hitting the night scene one more time. By this point, I was just ready to be on the plane. The inevitable moment of facing Emily weighed heavily on me. I wondered if I should just break it off with her and return the ring. The gossip heads on the trip were likely to spread stories like wildfire when we returned, so keeping it from Emily was going to be next to impossible. I thought to myself that she deserved better than me and questioned why in the hell was I considering marriage so soon.

The plane ride home was dissonantly silent. The tension from regret was well set in so many of us. The excitement we had on the plane just three weeks ago had dissipated like a mid-summer tropical storm. My whole body just decompressed and shut down trying to process all of the emotions, but it allowed me to sleep most of the way back. When I awoke, I took one more look at the faces of my group and saw unrest. It was evident that some of us were going to have to confess and face the consequences of the truth while some of us would continue to live a lie. After entering the terminal, I refused to look back or even say my goodbyes and headed into my improbable future.

My relationship with Emily was very uncertain as I stepped off that plane. I was torn between regret and elation that I had just had the experience of a lifetime. I wondered if I had committed myself too soon. I wasn't even through college, and there I was trying to commit to someone from the rest of my life. I was a hard person to love. At the time, I didn't even love myself. *How could I possibly commit myself to her?* As those thoughts consumed my mind on the car trip home, I convinced myself that I wasn't ready and made plans to return the ring.

That night, Emily and I finally got a chance to talk on a normal phone call. She expressed how much she missed me, but I couldn't convey the same sentiment. I thought about the way those women treated me over there and the euphoric sense of confidence it gave me. It was a confidence I couldn't emit once I stepped off that plane. It was as if the last three weeks of my life had been a complete façade. I wanted to go back instead of facing the life I had. Yet, I wasn't proud of the person I had become. Emily interrupted my thought process when she revealed that her parents were hit with a $482 bill from my collect calls. I promised to help her pay it back and told her I would see her in a few days.

After a couple days of reflection, it was evident to me that my life was slowly falling apart at the seams. If I didn't get control now, I was going to be destroyed by the same fate that had conquered my mother and so many alike in my biological family. I needed something to reinforce that the life I was trying to achieve was worthwhile although I had no idea what it might have been at the time. Just days and weeks ago, I was selfish and acted like an unrestrained fool throughout England. However, I knew that lifestyle wouldn't lead to the goals I had for myself. Emily was a sure thing. She was real. It was time to step up and become the man I knew I could be, but I needed my muse by my side. At that moment, I knew I couldn't let Emily go. I didn't know what to do about the lie, but I couldn't push her away. I needed her to know that I loved her more than I ever thought was possible.

Chapter Twelve

Lost in Transition

Taking my financial weight off Granny and Granddaddy and regaining some sense of dignity, I resumed the car payments and purchased new auto insurance. I felt a sense of relief from a different kind of burden that can only be referred to as a guilty conscience for reneging on my initial promise. That do-the-right-thing moment effectually cleansed my conscience; however, a different, darker guilt stained the brevity of my redemption.

I still couldn't find a way to bring myself to tell Emily the truth about that kiss. As I removed the ring from Granny's jewelry box, I knew this indiscretion was not the way I was supposed to love her. I thought if I committed myself to her, then I would remain faithful and never be tempted to do something so careless and stupid again. It wasn't my brightest moment, but I committed to the proposal. I called Emily to let her know that I was coming to visit as planned and started driving.

During the four-hour excursion to her house, I considered the best possible proposal scenarios that would convince her to say yes. Doubts interrupted my thought patterns as I reminded myself that I hadn't known her for more than six months and my carelessness in England. I doubted my readiness for such a commitment, and then I'd refocus to walking along her parent's meadow while suddenly bending down on one knee. That seemed so mundane. I wanted the moment to resemble a fairy tale or a dream, but I didn't have the money to whisk her away to the tropics. What I decided to do was the next best thing.

When I arrived that Friday, Emily and I embraced each other and just held on tightly. She made me promise never to leave her for that long again, and I happily agreed. Her father offered me a stern look and went on about his business around the house. I can only imagine that had to do with the exorbitant phone bill he received thanks to my collect calls. Her mother was more forgiving and greeted me with a warm hug.

It was a relatively quiet day around her fifty acres of nearly uninterrupted nature. Her home was simple and efficient taking as least from the Earth as possible. The house was powered by solar panels installed by her father, and he'd even laid every board in the house. Emily told me more about her childhood as we strolled through her meadow. The sunlight was beaming down on the redtop grass with just the two of us alone. The moment was near perfect. I thought about bending down on one knee there, but I hadn't asked her parents' permission. I usually balked at anything that would get in the way of what I wanted, but this was a matter of me earning respect from her parents. Bypassing my doubt, I sensed the magnitude of the situation. It wasn't as much about needing their permission as much as it was about gaining their acceptance.

The following Sunday morning, I heard her parents moving about the house and having conversation. I peered over at Emily, still asleep, and decided that this would be my only opportunity to properly ask her parents before proposing. I trekked downstairs convinced that I was doing the right thing. I loved her without a doubt, but the persistent nagging of England sat at the forefront of my thoughts. Nevertheless, I cleared my head and greeted both of them. There was no sugar coating it, so I just told them both that I loved their daughter very much and would like their permission to propose. Both stopped what they were doing and just looked at me like I was foolish. Their looks were probably justified since I'd only known their daughter since late January. Her mom told me that it was more up to Emily than her. If that's what she wanted then, she would always be in her corner. That was a relief, but I still awaited her father's answer. Once assured that I would take good care of her, he gave me his blessing, which subdued most of the doubts I had in my mind.

With renewed confidence in my decision, I pulled the ring out of the box and headed back upstairs. With Emily still asleep, I crawled back into bed. The way it worked out in my head, the proposal would've induced some sort of dream effect. Emily was supposed to think she was dreaming once I whispered, "Will you marry me?" into her ear. I would then kiss her on the cheek and slide down to the side of the bed holding the ring once she turned around. Instead, her response was, "I thought we talked about doing this in August. Are you serious?" Of course, she still had her head buried in the pillow facing away from me. I thought to myself, *you just had to squander the moment on the meadow.* She finally turned around as I gave a forced smile, still sitting on the edge of the bed and forgetting that I was supposed to slide down on one knee. *This worked out so much better in my head.* In reality, I went from Mr. Casanova to a greenhorn trying to make an elevator pitch. She eventually smiled and let me place the ring on her finger. This was just the start of our odd romance.

Later that day, we attended her church to break the news and continued that divulgence at her grandparent's house. I admired the depth of her family as we all sat down to enjoy her Granny's Sunday feast. I found her efforts every Sunday to cook for so many people awe-inspiring. *If she puts this much soul into her cooking every single week*, I thought, *then she must have a lot of love to spare.* Not once did I ever feel unwelcome in her home. Even Emily's grandfather, who she referred to as Pappy, broke the ice at the table by joking, "The only kind of intermixing I don't approve of is Democrats and Republicans. You're not a Republican are you?"

"No sir," I replied and couldn't help but laugh.

It was difficult to leave after being welcomed into such a large and loving family. Reality quickly set in as I had to start earning money. I was already a month behind due to my England trip. I still had that hanging over my head, which made the four-hour drive home seem that much longer.

The remaining summer life consisted of six-day work weeks and constant daydreams about Emily. My supervisor had moved me off the customer service front to the floor to control inventory in hopes of grooming a well-rounded future manager. I didn't mind since it was more hands on and got me away from the eight straight hours of customer complaints and selling cigarettes. It also allowed me to think about where Emily and I would live once we graduated. I loved the area and its proximity to D.C. I also enjoyed the respect from my managers and co-workers and the real potential for quick upward promotion. I didn't want another moment like the proposal, so I decided to wait for the right moment to bring it up. I was just satisfied with the thought of being happy regardless of where we spent the rest of our lives.

A few days later, Emily and I were having a conversation over the phone exchanging how much we missed each other. Much to my surprise, Emily brought up the idea of moving in with me right then. At the moment, I was uncertain since I was sleeping at my cousin Christine's house with nothing more than a twin bed supported with metal beams that made it seem like I'd caught a beat down the night before. I slept on the floor many nights. Plus, I didn't even know if Christine would go for it. I told Emily that I would run it by her and let her know. I was already paying rent, so the convincing part was fairly easy. Within a few days and agreement of $100 extra rent, Emily and I were together again.

With help-wanted signs all over Manassas, Virginia that summer, Emily had a job as a waitress at a local steakhouse within a week. I was relieved since Christine and her boyfriend weren't exactly the most cheery people to be around. After a full day of work, I would come home, and we would mostly stay to ourselves or go out. While I was at work, I encouraged Emily to take a risk going out to the city or go stir crazy as an alternative. It beat staying cooped up in a room lying on our twin bed without a television. When I was free, we traveled throughout northern Virginia dating and shopping. We eventually ended up at a bridal store in Centreville where she found THE dress, which she paid for after working extra hours one weekend.

Everything was going well until I came into the apartment complex one night and left my car doors unlocked. Emily kept telling me to detach the faceplate off of my 3-D display car stereo unit weeks before the theft, but I didn't listen as usual. The morning we went to get her dress, I was stunned to discover nothing but wires hanging out of the center of my car. We reported it stolen and rode in silence the entire way.

Luckily, I reinstalled the factory system a few days later, but it was a painfully expensive lesson.

With the exception of that one incident, I was proud of how well we assimilated to Northern Virginia as a couple. We even talked about the possibility of living in the area once we graduated. Eventually, I was working mornings, and she was working late into the night, so the initial set up wasn't as ideal as I had hoped. Plus, we were sleeping in a twin bed, but the objective was to make enough money to survive our new life together. After six weeks, we headed back to Harrisonburg, Virginia and agreed that was an experience we never wanted to relive again.

After being turned down for a residence just off campus for being unmarried, we found a one-bedroom apartment within walking distance of EMU. There was nothing glamorous about the place. With the rust-colored rug and green flower-patterned wallpaper, it felt like I'd stepped into a 1970's time capsule. With little concern for its aesthetic appeal, we were just relieved to find something within our price range. At $350 per month, it meant that I could pay the rent with the credit received for off-campus living for the entire semester. Of course, we had to consider the rest of the bills, so I continued my work-study position as an athletic trainer and Emily found a job at a nursing home within a mile of our new home. After last semester, she had decided not to return to EMU due to the financial strain it was putting on her parents, so she wrapped up her nursing degree at the local community college.

We were happy with our decision and confident in each other's ability to make the transition to a fully committed couple work. However, that mood didn't last long. One of our first major arguments occurred within a week of living together. I got the bright idea to purchase an unassembled entertainment center for the little 19' television and collection of movies we owned. It wasn't anything fancy; just some particleboard with an oak laminate finish and way too many nuts and bolts for someone who was engineering deficient and didn't like to read directions. I should have paid more attention during my high school shop classes, but it probably wouldn't have saved me in this instance. About thirty minutes into it, I grew frustrated and retrieved a hammer and nails to finish the project. Emily sat quietly on the couch, so I had no idea what she was conjuring in her mind.

Going solely by the picture on the box, I completed the unit in about thirty minutes. I had managed to place more than a hundred nails into the system. It was standing, which was good enough for me; however, the slightest touch gave it an off-beam lean, so I looked for spots I may have missed and hammered to my content. By then, Emily had had enough. With her having a father as a carpenter, the entertainment center was a far cry from the finished products she was used to seeing. She started shouting, and her overt hand gestures suggested she was doing everything in her power to refrain from physically attacking me. I was losing control of my temper, so I stormed out the front door. During the time I was gone to vent my side of the story to Reese along with my regrets of moving in with her, Emily decided that she would tear the center apart with the intention of putting it together with the directions. I came home and found her mid tear down and began to yell again. My anger and temper usually intimidated anyone who it was directed at but not Emily. She mounted atop a stool, looked me in the eyes and yelled right back eventually daring me to hit her. I was so dumbfounded and scared of what might happen next that I left our new home without saying another word. The only thoughts that went through my head were leaving her with everything. I would've given anything to reverse our decision to move in together and just be a normal college brat again. For whatever reason, I couldn't quit that easily. After a quick cooling off period, we decided to attempt to assemble the entertainment center together. Emily read the directions, and I did the work. Although the unit was splintered inside, and still leaned at the slightest touch, at least it could hold our television and movies without tipping over like a set of dominoes. Looking back, I undoubtedly deserved to be yelled at, but it was a sudden turning point in our relationship. Unfortunately, it coincided with about revelation about my misdeeds in England.

Within days of the entertainment center misstep, I was back at EMU for my junior year. I always looked forward to returning to campus, but this year was an exception. Almost immediately, I had people asking me how many girls I slept with in England and if Emily knew anything about it. The judgmental looks made me feel unwelcomed on campus for the first time. When some of her friends started overtly avoiding me, I knew the stories getting back to her couldn't be farther from the truth. The rumor mill was swirling in full effect around the England trip, and I knew it was just time to come clean.

I contemplated throughout that entire day trying to decide how to tell her. I decided to go home after a full day of classes and just lay it all out. After we had finished cleaning up from dinner, I sat her back down at the table as I fought back tears knowing our relationship could be over before the night's end. I finally revealed everything that happened and apologized for my behavior. Emily responded by telling me that she knew all along and that the lying was worse than what I actually did. As she got up to walk toward the front door, I took her hands, submitted to my knees and begged her to stay. I wrapped my arms around her waist and buried my face into her shirt crying, waiting for what seemed like an eternity for her answer. While I didn't necessarily deserve that chance, I couldn't just let her walk out of my life. I couldn't remember a point when I was weaker than in that moment, but I figured my shattered ego could be repaired later. Ultimately, it just proved that there was a wild streak in me that was never ready for this type of commitment. To my surprise she stayed, but the seal of trust had been broken.

During the next couple of weeks, the distrust was constant in the form of interrogative inquiries. I wasn't prepared for that type of pressure and questioned whether we had made the right decision to stay together. I missed my talks with Niko and Reese and just hanging out on campus overall. I wondered why I'd given up my college life and restricted my freedoms down to such a mundane routine. At one point, I was truly disappointed that I didn't let her go. There was absolutely no love in our new home. If it still existed, one of us was going to have to revive it. I didn't know who to turn to, or how to go about doing so. I internalized it and reluctantly accepted my new reality. I returned my focus to school and kept my head in the books. After all, it was still about me, and no one was going to stand in the way. Graduating was still the goal, and everything else was just part of the routine. That routine abruptly changed September 11, 2001.

That Tuesday started out as an otherwise normal day. I attended my morning classes while Emily waited for the cable guy to hook up our new receiver. When I returned from campus, I found Emily sobbing on the floor in the living room. Before I could even ask what was wrong, she pointed to the television. The correspondents were reporting on the plane that struck the first tower of the World Trade Center minutes before. We sat there glued to the screen in disbelief as the channel kept repeating the same footage causing a heightened level of anxiousness that slammed into my chest like a sledgehammer. I was trying to console Emily, but my fists clenched tighter with each replay.

As the events continued to unfold over the next couple of weeks, I skipped some of my classes to take in every bit of information even though I knew it was the source of my emotional drainage over that time period. My anger had once again numbed me to the point of blindness – a type of blindness that discouraged rational thought. I was in a constant dissonant state of mind, and the only thing that could've alleviated my unforgiving passion was vengeful death to whoever was responsible. I regretted not joining the Army back in the summer of 1999 when I had a chance because I, like so many other Americans, wanted retaliation.

Initially, the EMU campus didn't seem bothered by the event. I felt we were going on with business as usual with barely any meaningful discussion about what it all meant for our community. With such seemingly apathetic attitudes, I wondered if they even knew or cared that it had happened. I had grown tired of the pacifist's stand-still approach. I recall complaining to Emily about how they were only holding prayer sessions and expressed my doubt about it doing any good. It wasn't too long after hearing my rants that Emily handed me Mark Twain's *The War Prayer* and encouraged me to read it. It wasn't immediate, but I remember sitting on a bench and completing the book in less than 20 minutes. Although it read more like a long poem than a novel, it circumvented my fervent resentment to make a compelling case for pacifism. Afterward, I thought, *maybe killing a bunch of people across the globe who had nothing to do with the 9/11 incident wasn't in our best interest either.*

I'd finally begun to understand the tenets of pacifism. The basis of the philosophy wasn't the notion of avoiding conflict at all costs as I had originally interpreted from the turn-the-other-cheek rape professors. Instead, its foundation was based on mutual respect for humanity and a deeper reliance on our natural choice to arrive at an agreement that would ultimately prevent further violence. Instead of being feebly indifferent to all of the injustices in the world, pacifism was more intrinsic, more holistic than violent, unfettered, and unabated retaliation. Instead, it bravely confronted those injustices presenting a viable alternative directly in the face of evil.

After a while, I didn't want to live in a world wrought with viciousness; however, I pondered an alternative - there was always going to be evil in the world. How could we morally justify killing it off with eradication being the ultimate end game? I arrived at the notion that in order for one man to willingly take another's life, he must be willing to sacrifice a part of his soul as well. Ultimately, I don't think it was a choice I could've made on the battlefield. *The War Prayer* gave me a much more profound respect for life beyond my purview.

Beforehand, it was easy for me to advocate for a brutal retaliation while being so far removed from the violence I desired. The civilian people our nation was getting ready to kill had every right to be occupying the same Earth I did, and their innocent families were more valuable than collateral damage. Maybe it was all a foolish dream to think everyone could reach such an ideal state of mind, but no more foolish than an eye for an eye annihilation mentality. My head was on a swivel.

The fervor that had boiled up to the surface over the weeks following 9/11 was finally beginning to subside. I surrendered my unavailing anger to baptism by fire. While my entire philosophy based on reactionary anger was being reengineered, the stark reality was that I was powerless to do anything about my dilemma or retaliate appropriately. My relationship with Emily was still somewhat in disarray, and my grades were already slipping. I had to do something to get my mind off of the events, so I went on a television detox and began to refocus on FLED. It was time to get back to salvaging the life I once enjoyed.

I came up with the idea to sponsor an on-campus concert with different genres to get people back in the spirit of living. Music always did that for me, so I hoped it would do the same for anyone who attended. I delegated the coordination to Nick, a FLED member and good friend, who had better knowledge about event coordination than I did. After flyers and word of mouth advertising, rap and indie rock groups were set to perform.

After talking with both groups, they mutually agreed that the rap group would go first. I offered the standard best of luck and told the groups just to have fun. Even though I'd run into all of them around campus, I'd never listened to either group live before that point. One of the rappers reeked of weed smoke, and they even managed to bring groupies, but none of it concerned me too much. I was just hopeful they were going to be aware of their surroundings and not drop *nigga-this, nigga-that* lyrics the entire time. Thankfully, they only dropped it once. Since no authority figures showed up to the event, I didn't fret. I was satisfied with their show, and more importantly they got the crowd moving. The indie rock group went on stage and did a fine job from where I was standing. The music wasn't necessarily for me, but I could respect the talent they presented. They didn't generate as much excitement, but I was okay with the settled tone to end the night. One of the band's supporters suggested that they were missing groupies. I facetiously agreed, but reassured her by pointing out others in a corner who was feeling the vibe of her beloved group.

Hoping to build off of our success from the concert, my next FLED meeting focused on the topic of interracial dating.

With the exception of one outing, I had only dated white women up to the point of this meeting. Since I was engaged to Emily, it was just going to be my overall experience with women. I'd never focused solely on race as a criterion for dating, but I understood the cultural reasoning behind people doing so.

Unfortunately, this ended up being my least successful meeting – less than ten people showed up. I couldn't tell if I had the meeting on a bad night, had chosen a poor location, or if people just generally didn't care about the topic. Nevertheless, it required a lot of talking on my part, which meant the forum lacked the level of engagement in previous meetings. The black female students who attended were somewhat intrigued when I told them about my club experience at Jams, being related to most of the black girls in high school, and the one girl telling me I wasn't thug enough for her. I also expressed my feelings of rejection for being articulate and not being able to do things that were depicted in our society, such as being an avid baller or an aspiring rapper.

They openly expressed their trepidations with my inability to see the importance of color. Emily chimed in a few times throughout the discussion, but it didn't really help my case. I truly understood their frustrations and reluctantly told them based on my experiences with blatant rejection that I was afraid to approach black women at times in my life. It didn't help my case, but I felt that I was in a situation where I had to be transparent. I also explained that love was boundless, and I fell in love with Emily because of how I felt being in her presence. I didn't have to put up some front to impress her. The meeting didn't exactly end on a high note, and I left feeling like I'd just lost a jury trial. Unexpectedly, there was a level of mutual respect and acceptance of my relationship with Emily after that meeting. I continued to joke around and make conversation with them throughout the year. All in all, the meeting didn't go as bad as I had illustrated in my head.

Regrettably, I couldn't think about FLED anymore throughout that fall semester because I was struggling with another math course and needed to focus on my Business Law night course at the local community college. After I had received a D on my first test, I determined not to fail my College Algebra class the way I failed Statistics. Emily had a good grasp on the subject and managed to help me pull off a C+ grade for which I was grateful. She also encouraged my decision to retake Probability and Statistics the following semester.

I performed well in the courses I was interested in but only managed a C grade in my Sales and Retailing course. Even though it was my profession in the summer and winter months, I couldn't motivate myself to get up and just go on those Tuesday and Thursday mornings. Had I done so, I would have at least managed to pull off a B grade. It was a poor excuse, but I simply didn't care for the course enough to get up at

8a.m. to hear this guy drone on about nothingness. I'd clearly lost my drive that semester. Overall, I was satisfied with the outcome after taking on a new and compromising lifestyle living with Emily. After my most dismal semester up to that point, I just looked forward to spring.

The spring semester always excited me. I had the warmer weather to look forward to, and it signaled just how close I was to completing another year of college. The only thing deterring my newfound outlook from flourishing was the fact that Emily and I still weren't getting along as well as a couple should. Both of us were too stubborn to give in to each other's suggestions. It really came down to the will to be controlled and trying to change each other rather than just accepting compromise. She disliked my lack of communication, and I didn't care for her blatant sloppiness around the house. The list of irritations went on and on, but I was always picking up after her to satisfy my instilled high standards and grumbling every step of the way. In turn, she would argue with me over not knowing where I was going to be, and I kept it that way because I didn't want anyone having that kind of control over me.

Both of us were at a point of deep resentment toward each other. However, we did a great job of putting up a happy front for our friends and her pastor, who agreed to conduct his first marriage ceremony with us. However, before joining in our matrimony, he required us to go to pre-marital counseling. I can't exactly recall why the sessions were required, but by the end, it was the lowest moment in our relationship.

I had a great deal of respect for Pastor Loren after visiting Emily's church a few times. They were a semi-outcast group of the larger Mennonite community due to their willingness to accept others from all walks of life without judgment. I felt they had a better handle on the embodiment of Christ's teachings (specifically, the lack of judgment and condemnation) than other churches I had visited. They also spent most of their tithes on helping the local community with stressors such as utility bills and groceries when unfortunate families couldn't afford them. Even though I was at a non-denominational part of my spiritual journey, I had a profound respect for their seemingly uncanny ability to actually live the faith they were preaching. When Emily suggested Pastor Loren preside to over our wedding, I happily obliged without my usual rebuttals. Yet, I was still somewhat hesitant to proceed with his recommended counseling sessions given my previous experiences.

The sessions Pastor Loren suggested were on campus at EMU, and more importantly, were free of charge. Emily and I decided to get started right away if for no other reason than to get them over with. During our first meeting, Pastor Martin had us explain why we wanted to get married. At the time, I wasn't very in tune with people's intent, but I immediately saw that he disapproved of our relationship. He saw a black man and a white woman living in sin. If his head would've exploded, I would've walked away unfazed. His face was beet red the entire session, and we left feeling lesser than two people who loved each other.

The next session Pastor Martin asserted his agenda and dug a little deeper. Instead of discussing what we enjoyed about being together, we discussed what irked us about one another. We managed to rehash old arguments in order to justify our stances and quirks. Pastor Martin couldn't manage to hold back his smirk as we continued to bicker about issues that didn't matter in the grand scheme of things. Some novel advice about how to accept each other's idiosyncrasies would've been helpful. Instead, we left more irritated at each other and Pastor Martin for stoking embers that distracted us from what we were so desperately hanging onto.

We were supposed to have five sessions but could barely stand the idea of attending one more. We dreaded the third meeting and contemplated not even going at all. Out of respect to Pastor Loren, we decided to go ahead and complete the meeting requirements. For fear of upsetting each other, we walked around on eggshells and kept our conversations short in between that week. We entered his office holding hands before that third session and left in complete disarray.

Pastor Martin was more engaged in this session, almost to the point of directing my responses. With a series of negative leading questions, he finally asked, "Adam, is this something that you truly want to do?" No doubt, the thought of marrying Emily was an overwhelming commitment. I loved her, but the whole set up of moving in together was taking an emotional toll on both of us. The shift in expectations was almost cataclysmic and something I clearly wasn't mature enough to handle at the time. I missed hanging out with my friends on a regular basis. I hated disappointing Granny and Granddaddy because they were concerned that I wouldn't finish school. My grades had slipped to their lowest point in my college career because I'd lost the will to succeed. With pressure bearing down on me in the worst possible way, I reluctantly answered, "No, I can't do this."

Emily shrieked, "Adam, don't you know that I love you!" and started crying uncontrollably.

Pastor Martin gasped like a distressed debutante, and I truly considered slapping him to the floor. The situation felt akin to being entrapped in a Maury Povich episode. Sitting opposite from Emily, I wanted to console her, but couldn't move. Emily stormed out of the room and didn't return. I was numbed by the wrong answer I'd given and the fact that I'd hurt her yet again.

I don't recall much after that. Pastor Martin and I spoke for a bit, but I left after coming into being again. I had to find Emily and amend my mistake. Within a matter of minutes, fate would have us reconnect outside in the pouring rain. She had walked all the way home only to realize that she didn't want to give up on me that easily. I'm grateful she didn't. I looked her in the eyes to intake the hurt I had caused her and promised myself and Emily never to abandon her again.

After departing the session and getting to sort through the chaos in my head, I realized that she meant more to me than anyone. Falling that hard in love with her so quickly was overwhelmingly out of my control. It incited a level of vulnerability and trust I wasn't ready for. The walls I'd built over time were put up to protect me from reliving the experiences of abandonment and betrayal. The more she tried to overcome that wall with her indulgent love, the higher I seemed to build it to protect my case-hardened heart.

Even when Emily offered me a way out the previous semester, I outright rejected it. She even told me that we didn't have to get married right then. I don't know exactly why I responded the way I did, but I blurted, "We're getting married, or we're done." In my flummoxed mind, I just thought if we could get through this tough part, then everything would work out just fine. I didn't really think in terms of gray area or compromise back in those days. Plus, getting married later invited too much uncertainty, and I was too headstrong to accept anything less than absolute certitude.

I was still a lost boy in search of manhood. As turbulent as our relationship was, she provided a sense of security I may not have found again had we split after that dreadful counseling session.

After Emily had called Pastor Loren to discuss the sessions with Pastor Martin, he apologized profusely. He also revealed that Pastor Martin was not keeping his impartiality by making judgmental comments during their phone calls. However, Pastor Loren defended us while reminding him of his role as an objective counselor. Pastor Martin's incessant need to gossip didn't surprise or anger me. Instead, what irked me more than his loose tongue was the look he gave us the moment we walked through the door. It was no secret that I wore my emotions on my sleeve. I was definitely the less sure of the two of us for many reasons, but instead of helping me address my worrisome mind, he used my shortcomings to coax a desired response to arrive at his preconceived notions.

Thankfully, Pastor Loren didn't care about the last two sessions and was just happy that we were still in love with each other. As bad as the experience was, it happened to be a saving grace for our faltering relationship and brought us closer together. I was just grateful we didn't have to attend the last two sessions and released one more albatross I didn't need in my life. My grades were on the brink, and if I didn't gain some control over my outward misgivings, that could've been the year I failed out of college. In response, I revived my "no excuses" mindset because I wasn't going out like that!

I knew retaking the Statistics course would claim of my time, which would lead to some slippage in other course grades. It was a calculated risk I was willing to take thanks to

Emily's reassurance. However, I didn't expect my Managerial Accounting course to require so much extra attention. I was an A/B student in my accounting courses at Rappahannock High, so I assumed that I would catch on at the advanced level. Unfortunately, my professor couldn't make the connections many of us in his course needed to understand the material. Similar to my previous Statistics course, it was another professor who could apply the subject matter in a professional setting, but couldn't teach it to novices who didn't have the complete understanding of all of corporate accounting's inner workings. I may have been able to pull off a B had I not taken Statistics during the same semester, but I wouldn't dedicate more than five hours a week to the cause. I dedicated less than five hours to my other three courses mainly relying on prior knowledge. I ended up with two Bs and three Cs including one in Human Resources. I originally aimed for an A in the course, but it was a worthwhile sacrifice to achieve a C grade in Statistics.

I never set out to be the smartest guy in the classroom. My weak math background required me to use grit and self-discipline to achieve a passing grade. I had to work harder than most, and I accepted that as a fact of life when it came to complex math. However, with a more compassionate Statistics professor, I grew more confident over time and even passed the final exam. From the onset, I expressed my challenges from the last course and my weak background in math – not for pity or excuses, but to give her an idea for a tutoring start point. She knew I was determined to understand the material and pass this time around. Her willingness and patience to walk me through step-by-step allowed me to whisk away the dejected feeling. For the first few weeks, there was the "I can't do it" self-defeating voice I had to overcome. That C didn't come easy as I dedicated ten to twenty hours per week, but it was my absolute best effort. I was proud to have overcome another struggle and satisfied to be atop of my academic expectations.

My balancing act was never a thing of beauty. It was nothing more than organized chaos mixed in with some salty resilience at best. However, the time constraints meant that I had to sacrifice something, which ended up being FLED. I didn't have the wherewithal to lead anything since my life outside of college was in constant disarray. I only managed to have one event that year, which occurred during Black History Month. The coordination began during the fall semester when I ran the idea by my multicultural director. Once we put our heads together, the sparks ignited and we decided to host a Black Man's Think Tank. We invited students from all over the country specifically focusing on Historically Black Colleges and Universities (HBCUs), and we even managed to book civil rights icon James Meredith as our keynote speaker.

We were slated to discuss a multitude of challenges facing Black America, but the event wouldn't come to fruition due to blizzard conditions that affected much of the northeast region. None of the HBCUs were able to make the trip due to canceled flights and road conditions. Fortunately, Mr. Meredith made it, and I had the honor of escorting him from his hotel to the campus. I thought about the bullet he took during his infamous march through Mississippi. His courageous actions and sacrifices afforded me liberties I so often took for granted. I certainly realized the significance of the moment but took it all in stride. I even had the pleasure of introducing him before his keynote address. Embracing the spirit of Martin Luther King, Jr., my public speaking voice boomed through the nearly empty auditorium. Regrettably, we only had 30-35 people listen to Mr. Meredith's words of enlightenment.

The conversation I had with Mr. Meredith before his speaking engagement still intrigues me to this day. We were discussing race relations during the drive and managed to tie it into how it was affecting Black America. I was mostly nodding and agreeing in an effort to respect our generational differences, but he asked for my opinion on a single issue ailing the black community. There were and still are a multitude of topics to choose from, but I wanted his take on the word "nigger" in our daily conversation and the black community's acceptance of the word as a term of endearment. In my opinion, the matter warranted discussion, but there wasn't a public forum to bring such a debate to light. I told him that the number one issue facing the black community today was the acceptance of the "N" word. I went on to explain that referring to each other in such a disrespectful way meant that we have accepted a substandard role in our society. We inadvertently accepted a role as a second-class citizen role and couldn't positively aim to reach our potential as a result. I reasoned that so many sacrificed during the Civil Rights Era, and now we're not only taking it for granted, but were in a state of regression. Mr. Meredith's eyes widened and a vicarious pause ensued. Then he sternly told me, "Be careful what you take on! Some issues just aren't worth the effort." I was taken aback by his response, but I had to respect it since he was ultimately an authority on the essence of black culture. I let him lead the rest of the conversation through town.

Shortly after that day, EMU's Black Student Union invited me to the Brothers of a New Direction (B.O.N.D.) meeting over at JMU. I can't recall the agenda, but they were having a call to action sort of meeting. I listened intently and decided to respond during the Q&A session. I saw an opportunity to test the waters with my impossible mission to eradicate the word "nigger" from our vocabulary and psyche. I raised my hand and was called upon to unleash my spiel, "I think we can do a better job of respecting each other, and that starts by eliminating nigger, nigga, niggaz, or any other way you can think to spell it from our vocabulary and definitely stop using it as a term of endearment. What's wrong with using the terms "brother" or "sister" like they did back in the day? Our self-worth is hanging in the balance. Asians don't go around saying, 'Yo what up chink.' Hispanics don't go around calling each other spics and white don't go around referring to themselves as honkies. We have to ask, why are we the only race of people in this country deliberately doing this to ourselves?" The follow-on silence was eerily condemning. I set off a couple of snickers behind me and lit a fire of cognitive dissonance among the two black professors leading the meeting who quickly went on to the next question.

I thought to myself, *Damn, it's like that?* Both men taught courses at JMU and held PhDs in their respective subjects. They were at the apex of academia, yet refused to even acknowledge this shortcoming within our culture. I left the meeting disappointed as I failed to make my case. If I couldn't convince two intellectual men of my viewpoint, then I was only fighting a lost cause. I guess the great men of our time had retired long ago, and there was no evidence of succession from where I was standing. I asked myself, *what am I trying to salvage or prove anyways?* At that moment, one of BOND's brothers approached to let me know that he hadn't thought about it from my perspective before and would stop using the word. The fact that he not only heard me, but internalized my words gave me a sense of triumph over abject ignorance. That man will never know it, but he gave me confidence I needed to openly pursue my mission to make "nigger" dissipate from the American conversation even if it took a lifetime to change minds. I terribly wanted a FLED discussion on the word, but I knew it wouldn't fly on campus. Since I didn't have more time to dedicate to FLED, it ceased to exist. There were other matters that required my dedication and commitment. Track and field season was on the horizon.

I can't recall most of my track and field meets mainly because I was in a constant zone frame of mind. I would envision success and overcoming each hurdle while heedlessly ignoring chronic back pain. The hurdles signified my life course. There seemed to be all sorts of obstacles in the path toward my goals, and it was my effort that allowed me to glide over each one gracefully and in some cases gracelessly. Falling was inevitable, but what mattered was getting up and finishing what I had started. Battered, but undeterred, my objective was to cross that finish line. Track provided an outlet to confront the battle within. The self-doubts could be silenced with a victory or emboldened with defeat.

At the starting line, I'd kneel down to take my position, secure my spikes against the blocks, and the starting gun would catapult me into poetic symmetry of mind and body. My 6'4" long-limbed, 145-pound frame had no issue sashaying over the obstacles. Before my junior year, hitting one of the weighted hurdles could stop me dead in my spikes, and I'd have to spend the next few hurdles regaining my footing. However, during my junior season I managed to burst through two hurdles destroying the impediments and gaining a bloodied lead leg as my reward both times.

The 42" high hurdles and 36" intermediate hurdles were more similar to my life journey. I could have a plan in place, but I would undoubtedly have barriers to overcome along the way. I couldn't gaze into the horizon for much of my life because of the hurdles in my field of vision. In many ways, the 36" hurdles were more difficult to overcome. I could see them and plan for them, but if my step pattern was off in any way, I had to adjust to propel forward or fall flat on my face. The objective after the misstep was to either recover my step pattern or regain my forward motion to reach that finish line. Failure was temporary and gave me a chance to make corrections next time. There isn't a more perfect analogy for life than hurdling. The hurdles were always in the same spot; the destination was always the same, yet everyone's journey was different. The grand intention of hurdles and life itself was to add an element of unpredictability. It's exciting and fearsome at the same time. There were few accomplishments that could compare to the sensation of being a champion. My junior year, I finally earned first place in the 110 high and 400 intermediate hurdles at the outdoor Old Dominion Athletic Conference Championship (ODAC) meet.

I ended my junior year on a high note, but the moment of triumph quickly faded away as responsibility returned to the forefront of my mind. I couldn't just go home to work this year, so I looked for jobs in Harrisonburg, Virginia for a week before deciding that $5.75-$6.00 an hour wasn't going to cut it. One grocery manager even had the nerve to tell me that her $6 per hour offer was a lucrative deal. I didn't know if she thought I was born the day before or if she really didn't know the definition of the word. After that conversation, I commuted back to my union supermarket job in Manassas, VA that paid twice as much as those cheapskate retailers were willing to offer. Although I enjoyed the weekly paychecks, the four-hour round trip commute took its toll on me.

The summer of 2002 seemed hotter than hell's kitchen at times. Being pinned up in a car and stuck in Northern Virginia traffic on I-66 with the sun beaming down on me proved to be too much throughout the summer. To make matters worse, I tried to save on gas by keeping the air conditioning off. I kept the windows rolled down as much as possible, but the sweltering heat combined with the exhaust from the traffic made it impossible to catch a breath of fresh air.

There were too many days when I would be alerted by a horn only to find that I was drifting into the middle of the lane on I-81 going forty miles per hour. I inadvertently became suicidal in the name of the almighty dollar, but I didn't let near death experiences deter me. I wish that were the worst of it, but I also nearly rolled under a trucker's trailers more times than I could remember. There were too many days when I drifted off the side of the road only to be awakened by the vibrating along the warning tracks.

Looking back, it was a reckless sacrifice to make and shouldn't have lasted as long as it did, but I felt beholden to the company since they always welcomed me back. They even promised to get me in the management training program after college. The final wake-up call came when I startled while headed right toward a bridge pylon and managed to swerve back onto the road. I was only a car length away from certain death. Had I hit the bridge structure, it would have flipped me over I-81 and onto the road below. Luckily, I couldn't have been going more than thirty or forty miles per hour. From then on, I drove with the air conditioning on, music blaring and had something caffeinated for every road trip. I didn't discuss the near death experiences with Emily since she didn't need more stress in her life. The wedding was coming up, and I knew about midway through the summer that I was putting a lot of strain on our relationship.

As I realized that I had wasted so much of the summer we could have spent together in pursuit of money, I began wondering why she loved me so much. She deserved better than what I had to offer most days, but I had no idea how to love her on the same level. I wasn't sure of anything leading up to our wedding day. I was emotionally split up until the moment I walked up to the altar. My faltering thoughts had me to the point where I contemplated giving up everything, including school. Running away and starting over was tempting, but it was a coward's way out. I knew I had to face my challenges head on, but had no one trustworthy enough to turn to. Without dealing with my uncertainties, we were heading to get hitched in her hometown of Philippi, West Virginia.

I was well aware of the need to steer clear of the bride-to-be and her mother during preparations. It's a shame I can't recall who provided me with the advice since it was some of the best guidance I'd received about women who are on a mission. Both Emily and her mother had a clear set agenda. My only objective was to stay out of the way and do what they asked of me. The only concerns I had to manage were my friends and relatives. My brothers and cousins were eventually bored sitting around the church, so they took a walk down Main Street Philippi looking for girls.

Philippi is a small town resting along the Tygart River in north central West Virginia; one of many towns that had lost its luster after the coal mining companies abandoned the area leaving the local economy unsustained. Aside from having one of the few covered bridges in the country, it's not well known for being a tourist attraction. The sprawling rural community is mainly comprised of peaceful white folks who generally go about their business and kept to themselves. Now a group of young black men running their mouths and catcalling young women were destined to turn some heads. I'd taken my eyes off of them for a few minutes to help rearrange a table before Emily was telling me to rein them in. Thankfully by the time I had finished moving tables, they were on their way back. I reminded them of where we were and explained that it wasn't like our neck of the woods, but it fell on deaf ears. They had nothing but jokes, and I thought to myself, *y'all are gonna land me in some trouble.*

The rehearsal dinner and the rehearsal itself instilled a little more confidence in me. It was nice to have the supporting cast of Granny, Granddaddy, and the rest of my friends and family. One of my biggest worries was somehow messing this up in front of them. Of course, my other worry was the level of commitment. I was completely scatterbrained throughout the occasion and reminisced about my grand plan I kept in a trapper keeper in grade school. Even though I had started planning a family when I was sixteen, it only looked good on paper. Suddenly, my paper wife was becoming a reality, so the next thing was the twelve kids I even had names for. Six boys and six girls were going to be the start of a new Starks dynasty. However, my real wife didn't want to push out twelve kids. She didn't even like any of the names I had picked out. Emily had even suggested that she keep her last name. While I sympathized with her on the kids after recalling the pregnancy video I had to watch in my high school biology class, I stood firm on the last name issue. Being brought up Southern Baptist made me more of a traditionalist than I ever admitted to, but it was more or less about starting a new Starks' legacy. I'd pictured things going so much smoother, but decided to fall in love with a more independent-minded woman instead of the submissive, unperceptive one I had on paper. A lot of things on my list weren't going as planned. That wasn't necessarily a bad thing, but I needed everything else to go right that weekend. It seemed no matter how hard I tried, I kept messing up in some form or fashion. For my sake and Emily's, this wedding needed to go off without a hitch.

After a full day of preparation, it was time to get our party on. I didn't want a repeat of England, so I wasn't interested in the strip club scene. There was no reason to end up with an extra side of regret to go with the mixed plate of emotions I was already struggling with. Instead, Emily and I decided to have a co-ed bachelor and bachelorette party. Reese, Rex, and my best man Scott celebrated with some of Emily's bridesmaids and her maid of honor, Addison.

Emily's grandparents allowed us to use their garage apartment for the shindig, and it was the ideal size for our small group. The night was going smoothly with music blaring and watching the girls take tequila shots while I drank vodka like a Russian. Then I had to mess that all up by taking a couple shots of Jägermeister with After Shock chasers. That led to an immediate trip to the bathroom, which ended my alcoholic binge for the night. Afterward, Scott and I got too rowdy, and he ended up tripping and breaking his fall with an elbow through the drywall. Reese and Rex were laid back most of the night. However, Reese was too busy hitting on Addison to be bothered with us boys. They eventually hooked up that weekend, and we were in their wedding a few years later.

July 20, 2002. The day had finally arrived. I awoke that morning with my head on a swivel, but it wasn't due to a hangover. That would have been a welcoming morning ailment compared to the sickening dizziness I was experiencing. Upon reflection, I wondered what the hell I was doing. I'm not even 21 and getting ready to commit the rest of my life to someone I've done nothing but bicker with for over the past year. Why didn't I date and experience more women? Should I even marry a white woman? Why bother putting both of us through the stress of not being accepted by so many in our society? The line of self-defeating questioning trailed through my head right up to the time I outfitted my tuxedo. I was convinced that I had made the wrong decision, but it was too late to back out.

With my back up against the wall and no apparent way out, my body involuntarily went into full panic mode. In a small back room crowded with groomsmen, sweat began cascading down my back and drenched my shirt within a matter of minutes. The overwhelming doubt began invading my bloodstream until it reached my heart. I was looking for a door to get some fresh air or run; I really didn't know what I wanted, but the thought was interrupted by Scott asking, "Dude, are you alright?"

I replied, "I don't know, man." I sat down and tried to regain my composure. My chest was tightening up, but I sat silently trying not to cause a scene.

Scott affirmed what I was thinking, "It looks like you're having a heart attack, man. Are you sure you want to go through with this."

I mustered up, "Yeah, man. I gotta do this."

Just then, Pastor Loren walked in, "It's show time, gentlemen!"

I closed my eyes and reflected upon the first time Emily and I met. I thought about our intimate all-night conversations, and strangely enough the last thought had to do with her staying up and tending to me all night when I had violent food poisoning from a local pizza chain. That took some serious commitment! With that in mind I took a deep breath, approached the front of the church and gazed into the crowd. Exhausted from my manic episode, I was grateful to see friends and family smiling in anticipation of the event. Aside from the sweaty palms, the nervous energy had subsided enough to allow me to take in the processional. The dual harps produced a calming effect. I watched my groomsmen escort Emily's bridesmaids down the aisle at an unrhythmically fast pace, but I couldn't blame them. However, my three-year-old twin cousins and Emily's three and six-year-old cousins in tuxedos and cowboy boots stole the show.

Finally, the preeminence of Emily's arrival graced the church with her appearance. I admired her alluring figure and was reassured by her joyful, radiant smile. I delved into her deep green eyes and gave a genuine smile of approval in return as she glided down the walkway with her father's guiding escort. After her father gave his blessing one last time, I tuned in and out as needed. I spent much of that time affirming that life beyond that day was going to be okay. I visualized all of Emily's positive attributes. Inspiring. Supportive. Intelligent. Patient. Eclectic. Wild-spirited. Open-hearted. She opened up my world to a higher level of inclusion that I may have never had the chance to experience had I not met her that fateful day. For me, love was a learning process; one I didn't master until many years later. Up until I met Emily, I'd only experienced love on a superficial level. Her abundance of love was infinite; not overbearing but ever ready. I was overwhelmed with the love she exuded. In contrast, I thought love should be validated by action. When I fell short of her expectations, I'd always end our arguments by giving her permission to leave. I was indeed a hard person to love.

I tuned in for 1 Corinthians chapter 13 to hear "Love is patient." The element of patience in love exemplified Emily, but it was a trait I would need a lifetime to reciprocate. Emily was indeed worthy of that ambition.

Emily and I exchanged our own written vows to genuinely express our loving promise to one another. Her dedication was clear and wonderful. In anticipation of my exchange, the nervousness returned in the form of vengeful cotton mouth that made my mumbling seem unconvincing and probably unintelligible to the crowd. This was the commitment I conveyed:

Emily, today I stand before you and our families to commit my love you; to commit myself to your happiness and to always be there for you in your time of need. Just as you have always been there to inspire me during my times of strength and weakness, I promise to stand by your side in sickness and good health. I will remain faithful to you. I will support you in all of your endeavors and help you succeed in accomplishing all of your dreams. Emily, I am so thankful to have such a gorgeous, intelligent caring woman like you to be my wife; to do incredible things in this world, to see so many wonderful places and to spend the rest of my life with you, loving you until the end. I always want you to remember no matter what happens; my love for you will exist above all else.

My hands were visibly shaking as I put the ring on her finger; so much so that I needed Emily's assistance to finish the push. As soon as her hands embraced mine, I returned back to a calm state. Then Emily calmly exchanged her vow:

Adam I love you. I take you this day to be my husband and life partner. I promise to stand faithfully beside you; through success and failure, joy and sorrows, I will always be by your side. I promise to give you laughter; to bring a ray of hope into

your darkness with a smile; to help you know the healing
power of joy; and to share with you the joy that you have given
to me. I promise to love you; to love you with wasteful
abandonment; to give you unconditional, pure love
throughout; and above all else to give you the love that you
have given to me. I promise this to you today and for the rest of
my life. I love you

When Pastor Loren expressed that I could kiss the bride, I sensed our marriage was a sure thing. There was no messing this part up. I gently touched Emily's face and fastened my lips to hers. Pulling away, I looked into her eyes and finally embraced the reality of our commitment. Since the wedding centered on her Irish heritage, Emily wanted to literally jump the broom to honor my African American heritage. Once we hopped over the decorated sweeper, I strutted out of there like the late George Jefferson, with Emily by my side of course.

To this day, our reception was one of the best I've attended, but it definitely had its moment I had to learn to laugh at later in life. Once we were announced as Mr. and Mrs. Starks, we made our way to the head table through the applause and cheers. In an attempt to escort Emily past the support beam like a gentleman, I managed to step on her veil causing her to grab the back of her head to keep her hairdo from falling out of place. Scott teased me by lightheartedly claiming I had some real smooth moves. Whatever the case, I was just grateful to be sitting down. I immediately noticed the cake fortified with bridges and doves. Emily's cousin made the cake, and it looked brilliant. The display had different flavors on each tier, so everyone could find a satisfying flavor.

The only botheration that night was the DJ playing the wrong version of our wedding song. We were prepared to have our first dance to Alison Krauss' *When You Say Nothing At All* when Keith Whitley's twang-y voice cut through the speaker system. I thought to myself, *Aw, hell naw, man!* Generally, I could listen to just about any type of music, but I definitely wasn't feeling his flow at that moment especially when I was prepared to hear a more angelic voice gracing the airwaves. Emily expressed her disappointment as well, but we tried to make the best of a bothersome situation. Afterward, I walked to around to interact with the crowd and was amused by the segregated reactions to the song. Emily's family members patted me on the back expressing their love for it and my family asked what the hell that was supposed to be. Granddaddy, who was usually reserved when it came to cussing, revealed that he thought "Aw, shit" to himself as well.

The rest of the night went as planned. The music mix was excellent from that point on, and nearly everyone informed me that it was one of the best receptions they'd ever attended. My family stayed for the better part of the night, which was one of the reasons I felt secure throughout the first part of the night. I truly felt blessed to have so many supportive friends and family on that momentous day. The new in-laws were going to be fine for the most part. Of course, there were some members of Emily's family that couldn't accept me, and some were okay as long as we didn't have children. And some were just there for the boxed wine. Whatever the case, Emily and I managed to have a great time, but we were both exhausted.

When we arrived at the bed and breakfast, another gift donated from some of her local friends who also owned the business, we were more intimate with our pillows than we were with each other. Instead, my first official duty as a husband was to go to the local Sheetz gas station and get her a comb since she had misplaced hers. She wanted to take her hair down, so even though I didn't understand the importance of it, I started fulfilling my self-promise to treat her more deservedly at that moment.

It was after midnight, so there were just a bunch of redneck boys showing off in their trucks. I had to reiterate Granddaddy's "Aw, shit" before I stepped out of the car. They saw me and immediately started revving their overcompensating engines. I kept walking, and luckily a middle-aged officer came out with his coffee, and they stopped the intimidation tactics. I was grateful that I still had my tux on sans jacket, so I looked presentable and didn't worry him. I was also grateful that he wasn't a young, white cop with a chip on his shoulder. I'd run into a couple returning home from West Virginia but was more fortunate on this night. I bought

Emily's comb along with a pack of mints and high-tailed it out of there.

When I returned to our room, I told Emily about the run in. I had nothing left after that emotional roller coaster of a day and that last incident zapped the last ounce of mental stamina I could afford to give. Emily and I mutually agreed that we just wanted to sleep, so we kissed each other good night and passed out.

After that anticlimactic night, I was back on the grind working for another month before attending school. I worked right up to the end of the summer but took a day off to celebrate a life milestone. My birthday usually coincided with the start of a new college year; however, this year I was finally turning 21. To celebrate the special occasion, Emily wanted to take me to an amusement park, so we took a trip to one of my favorite spots, Kings Dominion near Richmond, Virginia. It took some coaxing on Emily's part because I was tired from working a six-day stretch, and the overcast sky didn't look like a fun day would be in store. We lucked out because no one was there due to the cloudy weather, so we didn't have to wait in line for more than a few minutes for any ride. We ended up having a great time, and I even managed to convince Emily to bungee jump with me.

On the way home, she took me out to a national chain restaurant for dinner and my first legal drink. After spending so many years drinking underage, I didn't even get carded for my amaretto sour. I had no desire to overindulge or buy cases to keep stocked at home. Maybe, just maybe I was finally starting to come of age.

Chapter Thirteen

Toward Self-Actualization

The positive aftermath that ensued after our wedding allowed my inner chaos to finally subside. Feeling vindicated and revitalized from the incessant drama that had overtaken my life throughout the prior year, I proudly accepted my dual role as a new husband and college senior. The class load I faced combined with trying to be a better man for Emily wasn't going to be an easy feat; however, it was time to focus on what mattered directly to me and to finally exhibit my full potential. I was better than the irritable person I'd become during my junior year. I was smarter than the grades I'd put up the previous semester. Emily deserved a better version of me. The pressure I placed on myself was enormous, yet it was due to goal-worthy burdens instead of the unrealistic expectations I usually had in mind. That mindset allowed me to thrive intellectually as I decided to dismiss my self-doubting ways and walk, talk, and act with the swagger of a champion. This was going to be the year I didn't strive to silence naysayers or make others proud of me. Instead, my energies were focused on achieving personal greatness. For my sake alone, it was my time to thrive academically and athletically.

Conversely, working throughout the school year, just wasn't going to be feasible if I wanted to take away anything meaningful from my classes this time around. Emily and I discussed the challenges, and we mutually agreed that the best course of action would be me taking the year off. In return, I gave up my leadership post in FLED and any other extracurricular activities I thought may be a good idea in exchange for being home more often. It was this decision that allowed me to finally showcase my intellectual capacity at the collegiate level.

The first semester wasn't a cakewalk by any means. Combining Macroeconomics with Corporate Financial Management was a wake-up call that I was going to have to hit the books hard. Realizing I only had the option of the same professor from my Managerial Accounting course meant I was going to have to learn this subject matter by myself. Thankfully, I managed to do well in both courses pulling off an A in Macroeconomics and a B- in Corporate Financial Management. However, the most memorable course was Sociology of Development. During the middle of the course, we were required to do a project in relation to our family tree.

When I expressed my discontent to Emily, she suggested that I borrow her family tree, which was traced all the way back to when her family arrived from Ireland in the early

1800s. Initially, I was embarrassed because I didn't have one, but most Americans with African lineage wouldn't have had one. Fast forward over four hundred-plus years to my plight of a distant part of me that's forever absent and complemented by the void of not knowing the whereabouts of my immediate biological family. My splintered an unknown history resulted in my constant state of wonderment. Nevertheless, I managed to ace the family tree project by presenting Emily's profound Irish heritage to my class. Being deeply engaged in the course throughout the semester, I also managed to pull off an A grade, yet that sense of belonging and knowing my lineage still eludes me to this day.

The first semester ended up being about as uneventful as I could have hoped for, but the results that came with it were tremendous; it was the first time I managed to pull off all As and Bs during a collegiate semester. Thanks to Emily picking up extra shifts, she made it possible for me to finally concentrate on school alone and have the money necessary to enjoy our delayed honeymoon in Fort Lauderdale, Florida.

After a long and arduous semester apart in the same house, Emily and I were excited about spending some quality time with each other. As two college students on a tight budget, we decided to drive down I-95 since it was cheaper than flying. We contemplated spending the night in a hotel about halfway down, but since we were making such good timing, I was determined to make it in one fell swoop. Sixteen hours later, we were finally in our hotel room. My sense of good timing had to do with making it to the northern end of Florida from Harrisonburg, Virginia in ten hours. I had no idea the remaining part of Florida would be six hours long. Yet, we made it through the extended day and night. I was exhausted the next morning, but I wasn't going to let that dissuade me from sticking my feet in the sand. Emily and I were finally in the midst of the intimate moments we had been anticipating without a care in the world. We walked along the beach holding hands admiring each other amidst the moonlit night.

One of my favorite nights during our honeymooning week was going to an upscale restaurant followed by a jazz club and dancing. Listening to the jazz genre was a new experience for me, but it didn't take long to find my groove and dance the night away with Emily. Our whirlwind trip continued the next morning as we ventured on a 3-day cruise to Nassau, Bahamas. On the way, we managed to pass Joe Robbie Stadium, which was the home of the Miami Dolphins at the time. I flashed back to always wanting to go to a game but never had the opportunity. I was just grateful to pass the venue and pay homage. Soon we were on board the ship and ready to voyage.

I recall being captivated by the vastness of the Atlantic. The mesmerizing sunset looked as if it were bending the curve of the ocean's horizon to its liking. Holding Emily's hand during those moments at dusk offered solitude as I closed my eyes and tuned into the waves. Completely revitalized and full of hope for our future, Emily and I knew we had unmistakably done the right thing by getting married.

During the start of my last semester, I was a glutton for punishment with Quantitative Decision Making and Research Methods and Statistics. In addition to four other courses, I knew that semester could prove to be my most challenging one yet. However, as I was determined not to go another day beyond the four years I had originally planned. The course load never discouraged me, and never once did I doubt my ability.

I ended up achieving a B grade in Quant as we called it for short and an A in Research Methods. While I didn't lack confidence in my aptitude, it was hard to believe as I realized consecutive A-B semesters. I was always capable, but never achieved a level of focus and balance needed to do so. While those courses were valuable in their own right, the History and Philosophy of Nonviolence course brought it all home for me. We went well beyond, Mahatma Gandhi and Dr. Martin Luther King, Jr. to discuss Lech Walesa and a multitude of other lesser-known heroes who used nonviolence to achieve a greater good. Consequently, this in-depth experience provided a life perspective on a much larger scale as I uncovered how to view not just myself, but the world. My courses were the most important aspect of my senior year, but the grades were far from my only high note.

While I considered myself going through the motions and learning some hard lessons over the course of four years, someone was pulling for me behind the scenes as I was nominated and selected for the prestigious Presidential Award. I attended the EMU Athletic Banquet without the expectation of any recognition as there were so many worthy athletes in various sports. I was always uncomfortable at fancy dinners, so my thoughts focused on making sure my napkin was in my lap and cutting my food just so. I would've given anything for a burger and fries that night. I also missed Emily at my side and thought about how she was doing at work. Granny and Granddaddy were in attendance, and I was grateful they could witness the moment.

The University President first announced the awards to two women, which was unusual since they traditionally honored one athlete. Next, he honored a male athlete with the award, and I was still clapping unaware I was the next recipient. After the first sentence, my heart began hammering as he reiterated words that had previously come from my mouth almost verbatim.

Our second recipient for the men's President's Award is Adam Starks. Adam and his wife Emily reside here in Harrisonburg. Adam is a business major with a cumulative G.P.A. of 3.0. Leader. Achiever. Student. Friend. Teammate. Advisor. All of these are words that describe Adam's involvement at EMU over the past four years. There were those who didn't feel as if Adam belonged in college. He will graduate in a few weeks with a very excellent G.P.A. There were those who said he was an introvert. He founded the student organization FLED and also served on the Black Student Union. There were those who said he was shy. He's now a family man, married last July. There were those who said he couldn't succeed in college athletics. He rewrote the EMU record book in track and field. Adam arrived at EMU four years ago as a shy, uncertain young man. Since then, he has grown in many ways. Spiritually, he is always willing to let others know how blessed he is. Academically, Adam made up his mind that he would succeed at EMU in the classroom. He has dived into his studies and is avidly pursuing his dream of one day owning his own business. Athletically, he has set his sights on the NCAA track championship, which he will participate in on May 22nd. These goals have been accomplished as Adam has held down a forty hour-per-week job, a ten hour-per-week work-study job and actively participated in several campus organizations. Adam has been a busy man. Adam has a stellar athletic career at EMU. This year, he capped that career by gaining national recognition in the 100 meter high hurdles and the 400 meter intermediate hurdles. Currently, he ranks third nationally in the 110 high hurdles and fifth nationally in the 400 meter intermediate hurdles. He will be pursuing All-American honors at the NCAA Outdoor Championships to be held at St. Lawrence

University in New York. Coach Pete says Adam has enjoyed a stellar career. He is an amazing student-athlete and an even more amazing individual. He will end his career at EMU owning six school records. He has been undefeated in the ODAC Championships since his sophomore year in both hurdle races. Adam has demonstrated what it takes to be a top-notch student-athlete. He has portrayed a Christian witness and shown leadership that has set a standard for others to follow. He represented ODAC and EMU with both pride and dignity. Coaches and members of the EMU track family will miss Adam's leadership, his friendship, and his performance in the coming years. Congratulations, Adam.

As the President handed me the silver cup with my name emblazoned on it and exchanged handshakes, I couldn't help but feel elated by the honor of being etched into EMU's transcendental history. All of the honorable winners had to give an acceptance speech, and I was grateful to go last since I had to thank so many people who were instrumental in my success. My nerves were on edge from speaking on the fly. I managed to thank my coaches, friends, Granny and Granddaddy, but regrettably I forgot to honor my beloved Emily. She was definitely on my mind as I wanted her there by my side, but the speech I prepared on the fly didn't go in the order I had so quickly deliberated. I momentarily froze as I peered across the tables and connected eyes with some of the unknown attendees. As I started speaking, it came across as surprisingly coherent and noteworthy enough to get complete strangers to make their way through the crowd to congratulate me.

I spent my final track and field season racking up wins in the hurdles and relays. I set the school record for the 110HH and even qualified for Division III national competition earlier in the season, but I couldn't manage to get neither the record nor qualifying time for the 400IH. Finally, I laid it all out at our next-to-last meet at Liberty University. I didn't care if I fell over any of the hurdles or what injury I might sustain. I was going to leave it all on the track. Running against one of the best fields during my entire collegiate career, I came within three-tenths of second of the school record and finally qualified for nationals. As a result, I was interviewed during practice and placed in the front page of the sports section in the local newspaper. I went out and bought five copies and sent one to Granny and Granddaddy. It didn't seem possible to feel more successful than I did at that moment.

At the onset of the ODAC championship meet, I was expected to win both hurdle races, and our relay teams were ranked high. Coach Pete even decided to throw me in the 100 meter dash to continue to work on my speed technique in preparation for nationals. I was curious to see my potential at first, but grew confident that I could medal in the event after pulling off gold medal wins in the 4x100 relays and the 110HH. I'll never forget the surprised look on my competitors and their coaches' faces at the finish line as I crossed in third place. I finished the meet with four gold medals and a bronze, earning me the ODAC Male Athlete of the Year, which I had secretly coveted all four years. At that point, I'd forgotten about giving up on my track dreams. I rediscovered my passion for the sport and had every intention of surprising everyone at nationals.

The Division III National Championships were held at St. Lawrence University. Florida, Georgia, or even California would have been better suited to my taste, but the event was awarded to a private university in Canton, New York. I was ill-prepared to deal with a 37-degree day and lacked sleep from the night before due to the excitement. The sun would peer through the clouds just to tease everyone down below while a cool wind reminded me that my windbreaker outfit didn't live up to its name this far north.

I made the best of an unfortunate situation, but in an attempt to stay warm and the constant shivering, I was worn out by the first heat in each of the hurdle events. I failed to qualify for finals in both races, and placed 10th overall for each race – just two places shy of a medal and nine places short of my expectations.

Four misdiagnoses for a twisted sacroiliac joint in my lead leg, chronic injuries, poor diet choices, and an inconsistent workout schedule ultimately led to me failing to realize my potential. There were a lot of external forces working against me, but on the trip home, I reluctantly had to accept the fact that it was a culmination of putting track on the back burner during past years to address my shortcomings that would hopefully play a role in my future success. The thoughts of what could have been made for a long van ride home down I-81. However, I went to EMU for a diploma, and that's exactly what I accomplished.

April, 27th, 2003 - Graduation Day. I achieved the unexpected; well, unexpected for some. I met the day with mixed emotions. Without my experience at EMU, I may have never contemplated forgiveness or discovered my inner peace. There were no regrets regarding my choice; EMU was the right destination at a destined moment. I thought, albeit naively, this day would be the pinnacle of my existence, but this achievement should've been defined as another major milestone. While it doesn't lessen the significance of that celebrated day, I nervously learned that I was only at the origins of my life journey. I assumed having a degree in hand would catapult me toward discovering my purpose in life. *Was I really supposed to go work as a supermarket manager with the hopes of pushing my way through to climb the unstable rungs of the corporate ladder?* It seemed so mundane and unfulfilling after thinking of myself as a worldly citizen.

My search would inevitably have to continue. As my friends would disperse to their next destination, I'd lost my sense of community. I simply didn't know where to pick up or begin. *Was I supposed to recover some semblance of my childhood by reconnecting with my lost family to fill that abstract void in my identity?* The whole ordeal left me somewhat scatterbrained, but I gravitated toward what I considered a more responsible option – working to establish a new family and just be present. I was a married man and expected to step up to do the right thing. I didn't have the luxury of going back to my parents' house or travel the world to sort out the meaning of life. As I draped the royal blue gown over my suit, I looked into the mirror, studied my eyes and grew confident that I would uncover the answer in due time.

The sea of royal blue caps and gowns were complemented by smiling parents, relatives, friends and alumni. While I didn't have it all figured out that day, my experience at EMU would be the foundation of every aspect of my being. No matter what happened, no one could take this from me. It was the kind of security that came with the struggle I grew to appreciate standing atop the community who deserved credit. This was my moment. My resilience had finally paid off. I happily accepted my role as an outlier to society's expectations. I was no longer a statistic condemned to failure. Upon hearing my name and grasping that hard-earned diploma, the feeling of triumph arose in my heart. Once again, I was proudly beaming as I reflected upon the notion that I belonged here.

In the pursuit of my degree, there's no doubt that I'd taken an unconventional path. Even though they couldn't join me on that stage, I thought of my mother, father, guardians, mentors, friends, coaches, and everyone who touched my life along the way. However, I was grateful to have Granny, Granddaddy, Emily and my brothers Chris and Noah to witness that extraordinary day. As a last ditch effort, I'd hope the events would inspire Chris and Noah to attend college to discover the same sense of self-discovery and elation I felt during the journey. As stated before Noah, opted out to work, but Chris proudly graduated from my alma mater. Both of them manage to overcome the odds, and I'm grateful that we were able to stay connected through it all. I'd like to think that our bond throughout those trying foster care years silently encouraged each other to persevere.

Despite my naysaying high school guidance counselor, the mere hope of going to college greatly altered my life trajectory. My well-deserved diploma afforded more than just the zenith of the moment culminating four years of knowledge and achievement. It afforded me something more essential; a liberation of my prospective future. Standing on the shoulders of my giant community, the world of opportunity was finally within my reach.

Author's Afterword

There is no passion to be found playing small in settling for a life that is less than the one you are capable of living.

Nelson Mandela

Nothing is impossible. The word itself says, 'I'm possible'!

Audrey Hepburn

A change of perspective may be all it takes to transform a painful experience into a powerful growth experience.

Iyanla Vanzant

Be the change you want to see in the world.

Gandhi

Two roads diverged in a wood, and I – I took the one less traveled by, and that has made all the difference.

Robert Frost

Born to a single mother with only a ninth-grade education, I came into this world without much of a chance for success. By any statistical set of societal norms, I should not be here. I should not have graduated high school. I should not have made it to college. I should not have graduated college and so on and so forth. Yet, I'm living proof that anyone can become an outlier, regardless of outside influences or test outcomes that cannot account for all possibilities. My greatest strengths have been my inward ability to persevere in the face of adversity. As a result, my magnificent trials and lessons have fortified a level of resilience I've grown to appreciate over time. It's important to understand that life is a constant series of tests and obstacles to overcome. I think of my challenges as gatekeepers to the desired end result. Without them, my accomplishments would be a little less sweet than if my goals were just handed to me. For that reason, I've provided a series of quotes throughout the book to express that inspiration can come from anywhere. Coming across each one of the quotes from all walks of life helped put my existence into perspective.

I didn't wait for a physical savior to rescue me from my plight. I was vigilant in everything I set out to do or wanted to do. While acknowledging the systemic pressures that manage to oppress so many, the will to do and overcome must come from within. Only then, will you ascertain others' readiness to support you in your endeavors. Throughout the book I hope you were able to internalize my struggles in comparison to yours and more importantly see that everything managed to work itself out in concert with my higher aims.

Regardless of scale, our troubles run deep and deserve merit; however, when you feel unneeded, unwanted, and unloved, reach into that deeper part that is your reason for being and embrace that value until your worth is realized. Hang onto that last thread of hope and know that something more positive is within your grasp. I encourage you to look outwardly for support during your roughest times and believe inwardly that your matters will eventually pan out to allow for better days ahead. Don't give up on your ingenuity, and more importantly, don't overlook the goodness within your community.

I've presented a lot of details that will give the critics plenty to judge and even condemn. For deeper thinkers, I challenge you to promote your energies toward making sure you do your part to ensure the success of our children. Be a mentor, a coach, a foster parent or a shoulder to lean on. The family unit has been deteriorating throughout this country for a long time. It's an issue that transcends race, class, and ethnicity. The future may belong to our children, but you are empowered to be there for them in this present moment. It truly does take a village.

I can gratefully acknowledge that amidst all of my triumphs and shortfalls, I achieved an upward mobility so many can only dream about or worse yet, not even know that a better life exists. My perseverant outlook and reliance on the spirit of community allowed me to achieve a continual apex of accomplishments throughout my life. Now, I feel that it's necessary to lend a hand back to help others elevate their potential and find their calling in this vast world of infinite possibilities.

I've chronicled my life in a way that shows how difficult it is to overcome poverty, uncertainty, and the psychological challenges that ensue while growing up in foster care. It doesn't take much to break the spirit of a child, but it takes the community to heal him or her if that broken soul comes to define their formative years. The trajectory of his or her life hangs in the balance of being loved or unloved.

As you likely noted throughout the book, I made a lot of reckless mistakes. Whether self-induced or externally influenced, it never meant that I lacked potential as a human being. Once I awakened and realized the need to better myself, a multitude of people came forward to support me without ever giving up. Now here I am at the summit of self-realization - an eclectic human being whose soul is on fire with a passion for knowing and doing more than I or anyone else thought possible. That level of potential is in every strand of our DNA. It takes a positive community to recognize it, but you must first realize it from within. The more I strive to help others learn from my trials, the closer I arrive at my search for peace of mind. It's important to understand that mending is a process of self-enlightenment and the will to embrace your community. The conscious endeavor takes longer for some than others depending on past experiences. With weathered eyes and salting hair decades too early, it's no doubt that this journey has taken a toll on me. As I approach my mid-30s, I'm finally gratified to discover what it truly means to be mended.

Pain is inevitable, but so is joy. Too many of us resort to abject fear or anger due to our sufferings or unknowns in life. Remain steadfast by approaching discovery and love so you can embrace the present moment. The past can serve as nothing more than a lesson and the future can serve nothing more than a notion.

Dr. Adam Starks resides in Philippi, West Virginia with his wife and three children. For more information, please visit www.adamstarks.com.